The Cornish Ordinalia

A Medieval Dramatic Trilogy

I Beginning of the World

II Christ's Passion

III Resurrection of Our Lord

Newly Translated

by

MARKHAM HARRIS

THE CATHOLIC UNIVERSITY OF AMERICA PRESS

Washington, D. C.

1969

PREFACE

The aim of this book is to introduce the *Ordinalia,* representing as it does about one-fifth of the surviving religious drama of medieval Britain, to a broader readership than it has hitherto attracted during its long yet restricted life. To this end, I have attempted to produce a version of the trilogy which is both responsible and responsive; responsible toward the letter of the Cornish original, responsive to the spirit of the work as a whole, which I have come to see as livelier, more various, and more appealing than that assigned to it by received opinion.

For all that pertains to the accuracy of my rendering, I am indebted to my colleague David C. Fowler and to my wife, Phyllis Pier Harris. The former not only supplied the initial impetus for the undertaking but also devoted the time and attention required for a close reading of the manuscript in draft. The latter, on a day-to-day basis over a period of many months, at home and in Cornwall, applied her command of Middle Cornish and her patient, scholarly exactitude to the testing and retesting of my results against her collation of MS Bodley 791.

Since mine is the sole responsibility for literary sins, whether of commission or omission, I absolve even as I thank my departmental associates, who were kind enough to interrupt their own pursuits in order to examine my project and give it the benefit of their reactions. They are Professors Margaret Duckett, James W. Hall, William F. Irmscher, and Lawrence J. Zillman. In addition, I take pleasure in naming a gifted student and his wife, Mr. and Mrs. Frank M. See.

It remains to acknowledge with no less lasting gratitude the hospitality and assistance of those in Cornwall who helped to further this book. Neither the research nor the writing carried forward there, on the native ground of the *Ordinalia,* could have been as fruitful without the good offices of H. L. Douch, the curator of the County Museum, Royal Institution of Cornwall, Truro. Minutely conversant with the resources of the museum's library, including its unique collection of Cornish manuscript materials, Mr. Douch extended aid and counsel of great value; to which should be added his knowledge of Cornish antiquities and the geography of the area with its bearing upon Cornish place-names, whose presence in the text of the cycle constitutes one of its distinctive features. It is, in fact, this lingering of the past under the surface of the present, in the very soil of Cornwall and in the sensibilities of its more aware inhabitants, which has helped to sustain my labors on the *Ordinalia* and now informs my wish to record these additional names, together with my thanks: E. G. Retallack Hooper, former Grand Bard of the Cornish Gorsedd, and Mrs. Hooper; Mr. and Mrs. L. R. Moir of Carbis Bay, St. Ives; P. L. Hull, archivist, County Record Office; Roger Penhallurick, assistant curator, the County Museum; P. R. G. Marriott, reference librarian, the County Library; and the late Mrs. J. Rolfe, who had retired from teaching but not from learning until the last.

For permission to quote from manuscript materials in its possession, I am indebted to the Royal Institution of Cornwall, Truro.

M. H.

University of Washington
Seattle, Washington

CONTENTS

Page

INTRODUCTION vii

I   BEGINNING OF THE WORLD..................... 2

II   CHRIST'S PASSION 80

III   RESURRECTION OF OUR LORD.................. 178

NOTES 250

BIBLIOGRAPHY 272

.

INTRODUCTION

Little known even today, the *Ordinalia* has come down to us from the Middle Ages in the form of a unique manuscript, the gift of one James Button to the Bodleian Library, Oxford University, under date of March 28, 1615. The MS, designated Bodley 791, consists of 7 introductory blanks plus 83 parchment leaves securely bound in leather, the leaves measuring 11 x 7¾ inches. Written in a script which the catalogue entry assigns to "the first half of the fifteenth century," the work is composed of approximately 8,600 lines of stanzaic verse in Middle Cornish, with stage directions and names of characters in Latin. Middle Cornish is a Celtic language closely related to Welsh and Breton and was formerly the vernacular of Cornwall, Britain's westernmost shire.

During its sequestered history, the *Ordinalia* has acquired various labels. Edwin Norris, editor of the only complete edition of the trilogy thus far published (1859), entitled his book *The Ancient Cornish Drama*—a dignified title but not overly informative as to the period or type of drama to be expected. On home ground in the Cornwall of the past and present, the *Ordinalia* is often referred to as a triad of "old miracle-plays." This label, while traditional in Britain, overlooks the useful modern distinction between the Cornish trilogy, a sequence of three interrelated dramas based mainly upon the Old and New Testaments, and Cornwall's *Beunans Meriasek* (The Life of Meriasek), the material of which is drawn not from Scripture but from the miraculous life history of the Cornish saint.

As viewed today, it seems most precise to term the *Ordinalia* a medieval mystery cycle, a characterization which serves to locate it roughly in time, indicate that its matter is dominantly Biblical rather than legendary, and signify that the work is composed of two or more semi-independent dramas that share, nevertheless, chronological progression and, in the case of the *Ordinalia,* a unifying theme. Whereas Britain's other extant mystery plays, the Corpus Christi cycles of the east and north, undertake to present the entire sweep of sacred history from the Creation to the Last Judgment, the Cornish trilogy concentrates upon the Passion (Play II) and the Resurrection (Play III), prefaced only by those Old Testament episodes (Play I) which account for the genesis of the earth, for the origin of man, for his Fall, and for the need and means of his salvation. The Cornish *Ordinalia* is, therefore, a Passion cycle, differing in both content and method of performance (see below) from the English cycles.

Author and Date of Composition

No direct evidence as to the authorship of the *Ordinalia* or its date of composition has yet been uncovered. Nor have we any means of determining how nearly Bodley 791 represents the original version of either the trilogy as a whole or any one of the three dramas taken separately. There are internal indications, however, that it is a version revised either by intent or through the accidents of copying.

The indirect evidence, much of which has been assembled and interpreted by David C. Fowler ("The Date of the Cornish 'Ordinalia,'" *Mediaeval Studies* XXIII: 91-125), is more promising and may be summarized as follows. When the approximately two dozen Cornish place-names mentioned in the cycle are plotted on a map of the county, the majority of them are seen to cluster near the southwestern coast in the vicinity of modern Falmouth. The spelling of these place-names is another clue. As they appear in the manuscript, they represent a roughly identifiable stage in the gradual evolution of their written form. The same holds true for the examples of Middle English which are distributed through the Cornish lines of the original and which can be approximately dated. There remains a less tangible yet pervasive factor, one which could be termed the intellectual and literary climate of the *Ordinalia*. Despite occasional ribaldries, of which too much can be and has been made, it is an educated climate, strongly suggesting a tutored mind employing the vernacular in order to reach, edify, and entertain a predominantly unlettered audience; a mind conversant with a considerable range of medieval learning, *i.e.*, the religious learning of the period, represented by the Latin of the liturgy, Scriptures, scriptural commentaries, sacred legends, and so on; a mind, moreover, sufficiently familiar not only with the area's geography and secular rivalries but also its ecclesiastical affairs and sensitivities to draw material for humorous thrusts from both sources; in short, a strategically placed cleric (or clerics), possessed of the motivation, literacy, and leisure to compose large-scale religious drama in elaborately patterned verse.

Taken together, these lines of inference converge upon an indicated time, place, and nurturing institution: time, the fourteenth century— probably its third quarter (see Fowler, *op. cit.,* p. 125); place, the town (borough) of Penryn, its outskirts now almost touching those of Falmouth to the southeast; institution, the former Collegiate Church of the Blessed Virgin Mary and St. Thomas of Canterbury at Glasney, the latter referring to the site of the college, now occupied by the houses, gardens, garages, and a playfield of twentieth-century Penryn. Beyond the borders of Cornwall today, Falmouth is, of course, better known than its smaller and older neighbor, Penryn. But in the Middle Ages, the reverse was the case. Thurstan Peter's estimate of the college's onetime prestige and influence is not an exaggeration. In the preface to his book-length study of the institution, *The History of Glasney Collegiate Church, Cornwall* (1903), Peter wrote:

> It was the foundation . . . of the Collegiate Church of Glasney, in 1265, that gave Penryn its chief importance, and made it a place known all over England, and, indeed, Europe. The following pages will show how men came hither from all parts, and how those who were connected with the college travelled to and from Rome and elsewhere on the Continent. For three hundred years Glasney was a favourite establishment of the bishops of Exeter, and many men of high standing in the Church held prebends therein. . . .

Glasney was a community of secular canons, and it is from the roster of those known to have been resident in the college during the middle years of its history, say 1350 to 1425, that students of the *Ordinalia* hope eventually to identify its author or authors; failing that, its reviser or revisers.

Prospects for the success of this endeavor are not, however, bright. Not only is there the preoccupation of medieval records with such solid matters as land, taxes, tithes, inheritance, rights, privileges, emoluments, crime, punishment, salvation, excommunication, and the like, to the exclusion of so insubstantial a concept as authorship but, further, Glasney College, like all other foundations of its kind in Britain, was suppressed by an Act of Parliament during the Reformation. Once terminated as an institution (*c.* 1549), even its stone fabric, massive and durable though it was, began to dissolve, until today, of Glasney's church, chapter house, refectory, dormitories, outbuildings, and encircling, towered walls, only a weathered fragment of masonry remains above ground, located a short distance from the point at which a brook that flows through the former college precincts now passes under St. Thomas Street on its way to the tidal waters of Penryn quay and harbor.

Of anything like a library no trace has survived, not even in comment so far discovered. Perhaps its contents were, in the natural course of things, lost; perhaps they were deliberately destroyed. The sole surviving contemporary Glasney record, the *Cartulary,* provides no useful clues.

Sources and Analogues

Tracing in detail the lines of influence among analogues and possible sources for the trilogy is beyond the scope of the present work. Certain probabilities should, nevertheless, be noted. The ultimate source supplying its narrative continuity as a whole and shaping the greater part of its episodes is, of course, the *Vulgate Bible* of Jerome. If the dramatist was a cleric, we can assume acquaintance as well with *Historia Scholastica* of Peter Comestor, which lends authority to such non-Scriptural events as the Infernal warning to Pilate's wife, the restoration of sight to Longius, and the inability of the soul of Judas to exit through lips whose kiss has betrayed Jesus; to these events should perhaps be added the Cornish trilogy's specification that the Holy Sepulchre was an alabaster sarcophagus rather than the rock-hewn chamber tomb of the New Testament (see note 3, *Resurrection of Our Lord).*

The various versions of the *Gospel of Nicodemus* (fourth century) supply details of Seth's quest for the Oil of Mercy, the origin of the Rood, and the Harrowing of Hell. However, for the first two of these themes a composite version, widely copied and translated on the Continent and in England, existed in the thirteenth-century *Legende* (see Meyer, in Bibliography), which presents the Seth legend in the developed form employed by the *Ordinalia,* including such embellishments as the indelible footprints left by Adam and Eve on their way into exile from Eden, Seth's visual report of the dry tree in the midst of the Garden, the serpent in the tree, the swaddled infant lodged high amid its bare boughs, and the three pips that Seth is directed to place in Adam's mouth, from which will rise, triple-stemmed, the Rood Tree. Jacobus de Voragine's *Legenda Aurea,* also of the thirteenth century, not only parallels much of the foregoing as found in *Origo Mundi* but also reinforces other extra-Biblical elements found in the balance of the cycle. Examples are the healing of Longius *(Passio)*, of Tiberius *(Resurrexio)*; and, again in the latter play, a linear calculation of the "great leap, which Christ made from earth to Heaven." Citing Rabbi Moses, Jacobus estimates the leap as equivalent to a human journey requiring 7,700 years at the rate of forty miles a day. The awestruck speech of Second Angel *(R.D. 2493-98)* exactly duplicates these figures.

Two extended vernacular works present close analogues to much of the Cornish cycle and may well have served as sources: *Cursor Mundi* and the *Northern Passion*. The former's full treatment of the combined Seth and Rood legends much resembles that of *Origo Mundi,* including the prophecy and martyrdom of Maximilla, while the poem goes beyond *Passio Christi* through the attention it devotes to the role of the Virgin Mary at the time of the Passion and after. *Cursor* omits the Death of Pilate, however, as does the slightly younger and less extensive *Northern Passion*. Recognized as a source for the York and Towneley cycles, the latter likewise parallels the Cornish trilogy at numerous points: the narrative order and detail of the Oil of Mercy and the Cross Tree, the episode of the smith's wife and the forging of the nails, the warning to Pilate's wife, and the healing of Longius.

Nevertheless, however much the matter of the *Ordinalia* may owe to any of the foregoing works, with the probable exception of the *Vulgate* they are rarely such as could be expected to have contributed directly to the composition of the cycle in terms, for example, of its stage directions, scenic chronology, dialogue, or, upon occasion, song. It is liturgy that becomes pertinent here. For an informed review of the liturgical aspect of the trilogy, the reader should consult Robert Longsworth, *The Cornish Ordinalia, Religion and Dramaturgy,* 1967.

Of the 89 episodes into which E. K. Chambers *(The Mediaeval Stage,* 1903, II, App. T) divides the story content of the *Ordinalia* and its cyclical English analogues (York, Towneley, Chester, *Ludus Coventriae),* the Cornish cycle shares somewhat less than half (36 episodes) with one or more of the others. Common to all five are such sequences as the Creation and Fall of Man, Cain and Abel, Treachery of Judas, Last Supper, Bearing of the Cross, Crucifixion, Descent from the Cross, Resurrection, and Ascension. The *Ordinalia* lacks

41 episodes found in one or another of the English cycles or in the later Cornish creation play, *Gwreans an Bys* (see below, *Staging*). *Gwreans* differs from *Origo Mundi* in dealing with the Fall of Lucifer (see note 2, *Beginning of the World*), Wanderings of Cain, his death at the hands of Lamech, and the translation of Enoch, while the English cycles treat the *Processus Prophetarum,* the parentage and early life of Jesus, the post-Ascension history of the Virgin Mary, Antichrist, and Doomsday, material omitted from the Cornish *Passio* and *Resurrexio*. In terms of the tabulation furnished by Chambers, the remaining 11 episodes are peculiar to the *Ordinalia*. They comprise Seth in Paradise and Death of Adam, David and the Rods, David and Bathsheba, Building of the Temple, Prophecy of Maximilla, Bridge over Cedron, Healing of Bartimaeus (by identity, not name), Cross Brought from Cedron, Release of Joseph and Nicodemus, Death of Pilate, and Veronica and Tiberius.

The Cycle as Drama

A conversion of the last paragraph's arithmetical values into rhetorical values would seem to reveal a principle of selectivity at work in the *Ordinalia* toward the inclusion of story material bearing upon theme and tone, and the exclusion even of Scriptural matter bearing upon sacred history merely for its own sake. On the whole, the episodes which are present in the English cycles but absent from the Cornish are oblique to the unifying concept of the Oil of Mercy and its instrumental symbol, the Rood. Again on the whole, the episodes which are not to be found in the Corpus Christi cycles, but whose presence is a distinguishing feature of the *Ordinalia,* are those, in *Origo Mundi,* which serve to anticipate the Passion; sustain the legend of the Rood (Cross Brought from Cedron) in *Passio Christi;* and, in *Resurrexio Domini,* give the final play, and reflexively the entire work, an extra measure of scope and reverberation. The sources of these qualities are the Death of Pilate and Christ's triumphal return to Heaven. The Death constitutes an innovation peculiar to the *Ordinalia* (see note 9, *Resurrection of Our Lord);* the triumphal return forms a coda to the traditional Ascension, a coda found in only one of the English cycles (Chester), where it is accorded nothing like so extended or powerful a dramatization as in the trilogy's ultimate and unique recognition scene.

To selectivity of story material may be added a sparing resort to extradramatic or semidramatic devices and a tempo that predominantly advances *en marche.* Except for the brief epilogue which concludes each play, the Cornish trilogy dispenses with the prefatory, expository, and homiletic agents made use of by two of the four surviving English cycles. In the misnamed *Ludus Coventriae* are three standard-bearers or heralds who alternate in delivering a general prologue (The Proclamation), a species of stanzaic table of contents covering 528 lines. The Chester plays employ both an expounder *(Expositor)* and an interpreter *(Contemplacio).* Between them these auxiliaries prefigure the action or comment upon it while in progress. Not only are there no such impersonal entities in the *Ordinalia,* but even the epilogues are assigned to working characters within their respective plays: King Solomon *(Origo Mundi),* Nicodemus *(Passio Christi),* and the emperor Tiberius *(Resurrexio Domini).* As for pace, aside from the low resistance offered by the *platea* of the Cornish round (see below, *Staging),* there is the fact that although the trilogy has an obviously didactic purpose, it neither slows nor suspends forward thrust in order to explicate or edify. Sermons are present, but they are implicit rather than explicit, a notably updated approach to message in so venerable a dramatic work.

The trilogy's departures from median tempo normally accompany a change of mode. Journeys, which in either Biblical or medieval times would actually have consumed weeks or months, are prone to giddy acceleration; that is to say, for the reader who, at best, must rely upon imagination to interpose the theatrical routine of a simulated journey across or possibly around the *platea.* As read, King David and his entourage ride their horses from Jerusalem to the Sinai Peninsula well within the time it takes the king to deliver a single speech *(O.M.* 1969-88). The messenger sent by Tiberius to Pilate returns to the emperor's presence between a pair of lines (see note 11, *Resurrection of Our Lord),* the first addressed to Veronica in Jerusalem, the second to the emperor in his palace at Rome *(R.D.* 1679-80).

Decelerations are commonly less spectacular but more artistic: loss of pace is balanced by a gain in dramatic effect. During the debate between the doctors of law before Herod in *Passio Christi* (1729-68), dialectical progress is substituted for spatial, while in the much expanded episode concerned either directly or indirectly with Thomas' doubt of the Resurrection *(R.D.* 893-1586), a gradual increase of tension takes the place of quickened movement. This extensive sequence, which has impressed some thoughtful readers as oppressively static and repetitious, reveals under closer examination the incremental structure and diction of what the twentieth century would recognize as a *progression d'effet.*

In drama, as in imaginative literature generally, a turn from discussion of action to that of character is widely held to involve no more than the shift from one face to the other of the selfsame coin. But since the Cornish trilogy's roster of speaking parts approaches two hundred (178 all told, including a small percentage of such carry-overs as Deus Pater and Lucifer), a full-scale analysis of characterization obviously cannot be undertaken here. Yet it should be noted that the cycle does not lack instances of dramatic portraiture which display individuality of profile or prove capable of the unexpected. The evidence begins to accumulate early in the first day's play and still occurs well along in that of the third day.

Genesis provides that after his expulsion from the Garden of Eden, Adam shall till the alien soil, earning his daily bread by the sweat of his brow. The Adam of *Origo Mundi* complies, but not until he has demonstrated the hardihood to bargain with Deus Pater for what he, Adam, considers an adequate allowance of acreage and has shown himself enough the persistent wheedler to enlarge his holdings from a spade's length until they embrace the entire arable world. Similarly, Adam's sons, Cain and Abel, are seen to do and suffer those things, and only those things, ordained for them by sacred history; at the same time, however, the Cornish playwright endows them with appropriately contrasted psychologies, whereby Cain is motivated, to begin with, by being too good to be true, while Abel ends through having been too guileless to have been false—nor does he stoop to suspicion of his brother despite his sensitive foreboding (in narrative terms, foreshadowing) of disaster to come.

The episode of Jesus before Herod in *Passio Christi* contains the first phase of a disputation between the two doctors of law (see above) who have accompanied Caiaphas on his mission to Herod's court. Their suavely punctilious exchanges, which are resumed at the second trial before Pilate, constitute an example of character-drawing through dialogue unaided by traditionally prescribed action. Identified simply as First Doctor and Second Doctor, they could easily be dismissed as no more than interchangeable mouthpieces of articulate pedantry. They are, nevertheless, clearly differentiated, although not merely because each clings to his point of view as the ground of contention shifts from the nature of the Hypostatic Union, Christ as both God and man, to the rights of an accused who has failed to testify in his own behalf. Before the *débat* is over, First Doctor has revealed the courage, breadth of mind, and humanity of spirit so often required of those who advocate an unpopular cause. Short on these heroic qualities, Second Doctor shows himself to be more the anti-hero: cautious, narrowly legalistic, herd-minded, smug.

Of the 639 lines in *Resurrexio Domini* concerned with the Incredulity of Thomas, 432 lines present him in direct conflict with Mary Magdalene, his fellow disciples, and Cleophas, who has met and recognized the Risen Christ on the road to Emmaus. This conflict, embodied in a series of confrontations, subjects Thomas to grueling psychological strain, an assay of character under prolonged and mounting pressure (see above). The result is a progressive revelation, not of a monochromatic figure, a "humour," but a human being at war with himself as well as with others.

As drawn by the playwright, Thomas has a skeptical mind but a compassionate heart. At first, the head predominates; he asks for facts, holding his feelings in abeyance. The core of his doubt is rational: lack of evidence. Little by little we learn what kind of evidence he demands. He rejects Mary Magdalene's eyewitness story because, to him, it is preposterous; because she has been a sinner, a great sinner who can hardly enjoy the Master's confidence; and, by implication, simply because she is a woman. He turns aside the arguments of the other disciples on the ground that their case is too abstract, or too theoretical, an attempt to substitute their wishful thinking for the direct evidence of his own eyes, which saw the "numberless mass of wounds," the thorns pressed through the skull into the brain, the spear-thrust to the heart.

Having resisted, twice around, the witness, reasonings, exhortations, denunciations, and outright threats of Mary Magdalene and the ten disciples, Thomas rebuffs Cleophas and his companion with a variation of the classic *argumentum ad hominem* earlier employed against Mary Magdalene. She had been a scarlet woman; they are itinerant rogues. The ultimate Thomas, who even in extremity will yield to no evidence other than the visible confirmed by the tangible, is, of course, a new Testament prototype. But the other Thomas—warm, excitable, suspicious, stubborn, combative, self-respecting, and plainspoken—belongs to the Cornish drama.

The same proprietorship extends to such non-Scriptural characters as King David's butler, the crozier-bearer to Caiaphas, and the jailor's boy. They are compact, efficient miniatures. Within less than half a dozen speeches, the king's butler reveals himself as the true snob, obsequious toward superiors and condescending toward inferiors. The crozier-bearer is a bland opportunist, quick to exploit official position as a means of lining his pockets, even with blood money. After Judas has given back the thirty pieces of silver and hanged himself, the crozier-bearer sees his chance and sells to Caiaphas a "good-sized piece of open land" (Cornish *goon vras* 'large down') as a burying ground for Christians; cost—thirty pieces of silver.

The jailor's boy comes through to the modern reader as a typical adolescent: rebellious, boastful, stubborn, loudmouthed, a cynic on the surface, an idealist under the skin, who seeks to bolster his insecurity with bursts of man-of-the-world language. In *Passio,* he proves hard to drive but easy to lead by means of an appeal to his better self. Appearing again in *Resurrexio* under the same nickname, Lashbutt (see note 12, *Resurrection of Our Lord),* with its past aura of whipping boy, its contemporary guise of the scapegoat, he remains adolescent. But he is now less the comic and more the youthful, impressionable witness at first hand of the horrors which abruptly invade the Death of Pilate interlude.

The presence of foreign languages in the dialogue of the *Ordinalia* makes its contribution to character-drawing also. The reference here is not, of course, to single words of a derivation other than Cornish—for those would occur without consciousness of their origin—but to units of a phrase or more composed of Latin, French, or Middle English. Although French was the courtly tongue of medieval England and functions as such in the Chester cycle, Middle Cornish takes precedence in the *Ordinalia,* where Deus Pater speaks nothing else, on station and in the *platea* a Britonic deity. French is usually reserved to the utterances of such lesser persons as King David's butler (see above) or else to such notorious pagans as Caiaphas, Pilate, and the Hebrew 'bishop' who orders the martyrdom of Maximilla. Exceptions to the rule, although of a very low order of incidence, are Joseph of Arimathea and Tiberius Caesar.

Latin colors the speech of the Old Testament patriarchs, Adam and Moses, and likewise adds a suitably clerkish flavor to the character of David, by tradition a psalmist as well as lover, warrior, and king. To these may be added the devout Cleophas of the *Resurrexio* and the supreme figure of the trilogy as a whole, Jesus of Nazareth.

The combined incidence of Latin and French is, however, far smaller than that of Middle English which, while thinly spread, is ubiquitous. In broad terms, English introduces the common touch. First spoken by the Devil as he tempts Eve in the Garden of Eden, its tags help to qualify the status of a long procession of messengers, artisans, soldiers, and torturers. It is frequently the language of exclamation, invective, and oath, through these modes reinforcing the mixed identity of a second roster of characters, whose social level ranges from high to highest, but whose speech lapses upon occasion into the foreign accents of English. These lordlings with feet of non-Celtic clay include not only Caiaphas and Prince Annas but also Pharaoh, Solomon, and Herod, crowned heads all three. Even Tiberius, by author fiat a convert to Christianity (see note 10, *Resurrection of Our Lord*), proves capable of employing a few English phrases, either exclamatory or imperative. Perhaps context is a resolving factor in the emperor's case, since in two of three instances he addresses underlings, the jailor *(R.D.* 2057) and the torturers *(R.D.* 2144). Perhaps it should also be borne in mind that the Death of Pilate, the episode containing the lines cited, may represent a comparatively late addition to *Resurrexio Domini,* itself not necessarily as old as either of its companion plays.

Advancing time may thus have done something to soften the impact of English on Cornish ears, since we have the presence in *Resurrexio* of the lament sung by the three Marys on Easter morning. The melody of their song has been lost, but the lyric text endures as a rhymed couplet in Middle English (see note 5, *Resurrection of Our Lord*).

Cornish Amphitheatres

There is documentary evidence that the Cornish mystery plays, unlike their English counterparts, which are generally thought to have been mounted on wheeled platforms or pageant-wagons, were staged in fixed earthworks familiarly known as 'rounds.' Nance (see below, *Editors and Translators*) held that the *Ordinalia* was repeatedly produced at Penryn, under the auspices of Glasney College, if not within

its close. To accommodate this view, he assumed that the Penryn
round was constructed of wood, no trace of which could be expected
to survive the passage of time as have Cornwall's two most representative examples, the one on high ground in Perranzabuloe, the other
adjacent to the town square at St. Just-in-Penwith (see note 13,
Christ's Passion).

Both these rounds are earthworks, erected on a level site and
originally encircled by a trench. The outer wall, rising from the
trench, remains more or less perpendicular and is topped by a rampart.
The inner wall, which was formerly terraced to form tiers of steps for
spectators, slopes down on all sides to the circular stage area: in
Cornish, *plen;* in the Latin of the cycle's stage directions, *platea;* in
English, plain. Several localities in Cornwall still bear the name
Playing-Place (Cornish equivalent, *Plen-an-Guary*) although the round
is gone and the source of the name a matter for antiquarians only.

Of the two rounds under discussion, Perran is the larger, by far the
better preserved, and very much the more impressive, due to the
lonely grandeur of its setting, isolated from human habitation.
As of 1934, the drop-off from the rampart to the bottom of the trench
—a surviving feature at Perran Round—was at least 12 feet, and the
plain measured nearly 130 feet in diameter, affording a stage area
in excess of 13,000 square feet. As recently as 1906, the indented
profile of what had once been seven or eight tiers of earthen steps,
faced with sod, could still be discerned, an arrangement estimated
to have provided standing room for approximately 2,000 persons. A
pair of openings through the bank are still located opposite each
other on the north and south sides.

The basic plan of St. Just Round duplicates that of Perran, and
their respective measurements are, or at least were, comparable. The
plain at St. Just has a diameter of 126 feet. The maximum height of
the outer wall is 7 feet, while before the trench was obliterated, the
total exterior height is said to have approached 10 feet. Today, houses
abut the perimeter at various points along three sides; a modern
wall forms a tangent with the remaining side, beyond which flows
the traffic of the town square. At one time or another, the area has
been a refuse dump, an informal children's playground, and a short-
cut for pedestrians. While continuing to serve the latter purpose, it
has now become a car park. The stone facings of the outer wall and
inner tiers, which were once a distinguishing feature of the St. Just

Round and might have been expected to give it added permanence, have long since disappeared through gradual appropriation for other, including private, uses.

Staging

A limited idea of how the *Ordinalia* was staged can be deduced from three principal sources of data: the standard configuration of the round; the stage directions supplied in relative abundance by Bodley 791, occasionally supplemented by the lines themselves; and the presence in the MS of schematic drawings, one for each play, which locate on a circle the positions or stations assigned to the regions of Heaven and Hell and to a few leading characters. The diagrams regularly locate Heaven in the east, Hell in the north, good characters to the south and west, evil characters on the flanks of Avernus to the northwest and northeast. The plan for *Origo Mundi* places Abraham, Solomon, and David (surprisingly, the pagan bishop also) at symbolically benign points of the compass toward south and west, Pharaoh and the Torturers toward the malign north ("Evil appeareth out of the north." *Jeremiah* 6:1). If these positions are related to the orientation of a medieval Cornish church, Heaven corresponds to the sanctuary at the east end; Hell to the north side; Abraham's station to the south side and porch; while King David has his home (the *domus* of the stage directions) at the equivalent of the west or tower end.

The stage directions reveal that the action of the trilogy had a vertical as well as a horizontal dimension. At a minimum, the vertical movement involved two levels, the one consisting of the *platea,* the other first indicated by the cycle's initial rubric, which provides in the following words that God the Father shall come down from Heaven to the plain: *Hic descendit Deus de pulpito,* 'Here God comes down from the platform.' Meaning in classical Latin not only platform or rostrum but also "the boards" of a theatre (Ovid), *pulpitum* came to signify during the Middle Ages both a pulpit and the gallery, itself a species of pulpit, running along the upper part of a chancel or rood screen. This gallery, known as the rood loft, served to separate nave from chancel, support the rood—large crucifix—itself, and afford an elevated position from which the officiating deacon read a portion of the service.

Assuming, as does Richard Southern in his study, *The Medieval Theatre in the Round* (see especially Ch. 11), that the other fixed stations were distributed along the circular rampart to the right and left of Heaven and at essentially the same level—though the rubrics of the *Ordinalia* are not specific as to these particulars—only two levels, rampart and plain, are incontestably assignable to the staging of the cycle. In order to postulate more than two, it is necessary to invoke again the symbolic analogy between a round and a parish church, whereby some critics have thought to increase the number of hypothetic working levels to three or even four. The full quota is then seen to match amphitheatre and church, level for level, after this fashion: *platea* and nave, lower platform and chancel, median platform and sanctuary, upper platform and rood loft.

Meanwhile the capacity of the horizontal dimension (the *platea*) to meet the demands of action in space and time, as if the plain could become the world in little, appears to have been due to nothing more conjectural than the inherent properties of a circular area. What must have been these capacities was borne in upon the present writer when he witnessed, during the summer of 1965 in Cornwall, an extremely rare event: a performance of native, traditional drama in the St. Just Round. The program consisted of the St. Sylvester and the Dragon episode from *Beunans Meriasek* (The Life of Meriasek), followed by Noah's Flood from *Gwreans an Bys* (Creation of the World).

The actors were primary and secondary school pupils, the scenery was confined to a raised platform for God the Father in *Gwreans,* and Deus Pater was impersonated by a teen-aged girl in white robes (who spoke from the demonic north rather than the angelic east, incidentally); yet both playlets were essentially viable. The action gathered and dissolved, and the lines (in English translation) were readily audible through the open air to the encircling audience, whose slight elevation above the arena was enough to aid perspective and encourage dramatic illusion. Regardless of what this small-scale revival may have lacked or did not attempt, the excerpts wanted neither pattern nor momentum, and the spectator came away persuaded that it was the circular stage, more than any other single factor, which both contained and sustained the plays and their players within its protean reaches.

Concrete evidence as to either the nature or amount of scenery employed by the Cornish cycle is meagre. At a minimum, however, there were the fixed stations and such token items as the Garden of Eden *(Origo Mundi)*, the Temple of Jerusalem *(Passio Christi)*, and the Holy Sepulchre *(Passio Christi* and *Resurrexio Domini)*. Henry Jenner ("The Cornish Drama," *The Celtic Review*, III: 369) speaks of "mountains, practical ones," but Southern appears to have rather the better of it when he argues for a cleared segment of the rampart as the setting for the opening of *Passio,* where the stage direction reads: *hic stat jhesus in monte quarentana videlicet in deserto inter jericho et jerusalem,* 'Here Jesus stands on the Mount of the Forty Days Fast, namely, in the desert between Jericho and Jerusalem.' Southern (p. 131) visualizes the solitary figure of the Christ outlined against the sky, the disciples grouped below on the steps of the inner slope temporarily free of spectators. As an example of powerful effect achieved by simple means, it is one of those happy inspirations which ought to have come to a medieval director whether or not it ever did.

Given the strong probability that the fixed stations were raised above the level of the *platea* and were established at various points of the compass around and partially on the rampart, what may have been their general design and appearance? The language of the stage directions refers to them as platforms *(pulpita)* and tents *(tenti),* occasionally also as houses or homes *(domus).* These labels combine to suggest some kind of tented, wooden platform or scaffold, its floor projecting inward from the rampart, the overhang supported on stilts. This purely verbal image derived from the rubrics receives a certain amount of pictorial confirmation, not through sources in Cornwall or elsewhere in Britain but from the well-known fifteenth-century miniature by Jean Fouquet in a French book of hours, *Le Livre d'heures d'Étienne Chevalier* (reproduced by Southern, plates 2, 3, 4). Depicting the martyrdom of St. Apollonia, the miniature presents half a dozen scaffolds, including one each for musicians and titled spectators, huddled close together in an apparent semi-circle. They differ as to details but are alike in their resemblance to a modern display booth curtained off on three sides and topped by a canopy with ornamental valance. Except for the consideration that the eight designated stations common to all three plays of the *Ordinalia* would almost certainly have been situated much farther apart (the perimeter of a round like Perran when measured along the inside circumference of the rampart exceeds 400 feet, permitting an average interval between stations of approximately 50 feet), the Cornish platforms could plausibly have resembled the French scaffolds. The chances in favor of resemblance are increased by the cultural ties between Britain and France during the Middle Ages.

The miniature provides a ladder for access to the king's scaffold, a cleated incline for that of Heaven. The shallow steps cut into the slope of a Cornish round (one-foot risers at St. Just in former times) should have met much of the need here. Southern estimates the floors of the scaffolds pictured by Fouquet as having been about eight feet square, an area roomy enough, assuming that the Cornish stations were at least equal to the French in linear dimensions, to permit a major character in the trilogy not only to have a quota of attendants about him on his tented platform but also to make an 'entrance' in conformity with the routine stage direction, *hic pompabit*, 'Here he shall parade' or 'walk about.' However much or little action is read into the words—at most the character could take no more than a few steps back and forth across the front of his platform—it must be borne in mind that an entrance of this nature normally took place on the level of the assigned station before, and not after, descent to the *platea*. The stage directions are explicit in this regard, thus affording the actor his moment of undivided audience attention as the spectators raise their eyes to where he stands on view in an elevated frame.

The scenic effects of the *Ordinalia* were not, of course, limited to those associated with the rampart. The *platea* undoubtedly accommodated its share. In the later analogue to *Origo Mundi*, Jordan's Creation Play *(Gwreans an Bys)*, the stage directions of which are in English, terrestrial Paradise is described as being "fynelye made wyth ii fayre trees in yt and an apell upon the tree and som other frute one the other" and "a fountaine in Paradice and fyne flowers in yt painted." The lines of *Origo Mundi* detail the progress made by King David, who begins what later becomes Solomon's Temple, and they carry its building forward to completion under Solomon, who comes down from his southern rampart station to be crowned and promptly thereafter to oversee the renewed work on the temple. It has been conjectured by Eleanor Prosser *(Drama and Religion in the English Mystery Plays,* p. 49) that this set piece was held over to serve as the Temple of Jerusalem in the second day's play, *Passio Christi*. A similar provision may have applied to the Holy Sepulchre, which figures at the close of *Passio* and again near the beginning of *Resur-rexio Domini.*

Further instances of what seems to have been fixed, simultaneous staging located in the *platea* are these: the prison where Pilate confines Jesus before the trial in *Passio (et tunc intrabit in carcerem pilatus solus et dicit ad ihesum,* 'And then Pilate shall go into the prison alone, and he says to Jesus'); near the prison house, a courtyard where Jesus is chained to a stake and scourged *(hic paratur flagellum per tortores et postis ad ligandum Jhm,* 'Here a whip is got ready by the torturers and a stake to bind Jesus'); and opening onto the court-yard, the doorway of the council chamber or court of justice *(et tunc vertit ad jhesum in ostio pretorii et dicit ei,* 'And then he [Pilate] turns to Jesus in the doorway of the court *[praetorium, pretorium],* and he says to him'). These examples do not, of course, exhaust the possibilities.

The internal evidence for stage properties is as comprehensive as it is restricted with regard to costumes. Properties range from Eve's apple to Pharaoh's horses (the latter would be entirely feasible on the plain of a large round), from Noah's shipbuilding tools to the iron chest which receives the corpse of Pilate and the small boat which carries it seaward. Contrastingly, the cycle specifies wardrobe at only a few points. When Solomon names his keeper of the privy seal as guardian and overseer of the temple, the newly created 'bishop' assumes his vestments *(hic consultor induit vestimentum clericum,* 'Here the counselor puts on clerical robes') and is handed his mitre *(hic dat mitram episcopo,* 'Here he [Solomon] gives the mitre to the bishop'). At the conclusion of the abortive hearing before Herod, the king ironically bestows upon Jesus a short, outer coat of fine satin, presumably of the kind worn over armor in the Middle Ages *(hic paratur tunica alba propter ihesum,* 'Here a white garment is made ready for Jesus'), which is later replaced by a purple robe at the hands of the torturers *(denudatur alba et paratur purpura,* 'He is stripped of the white robe, and a purple one is got ready'). The cycle ends with Christ's triumphal entry into Heaven clad in garments "red as blood." The comparison is emphasized in successive speeches from among the nine angels, commencing with the first, who asks: "Who may it be that in the perfection of his manhood and clothed in red has come so swiftly to the kingdom?" To which Christ answers, "Red is mine by right. . . ."

Presumptive allusions to the red garment of the *Resurrexio,* together with the purple robe worn by Jesus for a time in the *Passio* and the yellow and blue motley which appears to have been assumed by the four torturers who figure throughout the *Ordinalia,* are to be found in a pair of sixteenth-century documents. These are inventories of church goods taken at Bodmin, Cornwall (see Lawrence S. Snell, *Documents Towards a History of the Reformation in Cornwall, No. 2,* Exeter [1955], pp. 29-32). The earlier of the two inventories, 31 Henry VIII (1539), names two Jesus coats, one of them purple ("It. one Jesus cotte of purpell sarcenett,"), and four torturers' costumes ("It. 4 tormenteris cotes . . . made of a sewt of vestyments for goode frydayes"). The later inventory, 8 Elizabeth (1566), enumerates three Jesus coats, two of red worsted and one of red buckram, followed by three torturers' coats of yellow and blue satin and two devils' coats, of which one is new ("toe develes cotes wherof one ys newe").

Editors and Translators

During the 1690's, John Keigwyn, a Cornishman encouraged by Bishop Trelawney of Exeter and the antiquarian John Anstis, made a full transcription of Bodley 791 and an almost complete translation of it. Keigwyn is known to have brought to his task a considerable working knowledge of late seventeenth-century Cornish, but by this comparatively late date in the history of the language, a significant body of Middle Cornish vocabulary and syntax was lost to him, and he lacked the study materials through which to recover what had by then become obsolete. As a result of these handicaps, plus the difficulty he experienced in deciphering the medieval script of the manuscript, Keigwyn's transcription is far from accurate even by the standards of his own day, while his rendering of it into English is sometimes scarcely intelligible. That he was accustomed to proceed with translation not only word by word in total disregard of English syntax and idiom but also sought to reproduce the scribal pattern of the original is illustrated by the following excerpt from his rendering of *Origo Mundi* (597-605). God the Father is speaking to Cain:

Cain not shall it be soe } he shall find it seven times as much
for thee kill man if he shall }
of ye pains in ye earth world if remarkable hurt any be done thee
for all to be warrned I will in ye world man none not to kill
every hour work good happy world as many as doe it.

In a letter dated July 26, 1703, Edward Lluyd, a not inconsiderable Celticist for his time, says of Keigwyn's work: "As for the old MS, I find that Keigwyn, when he transcribed it, altered it as he pleased where he did not like it, or understand it, and then translated it; on which account his translation does but sometimes agree with the old copy." (MS Tonkin B, 197, Truro Museum).

A century and a half later than Keigwyn, Edwin Norris published *The Ancient Cornish Drama* (Oxford, 1859), a substantial and scholarly edition of the *Ordinalia* in two volumes. Although Norris made no claim to being a Celticist, he worked directly with Bodley 791 and was, moreover, an accomplished linguist. The accuracy of his Cornish text benefited, as acknowledged in his preface (p. viii), from the independent labors of Theodore Aufrecht, who, he testifies, "collated every line with the original manuscript." As for the English translation which Norris placed opposite the Cornish, it represents a very great advance over that of Keigwyn, as to both accuracy and intelligibility. On the whole, however, the like cannot be claimed for its readability, despite the fact that for upwards of a hundred years it has been the only complete version of the trilogy in English to have reached publication. By default, therefore, it has become a species of authorized version, in terms of which the literary quality of the cycle has been judged by subsequent generations and, not surprisingly, found wanting.

Norris' rather indifferent results as a translator are attributable to several factors. For one thing, his prime concern was linguistic; he sought to preserve the *Ordinalia* as constituting, in his own words (Preface, p. v), "the most important relic known to exist of the Celtic dialect once spoken in Cornwall." It appears, moreover, that preservation of the language was not merely his prime but his exclusive concern: "The object of the Editor in undertaking this work was simply to preserve from obscurity and possible destruction the most considerable relic of the language, existing in a single manuscript, which has not been consulted for perhaps a century, or since the language has ceased to be spoken in the more remote districts of the county." (*Ibid.*, pp. v-vi). And finally, when reporting on his method of translation, Norris wrote (*Ibid.*, p. vii):

> In preparing the manuscript for the press the Editor translated each line as he transcribed it; and finding the result to be better than he anticipated, he thought it might add to the interest of the

publication to print his version opposite the text. He made the translation like a school exercise, word for word, without attending in any way to English idiom; and he has printed it as he made it, only correcting mistakes of the earlier portions, by the help of the increased knowledge acquired as he went on with his work, and altering the diction here and there, where it was absolutely necessary to do so, if he would be understood. . . .

If the diction and phrasing of the Norris translation were less consistent than they are, less monochromatic, the comparison of a single stanza as rendered by Keigwyn (quoted above) and Norris would be pointless as well as unjust. But since, on the whole, both translators are notably self-consistent, what each is seen to have made of God the Father's final words to Cain in *Origo Mundi* can be viewed as representative of how greatly Norris improved upon the work of his predecessor while simultaneously suggesting the expressive potential of the drama which Norris chose to ignore. His version of the lines in question reads:

GOD THE FATHER

Cain, it shall not be so;
For if a man do kill thee,
   He shall get it seven times as much
Of pains on the face of this world,
   If any evil is done thee;

For I will mark thee
   In the world, that no man slay thee.
Always good works.
   Happy as many as do them.

No account of the editors and translators of the *Ordinalia* could afford to overlook the contribution made to it by the late R. Morton Nance (d. 1959), even though that contribution is, in a sense, oblique. Nance was a man of varied attainments: painter, masterly ship-model maker, dedicated student of the Cornish language and leader of the movement concerned with its revival in modified form. He was also a Cornish patriot, who became something of a county-wide institution during the later years of a long, influential life. It should be made clear that special circumstances surround his version of the trilogy, for the most part remaining as yet unpublished among the bulk of his papers entrusted to the care of The Royal Institution of Cornwall at

Truro. Although Nance possessed a photostat of Bodley 791, he appears to have employed it chiefly as a control against which, unlike either Keigwyn or Norris, he carried forward the development of new or Unified Cornish. It was his wish, moreover, that his parallel English translation be treated as inseparable from the simplified Cornish text to which it might serve as a learner's key.

Thus Nance produced not another transcription of the original, which had been the paramount aim of Keigwyn and Norris, but a systematic modification of the Middle Cornish text on linguistic principles of his own devising. Once again the Cornish language was the *raison d'être* of the undertaking, howbeit this time in terms of renovation rather than preservation, to the end that the old tongue might experience a revival and become a rallying-point, a renewed focus of ethnic and cultural identity. As for the accompanying translation, the more literal it could be kept, the greater its practical usefulness. Like that of Norris, Nance's translation proceeds line for line, with a similar, although not necessarily equivalent, loss of naturalness, flexibility, and idiomatic vigor. Nevertheless, Nance unquestionably succeeded in reducing the number of cruxes outstanding before he took the text in hand, and he left a more nearly readable version of the cycle in English than he had found because, while he is almost as literal as Norris, his gait is not so crabbed, and he confronts the occasional earthy passages with considerably greater candor.

The remaining work to be mentioned is that of Phyllis Pier Harris, who has in progress a new edition of the *Ordinalia,* of which the initial unit, *Origo Mundi, A New Edition,* is already available on microfilm (Ann Arbor, 1964). Her pilot project, a doctoral thesis, consists of a diplomatic text of the first play of Bodley 791, a literal translation, notes, and glossary, the whole preceded by an introduction oriented to both literary and linguistic considerations. When completed, the new edition, first of its kind to be undertaken since that of Norris a century ago, should make a valuable contribution to the study of the dramatic literature of medieval Britain and to the history of the Cornish language.

A Note on the Present Translation

The work which follows marks the fourth attempt to translate the entire *Ordinalia* into English, the first attempt to render it into modern prose (see F. E. Halliday, *The Legend of the Rood,* published in 1955, for a rendering in verse of thematic excerpts from the cycle). The aim of the present undertaking has been twofold: without loss of strict responsibility to the substance of the original, to replace Cornish-influenced idioms, syntax, and rhetoric by those native to English; to achieve, insofar as possible, a more various and responsive discrimination among levels of diction and tone than is to be found in former, literal renderings.

From the moment the choice was made not to follow earlier versions in forcing English to comply line by line and sometimes word for word with the Cornish, certain advantages were, of course, bound to accrue. Rigidity and awkwardness of phrase and clause, arbitrary ordering of sentences within a given stanza, were still only too possible but at least were no longer inevitable, once their alien mold was broken. And if a corresponding enhancement of clarity and naturalness, of emphasis, fluidity, and cadence has failed to materialize, the blame lies with the maker rather than the medium. Such gains are, however, to be looked for in a passable translation of any literary work.

In the case of the *Ordinalia,* there is a further obligation posed by its identity. It flourished as theatre and survives as drama, a genre in which the written word alone must assume the expressive burden otherwise shared by physical presence and action, speech, costume, setting, and the rest; the rest, where the Cornish trilogy is involved, including spectacle and music. As read in translation, therefore, the many-voiced dialogue of the cycle, if it is not to remain almost insupportably blunted and featureless, needs stylistic profile, textural recognition of the fact that its lengthy roster of speaking parts and procession of scenes quite literally runs the gamut from the ever sublime to the occasionally ridiculous.

Yet at this point the question arises as to whether it is possible to distinguish levels of style in the original language, whose spontaneous oral use died out in the eighteenth century and whose written remains are severely limited; and whether the dramatist himself left any traces of purposeful manipulation for the sake of defining character or controlling tone. There is evidence to show that he did.

One item of this evidence, located in the Cornish text itself, consists of foreign language interpolations (see above, *The Cycle as Drama*). As has been suggested earlier, there is a correlation throughout the trilogy between character status and language. This is not to imply that the present state of knowledge permits the dictation of a rigidly established order of precedence among the languages composing a hierarchy but merely that a hierarchy is perceptible. It seems likely that Cornish ranked first and English last on a parochial scale of values where the ethnic and the geographical were operative factors. Latin, with its liturgical echoes, presumably stood higher than French, whose flavor in the remote, separatist climate of Cornwall may well have been the ironic reverse of authoritarian and courtly. The incidence of these foreign tongues is not high, but the conclusion that their presence is no accident and that it points toward the linguistic delineation of character appears justified.

The credit for first recording the awareness of another means by which the Cornish text indicates levels of style goes to Norris. In the appendix to the second volume of *The Ancient Cornish Drama,* he analyzes the variations of stanza form encountered in the manuscript. Having established that the typical line is composed of seven syllables, the typical stanza of either six or eight lines, the latter predominating, he observes (Vol. II, p. 450): "All this is for the ordinary dialogue. The other varieties are used chiefly in declamatory or lyrical passages, and it is felt at once that we are on different ground." In her turn, Phyllis Harris (*op. cit.,* pp. 36-37) remarks:

> More notable as related to mood are his [the dramatist's] irregular stanzas. Some eight-verse stanzas are really extended six-verse ones, rhyming typically, *aaabaaab;* these serve largely for exclamatory, hortatory passages but also for moments of high emotion, as, for instance, when Abraham informs Isaac of the impending sacrifice and Isaac acquiesces, or when Abraham bursts out in gratitude at Isaac's reprieve. Some stanzas, six to ten verses long, have only four syllables to a line; these are usually the vehicle of rapid action. . . . Occasional stanzas of eight to eleven verses, of which some have only four syllables, tend to occur at key points, especially for opening or closing an episode; others, of six verses, have four syllables in verses three and six; these tend to be instructions, announcements, or exclamations, and hence point up, introduce, or report an action.

A broader index to the expressive range of the plays, registering the influence of situation as well as language, is the traditional element of humor. In one form or another it makes its appearance as early as the Serpent's cozening of Eve (*O.M.* 149-204), as late as Tulfric's obscenely jocular invitation to Beelzebub *(R.D.* 2355-57). Meanwhile, the varieties of comic effect introduced between these widely separated passages and the tonal spread involved make considerable demands upon a translator. A good deal of the verbal humor, entrusted for the most part to torturers, servants, and denizens of the underworld, is either simple and earthy or else openly sadistic, although there are also such exceptions to the straightforward as the undercurrent of sexual innuendo beneath the raillery of the smith's wife and the torturer *(P.C.* 2709-42) and, at a far remove in tone, the elaborately verbal thrust, parry, and counter-thrust of the doctors arguing before Herod *(Ibid.* 1729-68). At times, situation humor is broad and general, equally apparent, if not equally sure-fire, whether in the fourteenth or the twentieth century. The scene in which the jailor and his assistant, Lashbutt, go from dueling with words to dueling with swords *(Ibid.* 2253-2318) may be taken as an example. By contrast, there are ironies too narrow, too local ever to have survived export in their day and which must now, in consequence, be revived by means of a gloss; witness Solomon's ostensibly munificent inclusion, with his gift of Seal Rock, of the land, actually salt water, surrounding it (see note 23, *Beginning of the World).*

Ultimately, it is to scenes as dramatic units that the language of the present translation endeavors to be responsive. When the torturers converse among themselves while drawing lots for the seamless garment of the crucified Lord, their speech is rough and heedless, hence bitterly ironic under the circumstances. When Pilate tries to persuade Tiberius not to divest him of that same garment worn next his skin for its miraculous protective powers, his words are flatteringly adroit. Unlike the boastful and declamatory Herod Antipas of the York plays, for example, the Herod of the Cornish *Passio* neither brags nor raves, the little he does say being courteous, economical, and ironic. The rhetorical demands of such scenes as these and many more on the human level, plus even the gravely melodious discourse of Jesus during his earthly pilgrimage, can at least be undertaken if not mastered. But to follow the intrepid Cornish up the steep ascent to the kingdom of God the Father is a bold journey indeed. There, where the triumphant Christ imparts the story of the Redemption to the nine angels, one does what he can, heavy with the consciousness of all he cannot do.

I   BEGINNING OF THE WORLD

Principal Characters

in

Order of Appearance

God the Father	Japhet
Adam	Abraham
Eve	Isaac
Serpent	Gabriel
Cain	Moses
Abel	Pharaoh
Lucifer	Aaron
Satan	David
Beelzebub	Bathsheba
Seth	Uriah
Noah	Solomon
Shem	Bishop
Ham	Maximilla

Here Commences the Drama

of the

BEGINNING OF THE WORLD

GOD THE FATHER

I am God, the Father of Heaven, creator of all things that are made. One and three am I, in truth, the Father, the Son, and the Breath which is the Spirit, and this day, through my grace, I desire to begin the world, saying: earth and sky be they shaped to my intent.

Now since heaven is already made[1] and filled with the splendor of angels, I create the earth, no less nobly and royally, even as we are three persons in one God, our work according to our will.

Because that which I made on the first day seems to me good, on the second day I make the firmament, the sky. Let it be the roof over all things else, holding the rain on high, whence it may be sent forth to the earth.

On the third day, I make a separation between the sea and the land, and on the land I ordain the growth of plants and trees. The trees shall stand upright, bearing leaves and fruit and, against summer, the plants shall bring forth seed in gardens.

On the fourth day, let there be lights for the whole earth, namely, the sun, the moon, and the stars, each one a bright perfection. Above the trees, high in the midst of the heavens, I place the moon by night, by day the sun, that their light may shine.

On the fifth day, I will that there be created by my power beasts, fishes, and birds to fill both land and sea, for the time shall come when the earth will be the better because of them, whom I command to multiply and live long.

(Here God descends from the upper stage and says:[2])

Today is the sixth day since my work began. I have made the world,

3

sky, water, and land: lights, trees, beasts, and fishes. As far as in them lies, they shall be obedient to me. And now I create a son, man himself, creature of clay entire.

(Here God makes Adam and says:)

As I am three persons in one God, I make you, man of clay, after my own image. Into your body I breathe spirit in order that you may have life; and when you lose that life, to earth you shall return.

Adam, become flesh and blood and arise in meekness, fashioned as you are from dust. Yet also consider how like myself I have made you, head to foot, and that I give you dominion over all that are on land and in the sea. And you shall live until your head is whitened with years that you may bring children into the world.

As I am a gracious God, I bestow upon you, Adam, the guardianship of paradise, and I leave you to rule over all seed and fruit that may hereafter grow in it, except the fruit of the tree I have named the tree of knowledge, which alone I forbid to you. Honor this prohibition in remembrance of me.

But if you eat of the fruit I have named, you shall go forth an exile from this place, and a death which is death indeed shall be your portion.

ADAM

Praise without ceasing, O Father, Son, and Spirit holy, to your dear person! In fashioning me a creature of unblemished beauty, you have made me very like yourself and therefore able to order my own days and ways, a thing greatly to be desired, as is also my most fervent wish that you obtain for me a helpmeet.

GOD THE FATHER

Of a certainty it is not good that a man should be alone among his kind. Go, then, stretch yourself upon the earth, and sleep, not to rise until the work is accomplished.

(Adam shall sleep. God makes Eve and shall lead her to Adam, and he shall receive her at his hands, and God the Father says:)

Forthwith from one of your ribs I make for you a fellow to be your constant helper. Look upon her, Adam, and naming her, take her for your mate.

EVE

Lord and Father of Heaven, full of grace, may you be glorified forever! Exceedingly great has been your work in my behalf by which I am made after your likeness, O triune God!

ADAM

Father, you have brought to me, bone and flesh from my body, a fit companion. I will name her Virago. All honor to God, who bestowed her upon me for my benefit.

GOD THE FATHER

Direct your attention now, Adam, to the birds of heaven, to the animals both on land and in the sea, and to the fishes: give them their names. They will come at your command, but do not ever misuse them.

ADAM

I name cow and bull. I name horse, beast without equal as a help to men; also goat, hind, stag, sheep. In brief, let each kind take its right name.

Now I name goose and hen, which I consider peerless food-birds; duck, peacock, dove, partridge, swan, kite, crow, and eagle I name in addition.

I will likewise give names to the fishes: salmon, porpoise, conger, ling, cod, all shall obey me. And if I worship God perfectly, not a one shall escape from before me.

GOD THE FATHER

Inasmuch as the whole of my six days' labor of creation is found fair and good, I give it my blessing, and in order that this, the seventh day, may be hallowed, I proclaim it the day of rest for every man who shall be saved. As a token of this, moreover, I, too, shall rest.

(Then God the Father shall go to heaven, and afterwards the Devil, like a serpent, speaks to Eve from the tree of knowledge, and he says wickedly to Eve:)

SERPENT

Eve, why not come closer so we can talk? There's something I know which, if you knew it, would delight you. For sheer joy, you'd laugh and laugh and laugh. For all the world like a goddess, you'd ascend to heaven.

EVE

What thing? Tell me right now!

SERPENT

I can't, Eve. You'd give me away.

EVE

I may be only a woman, but you can tell me because nothing would ever make me betray you.

SERPENT

I've come down from heaven, no less, to better your situation, sweet Eve, and the point is this: don't ever hesitate to eat the fruit of the tree of knowledge.

EVE

Get out of here at once, and don't say another word! Nothing could be further from my mind, and besides my dear Lord has forbidden it.

SERPENT

There's where you're being mighty foolish, woman, in not believing what I say. All you'd have to do, you and your husband, to make yourselves like gods on the spot, would be to taste an apple from this tree. I'm not lying to you, Eve. Just step up and take it.

EVE

The one who made us, me and my husband, told us flatly we weren't to go near the tree, let alone eat any of the apples.

SERPENT

I know why he's like that about it. Seeing it's a tree which carries divine favor, anybody who eats its fruit will be able to understand the Father's eternal plan. There isn't anything in God's world such a person wouldn't be able to explain. The man's an utter fool who'd let slip that kind of fruit.

EVE

I'm almost out of my mind, trying to figure what to do about the apple, as much as anything because I'm afraid there might be some trick.

SERPENT

Let the risk be mine, then. Go ahead, pluck and have done, and include your husband while you're at it.

EVE

If I'm going to reach the branches, you'll have to bend them toward the ground.

SERPENT

All right, but no more quibbling. Pick a handful and be on your way.

(Eve shall take the fruit and carry it to Adam, and Eve says:)

EVE

Adam, put out your hand and take this. Now eat it, only quietly, without blowing your horn.[3]

ADAM

Suppose you tell me, you woman you, exactly where you got this fruit, in case it happens to be the forbidden kind.

EVE

While I wandered about, I heard an angel singing in a nearby tree. From above, he counselled me to gather fruit from it, fruit that should make us like gods, untroubled forever.

ADAM

You wicked woman, the devil take you for listening. That was no angel. It was a most evil bird which could easily mean our death unless we draw back in time. We must think of our last end and how it could be.

EVE

Oh, hush! It was an angel, I tell you, and he held forth to me about the tree and its power exactly as I've told you.

ADAM

I can't and won't believe you. Our prayer should be that we remain the Lord's servants. Forming us from the dust of the earth, he commanded us not to eat the fruit of the forbidden tree, ever.

EVE

Not to believe me is to lose me and my love. You'll never see me again as long as you live.

ADAM

Oh, Eve! Rather than set you against me, I will do anything you want me to do. Give me the apple. I'll eat it.

(And then he eats of the apple, and sees that he is naked, and says with a groan:)

Ah, woe, woe! I have sinned; I have broken God's law. Evil and graceless as you are, you have mindlessly deceived me. We are become naked and with leaves must cover ourselves. I see beyond all doubt that your woman's act has angered God, our Father.

(Adam hides himself in Paradise. Then God the Father shall come to Adam, and he says to him:)

GOD THE FATHER

Adam, Adam, what have you done and what is it you do now? Why don't you come to welcome me?

ADAM

Because I am naked, I went and hid myself from you.

GOD THE FATHER

What revealed to you your nakedness, unless it was the fruit you are not privileged to taste and yet go sinless?

ADAM

The woman you gave me for a wife, she is to blame, entirely to blame, for it was she who plucked the alluring apple and brought it to me to taste.

GOD THE FATHER

Because you have listened to her and, in listening, broken my commandment, I curse the earth in the name of your deed. From this time forward to the day of your death, you shall labor, in sweat and sorrow, among thorns and briars, in order that you may live.

(To Eve:)

Why, Eve, did you deceive your husband, with such folly plucking the apple after I had forbidden you to do it? You have sinned, and in causing him to taste of the fruit of the tree you have visited great affliction upon him.

(Here let the Devil be present.)

EVE

O Father, enlightened and beloved, I was deceived by the serpent. I believed its falsehood, and my greed has ruined me. The serpent said that if I plucked the fruit, I should become an immortal. If its words were evil words, cut it down with your sword.

GOD THE FATHER

Forasmuch as you have permitted yourself to be seduced by the serpent and have betrayed your faithful spouse, I ordain that a woman must always obey her husband and, made increasingly acquainted with suffering through her disobedience to my commandment, she shall ever bring forth her young in sore travail.

(God the Father speaks to the serpent.)

Answer me this, Devil. Why did you delude her without reason, why did you tempt her to taste the forbidden fruit?

SERPENT

I will tell you why. Every hour while he and she had such great joy, I burned. That is why I tempted them to sin, so that the burden of their song might be, like mine, "Alas! Alas!"

GOD THE FATHER

Above all the beasts that walk on the earth, you are accursed then, and your seed and her seed shall be enemies forever.

(God speaks to Adam and Eve. The Devil leaves.)

As for you twain, you may no longer abide here. You must depart forthwith, forfeiting my bliss which I gave to you in Paradise. Nor, Adam, can it avail you anything to attempt to excuse yourself by saying that our covenant was violated through your wife. Because you heeded her, a thousand mothers' sons shall be damned.

ADAM

God and Father, in your infinite enlightenment, hear my prayer. O grant to me, your handiwork, something of the oil of mercy.

GOD THE FATHER

Adam, at the end of the world I will grant the oil of mercy to you and to Eve, your wife.

(Then God the Father ascends to heaven and says to the cherubin:)

Take a sword, Cherubin, hasten to Paradise, and drive out the human couple you find there. Their lot and the lot of those who come after them, I shall make exceedingly hard. They will live to curse this day of their transgression.

CHERUBIN

I go at once to do your bidding. Any person I find in Paradise, I shall expel.

(The cherubin goes down.)

Adam, you are ordered to quit this region. You will proceed to another country and make a new life, you by tilling the soil, your wife by spinning and weaving. And because you have angered the Father, your penance will be both great and everlasting.

Make haste toward the portal, for here you may not remain.

(The cherubin remains in Paradise. Adam and Eve depart from Paradise.)

ADAM

Alas, that I should see the time when I made the Lord angry and when, acting contrary to his command, I lost my inheritance! Without clothes or shelter, I don't know where to go. My heart breaks for sorrow and homelessness.

With not a stitch to our backs, no roof over our heads, we shall all but perish from cold, astray amid terrors and parted far from the joy and pleasantness that were ours. In our wretchedness, we have no idea where to turn, whether to field or forest. In dire need of food, our bellies empty, we may starve.

Therefore, Eve, take the distaff, spin clothes for us, while with every ounce of my strength I start to work the soil.

(And he shall dig, and the earth cries out; and again he shall dig, and the earth cries out.)

I'm dumfounded! The earth won't even let me scratch the surface so I can raise a little grain. I've got such a crick in my back, I can hardly walk. Exalted Lord, I beg you, before it kills me, to let the land allow me to seek food in it.

(Here God the Father comes down.)

GOD THE FATHER

You have my permission, Adam, to cut the earth a full spade's length. Earth, I order you to open to Adam.

ADAM

O sire, omnipotent Lord, that's not very much, not for the two of us. My wife and I would eat the whole crop in a day.

GOD THE FATHER

Then take two spade lengths for you and your wife.

ADAM

It wouldn't be enough, Lord, if we have a child.

GOD THE FATHER

Since you have need of more, take three lengths of your spade one way and three breadths the other, but see to it that you do not cheat.

ADAM

My dear Lord, even though I make use of every last inch of an allotment of three spade lengths, it will be difficult to support myself, my wife, and the little one, and if more come, they will faint from hunger, having nothing with which to sustain themselves. Should that time ever come, bitter would be the tears I shed in my misery.

GOD THE FATHER

Very well, Adam, go and take possession of as much of the world as you desire. You will find that it serves you well, you and your descendants.

ADAM

Oh, thank you, Father of Heaven, may your precious person be glorified. Eve, the mastery of the world is mine!

EVE

We are fortunate, my husband, that our Father and sublime Lord has granted us his permission to delve and cultivate. As for me, I shall at once take my distaff and begin to make us clothes.

GOD THE FATHER

It was not good to have shaped man so nearly after my own image. As a result of listening to a woman, he has utterly lost the paradise which with my right hand I made for him, a place he could have kept had he not fallen from grace. But seeing that he disobeyed my commandment, grievous is my anger against him.

Adam, of all that you produce, you are to set aside a tenth share as an acknowledgment in kind of what I have done for you. Of your free will and without grudging, take it to Mount Tabor, there to burn it in honor of me.

ADAM

Be it done according to your will, Lord, and if you want me to sacrifice more than a tenth part, I shall burn it faithfully at your pleasure. For fullness of love and mercy, where is your equal in all the world? . . .

(Here God the Father shall pass to Heaven.)

And now, Cain and Abel my sons, go at once to the mountain and make your sacrifice to the Father of Heaven. Be sure that each of you offers his full tithe, burning it as God has enjoined.

CAIN

Dearly beloved father, I will, and may the Lord of Heaven grant his blessing upon all my future work. Abel, dear brother, let's get started on our way to worship the supreme Lord, as our father commands.

(Cain retires.)

ABEL

I will go to the mountain with you gladly, brother, very gladly. But before I go, my dear father, give me the fullness of your blessing, your benediction before I depart. It will please me very deeply to have it, yours and my mother's as well.

ADAM

You shall always have it, as much by night as by day, and may the world be yours and everything that's in it.

EVE

This is my prayer: a mother's blessing be ever upon you. Amen.

ABEL

And mine upon both of you in return. Happy is my lot, O God, for I am truly blessed.

(Then after the four benedictions, let Abel go to the altar, journey-ing in the platea, and Cain says:)

CAIN

What took you so long, Abel? When you're going to the sacrifice, you're supposed to be on time.

ABEL

Cain, it couldn't have taken more than a minute to get Father's blessing and Mother's.

CAIN

I swear we're a couple of fools to go out and burn something on which a man can live. So we take a tithe and reduce it to cinders on the rocks. Where does the honor to God come in?

ABEL

Think of your soul, dear Cain, and mindful of the Father, God of Heaven, perform his commandment. That way we can't possibly be sorry since it's surely his will that we burn it without fail.

CAIN

Get rid of that idea, Abel. I'll never do it. I'm thinking up a dodge instead, that will let me keep the ten percent for when summer comes.

ABEL

Have you gone mad? If you don't do as I say, it's my belief you're headed for the constant and dreadful torments of hell.

Through his boundless love and favor, God gave us nine parts out of ten to live on. Do we then grudge him the sacrifice of a tenth part since that's his wish?

(Here all shall come onto the platea. Let Cain offer a part of the tithes that he may retain the other part, and Cain says:)

CAIN

Speaking confidentially, I'm not going to offer my whole tithe, that's for sure. . . . O Father God, full of compassion, take, receive from Cain's hands the tithe, his offering, pure and complete.

(God does not accept it.)

Heed me, Lord! Look upon my sacrifice and accept my tithe, for if you do not accept it, I shall take it home with me again.

ABEL

O exalted God and Father, I worship you with all my heart and my strength. Here and now I lay before you the full tenth part, my true tithe, that it may be burned in honor of you.

GOD THE FATHER

Because Abel's sacrifice is a true tithe, he shall have at the last the joy that never fails and in my kingdom, rest.

CAIN

Since God chooses to disregard me and won't prosper anything I undertake, while everything Abel touches will thrive a thousand times better, little brother is going to pay for that!

ABEL

Let's go home, gentle brother, for my heart grows very heavy, whatever the reason. May the Father in heaven, who created me, shed his grace upon the offering I made. And when I quit this world, may he bring me to his kingdom in the next.

CAIN

Dear Abel, don't worry. With the Lord's help, all will be well. As you love me, lead on. . . . And now, by God, to make sure that you'll never know success, take this in the chaps!

(Then he shall strike him on the head, and he shall die, and Lucifer says:)

LUCIFER

Satan and Beelzebub, as you love me, your god, go at top speed and fetch the fellow home so that he can warble his "Alas!" in the utter dark forever.

SATAN

We'll be only too glad to bring him to you, Lord Lucifer, and that without delay. In requital for his father, Adam, he'll never get so much as a glimpse of precious light.

(They shall go to Abel.)

BEELZEBUB

Our pleasure is to take you at once to terrors and to pain. Like us, Abel, you're to inhabit the night, black, joyless, and endless, all your true tithe notwithstanding.

SATAN

Let's whisk him home with us to Lord Lucifer. I'll stick to the plainsong while you improvise the descant[4] above it.

BEELZEBUB

Hail, Lucifer, sire and lord! I have brought you the son of that deceiver, Adam, that he may dwell with us.

LUCIFER

Abel, in spite of that precious offering of yours, you're to settle down with us on a permanent basis, the snarling of numberless devils your hour by hour entertainment.

(Then God the Father shall come to the earth: he speaks with Cain, and God the Father says:)

GOD THE FATHER

Speak, Cain! Where is Abel, your brother and my loyal servant? Why is he not with you?

CAIN

You gave him to somebody to keep. Ask that somebody. Since when was I his keeper?

(A voice calls.)

GOD THE FATHER

Behold, the voice of your brother Abel's blood this moment calls upon me from the ground near and far. For what you have done, you and the earth you call yours are cursed in perpetuity.

My wrath and the wrath of my angels be upon you, and may your ground never come green nor bear good fruit to the end of the world.

CAIN

Lord, I hear your voice, but your face, to my sorrow, I cannot see. Only this much, wretched as I am, do I know: my sin is greater than God's mercy. Supremely among men, I am the empty one, the dispossessed, unable to say why he should not meet death at the hands of any man alive.

GOD THE FATHER

Not so, Cain, not for you. It shall be instead that if any man harms you in the slightest, much less presumes to kill you, he shall pay a sevenfold penalty, for I shall set my mark upon you in order that no man may take your life.[5]

(Here God ascends to heaven. Then Cain shall come to Adam his father, and Adam says:)

ADAM

Where has your brother gone, my son, and why hasn't he come home with you?

CAIN

If you're anxious about him, ask his keeper.

ADAM

By my faith, you have killed him, and he so precious to me! May you and your abominable deed be damned forever.

Ah, misery that I should ever have lost him, sweet Abel, my most dear son; that I was ever created to suffer a calamity the equal of this; that Cain was ever begotten! What a retribution has fallen upon me through a woman! Ever to have looked on Eve, that is my woe!

As God yet lives and rules, I'll never mate with Eve again.

EVE

Alas, to think that I listened so believingly to my enemy! Without a doubt, all this misfortune, both early and late, is enough to make me weep tears of blood. Merely to be alive is an affliction when you endure such a burden of grief! . . .

GOD THE FATHER

Seraph, go to Adam and charge him by my command to lie again with Eve his wife. The son born to him cannot fail to be good.

SERAPH

Lord, I shall do your bidding, as is everywhere incumbent upon me. I go to the world forthwith and to Adam, in order that I may advise him.

(And then he shall go to Adam, and he says to him:)

Adam, God the Father commands you to lie with your dear spouse, Eve, to have a child to serve you.

ADAM

Since the Father ordains it so, it is needful to do it, most needful. If God commands, what is done will, I trust, be for the best.

Come, Eve, my companion, and extend yourself at full length on the bed. Above all things, a command of God needs must be fulfilled, even though it's now been some two hundred years since I last had to do with your flesh.

EVE

When the Father of Heaven expresses a wish, it is necessary to conform, no matter what's involved. Through the favor of our sublime Lord, we'll beget a worthy child to be a help to us.

ADAM

In the name of God, let's hope it turns out that way. Lord, we beg you to favor us.

(And then let him go away from her a little while: and again he shall come to her.)

EVE

Adam, there's no hiding a thing that's destined to happen. I have a child, born by the will of the Father. I bless the time which brought us together again. What are we to name him? Tell me.

ADAM

The right name for him is Seth, and may God give him grace to serve. As for me, I'll go dig in order to keep us alive. To work is essential, absolutely essential.

(Here Adam shall go to his work, and here he sighs, saying:)

Dear God, how tired I am! What a stroke of good fortune if I could just catch one glimpse of the end of my labors! But the briars are strong. Their roots break my arms as I ceaselessly tug and tear.

I'll send my boy, Seth, to the gate of Paradise, to the cherubin who guards it. Seth can ask him whether in the end I shall have the oil of mercy from God, the gracious Father.

SETH

At your command, my dear father, I will go to the cherubin at once. But I don't understand what you want me to ask him, nor have I any idea of the route I should take.

ADAM

Say to him that I, being weary of life, entreat him to tell you the truth concerning the oil of mercy which was promised to me by the Father, in his compassion, at the time the angel drove me from Paradise with such relentless zeal. We were expelled together, your mother and I, and that speedily, for our foolish disobedience.

Follow the scorched trail made by my feet. Neither grass nor flowers of any kind grow in the road I walked when I and your mother came from that place. You'll note the tokens, and though you see a great radiance, don't be afraid. Nothing bad will happen to you.

SETH

I'll gladly see your errand through, dear father, and won't delay any longer, except to beg your blessing before I set out.

ADAM

My blessing ever goes with you, my son, and I pray that you will unfailingly accomplish your mission before you return.

SETH

Father, you have nothing to fear. I'm on my way this instant, asking God in his mercy to help us.

(And then he shall go to Paradise, and the cherubin says:)

CHERUBIN

What's the reason for so long a journey, Seth? Tell me straight.

SETH

Angel, I will. My father is old and weary, and since he has no wish to live longer than he already has, he implores you through me to reveal the truth in regard to the oil of mercy which was promised to him, come the end of the world.

CHERUBIN

Put your head in at the gate but make sure it's only your head, no matter what you may see. Look in every direction and carefully examine everything in sight.

SETH

I'm overjoyed to do so, considering myself indeed fortunate to have permission to learn what's there and tell my father.

(And he looks and turns around, saying:)

God in heaven, how lovely it is! How great the sorrow of him who lost it! But the one tree—I'm very much surprised to find it dry. Yet I suppose it's in that state, completely bare, because of the sin my father and mother committed. The tree and their footprints, both are as dry as ashes. Alas, that ever the morsel was eaten!

CHERUBIN

Ah, there you are, Seth. What did you see inside the gate of Paradise? Give me an account.

SETH

No tongue of man on earth could tell of all the beauty I saw and heard.

Luscious fruit and exquisite flowers, sweet song and minstrelsy; a fountain bright as silver with four great springs running from it that made one long to gaze on them.

There's a lofty tree that spreads its many branches over the fountain, but the branches are utterly bare of leaves and of bark as well from trunk to crown.

CHERUBIN

Look again, and you'll see the rest before you come back.

SETH

Your permission makes me happy. I'll return to the gate at once, and perhaps I'll be able to see something more.

(He goes and looks again, and returns.)

CHERUBIN

Well, did you see more this time?

SETH

There's a serpent in the tree, a frightful beast and no mistake.

CHERUBIN

Go back still a third time and look closer at the tree, both roots and branches. Observe every detail.

(He goes again.)

SETH

Cherub, angel of the God of grace, on a high branch of the tree I saw a child, small, newly born, wrapped in a garment and bound fast with swaddling-bands.

Gazing at the base of the tree, I perceived its roots piercing down through the great dark even into Hell, while its branches, high aloft and radiant, extended even to Heaven, the whole stripped clean of bark, both stem and boughs.

CHERUBIN

It was the Son of God you beheld, swaddled like an infant. When the time shall come, it is he who will redeem, equally with his body and blood, your father, Adam, your mother, and all the righteous.

He is the oil of mercy which was promised to your father. Through his death, in very truth, all the world shall be saved.

SETH

May you be ever blessed! To know the whole and certain truth is to be happy, O God. And now I will leave you, Cherub.

CHERUBIN

Take with you three seeds from the apple that Adam, your father, ate. When he dies—he won't live beyond the third day after you reach home—put the seeds without fail between his teeth and his tongue. In a short time, you'll see that three trees have grown from them.

SETH

May you be daily blessed! I will ever honor you most faithfully. And my father, what joy will be his to pass from earth so soon.

(And then he shall come to his father, Adam, and says to him:)

Dear father, in Paradise I saw a mighty fountain of water and over it an immense tree, and in the midst of its host of branches there was a child wrapped in swaddling clothes.

That child is the oil of mercy which was promised to you by the God of Heaven. And the angel told me that when three days have passed you will yield up your soul.

ADAM

Great honor to you, precious Lord! The years of my service are very many, and I have lived long enough. Take my soul unto yourself. I have conquered the world's labor and its sorrow and am grateful.

It is useless to hide from destiny, my son. I have become old and fearfully weak. May God the Father, Lord on high, put me to rest, body and soul. This is my secret prayer. Amen.

(And then Adam shall die, and Seth says:)

SETH

Ah, what grief is mine, alas! Adam, the father who begot me, is dead. Because he was a good man, I will dig a grave in the earth for him, that there he may be covered.

(Seth makes a grave and buries Adam.)

I'll make it long and deep, the least I can do in my bitter distress at having to bury him so quickly.

(Here Seth puts the three pips of the apple in Adam's mouth and says:)

And faithfully, as I was commanded, I place the three pips in his mouth, for such was God's will, once my father had passed from this world. Surely he was made in God's image even though his taste of the forbidden fruit angered the Lord of Heaven.

LUCIFER

Aha, Beelzebub! Aha! Here's a neat turnabout. Regardless of all his assets, Adam's about to be ours, fetched in one leap.

SATAN

I'll grab the fellow right now, to lie with us in darkness for good. Beelzebub, as you love me, stir yourself and help me lug the foul wretch.

(Here they descend.)

BEELZEBUB

I'll help you carry him to hell, just like a lamb on a big dog's back.
In spite of all your bragging and noise, Adam, your throne's to be with us in misery forever.

(Here he shall take the soul and carry it to hell.)

SATAN

You were proud when you were in Paradise, lording it like a rogue. For that, Adam, we're going to transport you to a place where you'll feel nothing but pain until the world's end.

BEELZEBUB

Hail, my lord, in your see![6] Cast your eye on the great rogue we've brought home to your domain, loathsome Adam, who yearned to be our master for always. Now he's our slave.

LUCIFER

I'm perpetually grateful to you both, seeing how willingly and efficiently you execute my business no matter where it takes you. And now without delay transfer the false scoundrel to his appointed place at Abel's side.

HERE BEGINS CONCERNING NOAH AND THE ARK

(God says:)

GOD THE FATHER

Of a certainty I regret that I made man so altogether like me. As the result of listening to a woman, he has forfeited outright the place which I fashioned for him with my right hand. He acted contrary to my prohibition, and the angel forthwith ejected him from joy-filled Paradise.

Nor am I willing that my spirit should lastingly inhabit the body of any son of man anywhere in the world, and the why and the wherefore is this: the flesh from which I fashioned him is soft. Moreover, I do not believe there is a single human being in all the world who serves me faithfully and truly except Noah, his wife, and his children.

(Then God the Father shall come to Noah, and he says:)

Noah, my cherished servant, rise and accompany me for a space while we stroll, and I will inform you about matters private to you and me.

NOAH

O Father God on high, ever holy, my labor is at your disposal anywhere and everywhere.

GOD THE FATHER

Now, Noah, the present world is so full of wickedness that the end of all flesh is at hand. Man is universally tainted with such great sin that I can no longer refrain from visiting swift punishment upon the whole of human kind except you.

Hasten, therefore, to go and build a ship made of smoothed planking and composed of numerous living spaces, which shall be known as rooms. Make it watertight by means of a good application of pitch both inside and outside, and let it be three hundred full cubits in length. Give it a beam of fifty cubits, and I want it to have a height of thirty. In the stern, locate a small door, called a port. Reinforce it with nailed cross-members to prevent springing.[7]

NOAH

Of course I'll make the ship, Lord, in exact accordance with your wishes, but what is the need of our laboring like that? Since you desire to kill everybody on earth, save only my people and me, just do away with us as well.

GOD THE FATHER

Because of your great goodness, you shall always have my favor, Noah. So take your wife and your children and their wives and put them into your ship, also being careful to take with you two of every kind of beast and useful bird in the land, for I shall bring a mighty flood. It will cover the entire world so that, before it is ended, all who are left on earth will have drowned; no trace of that former life will ever be seen again. Be at pains, therefore, to follow my instructions, and when they have been carried out, I shall return to you.

I repeat: you are to place in the ark a male and female of each species, together with every kind of edible food for man and beast alike.

(Then let God the Father pass into Heaven, and Noah says:)

NOAH

My duty, precious Lord, is to execute your commands. Without urging, I shall set about it.

(Then Noah shall go to his wife, and he says to her:)

Reach me my axe quickly, my auger and my hammers. I've got a job to do.

NOAH'S WIFE

Right away, husband, and may all our work in this world be pleasing to the beloved Father of Heaven.

(Then he shall go to build his ship, and Noah says:)

NOAH

Sweet God, but I'm weary cutting these oak timbers! Seems I'll never get a rest. What with my arms and legs battered like this, if the word to quit ever comes, that will be a happy day. Take pity on me, Lord, since great trouble is in store for the man who incurs your wrath.

(And then God the Father shall come to Noah and says to him:)

GOD THE FATHER

Now, Noah, go into the ark, you and all the members of your house, and because you have served me fully, my peace abides with you always. Of every kind of beast and of all the birds that fly take along matched pairs, male and female, in order that their seed may be preserved alive from the forty days of rain which, within a week's time, I shall allow to fall from the heavens. Every living thing on earth, whether human or non-human, save only you and your children, I shall cause to be slain by flood.

NOAH

Your command, O blessed Father, I will obey, going quickly from this place to my wife and children.

(Noah says to his wife:)

Wife mine, sons and daughters likewise, by the unfailing will of our beloved Father, there has been ordered a strong ship. Let us hasten to board it, for a flood is coming upon the earth, such a flood as will drown together both man and beast.

WIFE

I'll do everything just as you want it done, dear husband and master. Let's all head for the ship, fast, so we won't be drowned by the flood.

SHEM

As ordered, I'll get the beasts and the birds into the ark, and Ham can fetch the food.

HAM

You see the load of food on my back. I call on Japhet to shoulder another, and let's get a move on, for God's sake, as I'm scared nearly blind.

JAPHET

I've got a good load of mixed hay and corn, enough to last all the animals on hand for a year.

(And then let all go in, men and cattle, and Noah says:)

NOAH

In the name of the sublime Father, get into the ark at once before the rain fills it from above. You'll have to lead the horses, cattle, pigs, and sheep, but the birds will fly in quickly and readily enough, bless them. O Father, to us your handiwork, which you fashioned from clay and from mire, grant strength and help, for our prayer is ever to you.

SHEM

I'll now cover the top of the ark with a canvas, which will keep the rain from coming in.

HAM

Praise be to God, cover it, or we'll be in trouble! Faith, here comes a fierce shower right now.

JAPHET

The cloudburst, look at it! Frightful! No man can endure it for long. And those rivers, huge ones, breaking through, smashing through, from underground!

NOAH

By the grace of our heavenly Father, we shall come through, be the flood ever so deadly. Our ship floats! May she save us, O Lord on high. . . .

GOD THE FATHER

Everything in which there was the breath of life is dead. I now command the rain to cease and let the savage flood withdraw and return to its former place, that Noah may again till the soil.

NOAH

The rain has completely stopped, and it seems to me the water has subsided. It would be a good idea to send out a raven to see whether there's dry ground on the earth as yet.

SHEM

I'll send it out, and I don't think it will come back. If it finds any dead flesh, it's certain to stay with it.

(And then he shall send out a raven, which returns no more.)

NOAH

You were right when you told me the raven wouldn't return. It has lighted on some great chunk of carrion, where it pitilessly gorges itself. This time release the gray-eyed dove into the open. By the Lord, I can't say where there might be a more faithful bird.

SHEM

I'll do so at once, beloved father, and it will see whether there's dry land anywhere.

(And then he shall send out the dove, which shall immediately return to the ship and be taken in.)

HAM

This time I'll sent it out in God's name. Go now and look carefully for dry land, look everywhere.

(Here the dove comes, bringing an olive branch in its mouth.)

JAPHET

It's come back, and there's a branch of green olive in its bill. I'll quickly take it inside the ship.

NOAH

All honor to God the Father, great is our obligation to love him. The flood waters are now abated, for the trees have begun to dry. My sons, pray send out yet a third dove. If it finds dry ground, I'm confident it will not return to us again.

JAPHET

Your wish is my command, father. Gentle dove, you of the blue eyes, go, fly over many a country, and if you really find dry land, whether in field or meadow, don't forget to look for food there. Search carefully for your breakfast and dinner.

(And he shall send another dove.)

SHEM

Since I don't see it on the wing anywhere, it must surely have located dry ground.

NOAH

In the name of the Father on high, let us uncover the ark. The weather is dry and fair, for which it behooves us to give thanks to God.

(And then let them uncover the ship, and Noah says:)

Praise and thanksgiving be to you, O Father, that the flood waters are gone from the world and that we, among all men who inhabited the face of the earth, are left alive.

WIFE

God's will be done and whatever is pleasing in his sight. Surely his power is great on earth as it is in heaven.

(And then God the Father shall come to Noah, and, standing in the platea, says:)

GOD THE FATHER

Noah, I command you to disembark without delay, your wife and your children also, and all birds, beasts, and reptiles. Multiply and fill the world as before, every son of the breast. And in order that you may be sustained, go till the fields and the unploughed land.

NOAH

Wherever I may be, Lord of Heaven, I shall do your will, quitting the ark at once, I and my wife and my children. And in honor of God, praise his name, let us raise an altar, well-made and beautiful on which we can sacrifice to him.

HAM

It's right, certainly, to make an altar and offer up our bullocks to God that our prayers may be strengthened.

JAPHET

A man couldn't hope to see anywhere a lovelier altar than we have right here on the top of Mount Calvary.[8]

(Here an altar is made ready, and let God the Father stand near it.)

NOAH

I offer a tithe of all our birds and beasts in homage to the sublime Father.

HIS WIFE

I offer a cow, that the Father God, who made all things, may send us his grace.

SHEM

I have a dove. I place it on the altar in honor of God.

HIS WIFE

To the Father of Heaven on high, I offer a pheasant, plump and goodly.

HAM

Kneeling, I offer to God a prime goose, placing it on his altar.

HIS WIFE

God is worthy of all your sacrifice. I proffer a choice mallard in homage to the Father.

JAPHET

In honor of God the Father, I put upon his altar a fine partridge and a lark.

HIS WIFE

I offer in my turn another lark and add a first-rate capon.

(And then God the Father shall come to Noah and says to him:)

GOD THE FATHER

For your sake, Noah, I shall never again take heavy vengeance upon the world as a whole nor, as retribution, bring death to all that lives. Therefore multiply and repopulate the earth, taking power over bird and beast.

All four-footed creatures and those with wings, the fishes likewise, are to obey you and are ordained as food for you. However, I command you not to eat flesh with blood as long as the world endures. Go, therefore, and till the soil with prolonged and unceasing diligence.

NOAH

If you were ever to become angry with mankind again, Lord, what would we have gained by cultivating the soil? No matter how long and hard we'd worked, it would end in failure. All would perish under the weight of your retribution. As for me, I might as well die quickly before that day of sorrowful disaster arrives.

GOD THE FATHER

Noah, because of my love for you, I will establish a covenant between us: never again will I inflict total punishment upon the world.

NOAH

There is no appeal from an agreement made with the all-powerful. Though it were broken merely in the heat of anger, I would be powerless to do anything about it.

GOD THE FATHER

The accord now made between me and the race of man, I shall not break. It stands forevermore, and on record as a sign of good faith that cannot be broken, I shall set my rainbow aloft in the midst of the sky. It shall be an unfailing token of our covenant, so that even should I wish in future to avenge myself upon this world, I will cast my eyes upon that token and remember my vow never again to destroy by flood a living creature, whether man or beast, wild or tame.

(And then God the Father goes away from Noah, and Noah says:)

NOAH

Your will be done, O Lord most high. I and my wife and my children will set to work. . . .

HERE ABRAHAM SHALL PRESENT HIMSELF

(Then Abraham says:)

ABRAHAM

It is fitting that I should go to the temple and worship God, for he is Lord of heaven and earth, as I believe with my whole heart.

(Here he comes down.)

GOD THE FATHER

Abraham, Abraham, it is my wish that you make haste and come to me at once, the truth being that you must shortly undergo an ordeal.

ABRAHAM

Here I am, obedient to your command. At the last day, Lord, remember my soul. Now you have only to tell me what I must do, and when the time comes, I will do it with zeal and devotion.

GOD THE FATHER

If you are to obey me fully, which means no hanging back at any point, you must offer up, on a mountain that I shall show you, none other than Isaac, the son you love. And I say this: if you sacrifice him to me, I shall never forget it.

(Here God goes up to heaven.)

ABRAHAM

The sacrifice which you demand, precious Lord, shall be made. I will offer up my son, Isaac. I will lay him on the altar and burn him in the flames of kindled wood, refusing nothing that you require of me.

(Here he shall come to his son.)

Isaac, seeing that it is necessary for me to make a sacrifice to God, the Lord of heaven and earth, take a load of firewood, rope it together, and carry it on your back.

ISAAC

I've bundled the wood, father, and here it is. Let's be going to whichever mountain God has chosen.

ABRAHAM

Since we have both firewood and sword ready to hand, we are free to proceed from here to offer up the sacrifice.

ISAAC

I'm wondering about one thing though, father.

ABRAHAM

What does my dear boy want to ask me?

ISAAC

Here's the wood I've carried from home to make a fire, no doubt about that. But where is the offering, father, that's to be burnt in worship of God?

ABRAHAM

God will surely send it to us from heaven, my son, in accordance with his purpose. First, however, I am placing the wood on the altar in order to burn the sacrifice.

(Here he puts the wood on the altar.)

And now, my son, I am resolved to tell you that God himself has commanded me to offer you upon the altar as a sacrifice to him.

ISAAC

If it is his will, I shan't resist. If I'm to die now, I accept my death.

ABRAHAM

Climb up, then, and lie flat on the firewood so that you can be burned. O sweet son, I am deeply grieved and sick at heart, yet I say to you that I will not oppose God for the sake of anyone in the world.

ISAAC

Don't be sad. Since this is how God wants it, I'm ready to die. Only, dearest father, tie my hands and legs with the rope, tie them tight, so I won't be able to get to my feet. For unless I'm tied down, I might run away when I feel the bite of the flames, which would disgrace you forever. The pain will be cruel, father beloved, before I'm burned to ashes. O God, keep well my soul!

ABRAHAM

My son, my son, you mustn't distress yourself so. God will help you, the God of grace will never forget you.

In haste I bind you fast, and in another moment my sword will quit you of this life.

(Here Gabriel comes down and shall come to Abraham, whose sword he arrests.)

GABRIEL

Abraham, Abraham, heed me this instant and listen to what I have to say.

ABRAHAM

Who are you that speaks to me so loftily? As you love me, pray be open with me.

GABRIEL

I will, Abraham. I am an angel from heaven, sent to preserve from death Isaac, your son and your joy. God truly understands all the wish of your heart. Therefore, withhold your hand.

ABRAHAM

Ah, God be praised! My son is saved; my heart is healed. There is no lord but my Lord. In worship and thanksgiving, I offer up this sheep in Isaac's stead and place it on the altar to burn.

ISAAC

I hurry to set the wood afire, and I blow upon it. O God of heaven, hear the voice of our prayer.

ABRAHAM

Now that the sacrifice to God is made, my son, let us go home. Come away at once, Isaac, and follow me.

HERE MOSES APPEARS AND SPEAKS

(And let God the Father stand before him.)

MOSES

I am astonished by what I see: the bush burns, yet is not consumed. I'll have a closer look and find out what's happening before leaving it. This is very strange.

GOD THE FATHER

Stand where you are, Moses! I forbid you to come any closer. And take off your shoes immediately, for you are on sacred ground.

I am the God of your fathers, of Abraham, of Isaac, and of Jacob likewise.

MOSES

My eyes cannot endure the brightness of your countenance. I lack the grace needed to look upon you even for a single instant.

GOD THE FATHER

Trouble has arisen in Egypt, where my people, very grievously afflicted by Pharaoh, the accursed, cry out to me from the midst of their suffering. Since they will never be able to improve their condition without help, you must go to Egypt and to Pharaoh and warn him, in my name, that he should cease his oppression of my people, lest disaster befall him.

Thereafter, you are to lead them out of Egypt and to that land which pours forth its abundance of milk and honey. I will not allow my people to remain long in misery, and I give you my word, Moses, they shall follow obediently in your footsteps.

MOSES

Lord, despite anything I say to them, they will neither listen nor believe. The fact that God himself has appeared to me will never be believed either, whether among the great or the small.

GOD THE FATHER

Answer me promptly and in the light of your faith. What are you now holding in your hand? Speak, Moses.

MOSES

As I fully believe you to be our chieftain and our Lord, I am holding a wooden rod.

GOD THE FATHER

Then throw it on the ground, and you will witness an honest miracle.

MOSES

God of grace, it has become a serpent, a fearful sight! I tremble and am afraid.

GOD THE FATHER

I order you to pick it up by the tail and hold it in your hand without a word.

MOSES

Even as I take it up, Lord, it turns into a rod again.

GOD THE FATHER

Guard this rod well, and no man will harm you. Now also I shed my grace upon you so that, for as long as it remains yours to command, no earthly evil shall prevail against you.

Be neither downcast nor afraid, since I will be ever at your side, your help at all times and in all places. And now get you gone from here at once, carry out my instructions to the letter, and my blessing go with you.

MOSES

My journey to Egypt will be swift, O Lord, in order that I may fulfill your wishes. For the man who is permitted to serve you, just to be alive is sweet. His Lord does not forget him.

(Here God ascends to heaven, and King Pharaoh appears and afterward Moses says:)

God has sent me to you, O Pharaoh, man as well as king, to ask how you can find it in your heart to punish so harshly those of his people who are dwelling within your borders. He is astonished at your conduct.

PHARAOH

Bah! What does this god of yours amount to that I should have to listen to anything he says? This much is certain: I don't know him. As for the Israelites, I won't allow them to be taken off hard labor.

AARON

And God orders you to let his people make sacrifice to him. If you hinder them so that they cannot serve him faithfully, I tell you now, a mighty vengeance will descend on you, for the Lord is exceedingly powerful.

PHARAOH

You two savages disgust me, the pair of you! What, you have the impudence to lecture me in my own court? Your people will be kept under strict control as long as they're in my kingdom. As for you, you're a couple of nothings.

MOSES

Ah, will you not obey the God who created you and who likewise created both heaven and earth? Unless you believe in him and put your whole trust in him, you will be damned.

(Pharaoh goes down.)

PHARAOH

You appear to me to be crazy, utterly irrational. The Israelites won't be spared on account of this god you talk about. Night and day, they'll remain abject.

And I shall keep a sharp eye out, seeing to it that not a man among them makes a sacrifice to his god. If he does and it's discovered, he'll be destroyed forthwith.

AARON

You refuse, then, to heed God's voice and are determined to carry on in the hardness of your heart, great hardness. Yet, unless you mend your ways, the Lord will punish you so severely your wail shall be, "Oh, wretched!"

PHARAOH

You sicken me, you scoundrel, you blockhead! Get out of here, out of my sight! Now! Leave my court. By Jupiter, if I find you, I swear I'll kill you with my own two hands before morning.

(Moses walks in the platea.)

MOSES

Regardless of what is said to him, this man will never turn to the Lord on high.

AARON

We can do nothing with him. That's as certain as it is that evil will fall upon him and soon.

FIRST MESSENGER

Hail to the flower of mankind! A great calamity has occurred among your people. The dead cannot be numbered. Surely this God of Israel is displeased.

PHARAOH

Out upon it! Oh, out, out and alas! To think that it should happen in my kingdom, a misfortune the like of this! Before you go, tell me where Moses is. Where can he be found?

FIRST MESSENGER

Amid the children of Israel he teaches the laws of their high God,[9] by day and by night. He and his people make sacrifice to this same God, raising a great clamor, and, meanwhile, the inhabitants of your kingdom, both man and beast, perish in hordes from poisoned water and poisoned grain.[10] Assuredly the God of the Israelites is aroused against you since you and your people are so harshly punished.

PHARAOH

What now, alas, shall I do? Noble counselor, I entreat you, give me good advice, for it makes me heartsick beyond belief that an evil such as this has descended upon my realm.

COUNSELOR

If you are to be free of trouble, you must get Moses and Aaron out of your domain and all their tribe with them. Include the women and children in a general exile, and do not permit a single one of them ever to return and live here.

PHARAOH

Bless you, counselor. I will follow your advice at once and in every particular. I shall go to Moses and Aaron and speak firmly to them, you may be sure.

(Here Pharoah goes down.)

Moses and you, too, Aaron, I command you both to leave my kingdom. I tell you straight, not a man, woman, or child of you is to remain behind. Each man is to take as much of his goods as he can carry on his back, for I will no longer tolerate your presence among my people. Get out and go to some other country.

MOSES

No matter where we were to settle in your land, you wouldn't let God's people live in peace. Soon, therefore, the Lord of heaven will mightily chastise you for your evildoing.

AARON

We've got to get away from this place. It's not possible to live here any longer, it seems, because we're never going to be left undisturbed.

MOSES

O God on high, with a full heart I beseech you to help us and protect us from the wickedness of Pharaoh the abominable. . . .

FIRST MAN

More than a hundred thousand people are assembled at this spot, carrying their possessions with them. All who worship our dear Lord shall have unhindered passage.

SECOND MAN

My back bears a stout load, surely. Hear our voice, O God, and keep us in your care.

MOSES

Men, women, and children, in the Lord's eyes you are precious. Let us journey forward to the Red Sea and beyond, there to inhabit the land of promise, which the God we love has given us. . . .

PHARAOH

Moses and his entire clan have taken themselves out of my kingdom. So much the better and that's the truth, upon my soul. I'll follow them and before I return home, kill every last one of them.

(He mounts a horse.)

FIRST SOLDIER

It's imperative that you move swiftly before they can ford the Red Sea.

(Here Gabriel comes down.)

The truth is they're already long gone, so I say now is the time to be resolute.

PHARAOH

Knights and squires, forward in speedy pursuit of the Israelites. I want them totally destroyed, sparing no one. All will be dead before daylight.

FIRST MAN

I'm telling you, Moses, you've made a mistake in bringing us out of Egypt at this time. My life on it, we'll never be able to get across this sea. There's absolutely no passage for us.

SECOND MAN

And I'm telling you King Pharaoh is about to arrive, accompanied by a great host. Miserable wretches that we are, what are we to do now? We'll be killed, every one of us. There's no escape.

MOSES

Do not lose faith in the God of heaven, for he will hear your voice. Trust in his grace and leave off grumbling. I say to you that he will fight on your side.

GABRIEL

Moses, God commands you to take your rod and strike the sea with it. The waters will open wide enough to allow you and all your people to walk through them with ease.

MOSES

To you the praise and thanksgiving, O God of grace, who has sent your messenger to preserve us from Pharaoh. O good people, from the youngest to the oldest, I address you, saying, follow me.

(He smites the sea.)

In the Lord's name, I strike you, crystalline depths, with my staff. Open a broad path for us that we may go to the land which God has ordained.

SECOND SOLDIER

Even as I speak to you, my lord Pharaoh, Moses is advancing far into the sea, marching forward rapidly while the water, it appears, rushes to divide before him moment by moment.

SQUIRE

The entire body of his Israelites has fallen in behind him, and the sea stands like two walls on either side of them. They are sheltered as by an enclosure and certainly cannot be drowned.

PHARAOH

I will pursue them, then, and annihilate them, regardless of age, sex, or station. No one shall be permitted to survive, no matter what the circumstances. . . .
The sea! The sea! Oh, disaster is mine! The mighty flood descends upon us and we drown. The God of Moses has done this, ending our lives in utter destruction.

SQUIRE

Ah, my fate is miserable! We shan't escape the smothering waters. Our stars are deadly, our death is now. . . .

(And Moses and Aaron shall come and build dwellings for their number, and Moses shall say:)

MOSES

I will establish a village and build for myself a permanent dwelling. King Pharaoh and all his host being drowned, we shall have peace in which to live.

FIRST MAN

Dear Moses, we'll construct a house which will serve us for some time to come and, while we're waiting for it, we can put up a tent.

SECOND MAN

Look, here's a good one already at hand. Give us your blessing before we take shelter.

MOSES

The Father's blessing be upon you, and may he preserve you in peace forever. May he grant you the grace always to bow down before him, in the beginning and in the end. . . .

(He goes up on a mountain.)

I see three shining rods, nor, in faith, have I ever seen finer since I was born. Truly, these rods are an evidence and a token of the three persons in the Trinity.

(He cuts the rods.)

Come what may, I will cut them and bear them into the house that worship of God the Father may be present there.

AARON

These rods are holy since they yield so sweet a savor. It's my belief that such perfume could never rise from all the plants of the world in flower.

MOSES

Hallowed be the Father who would reveal to us a triple sign so filled with virtue that grace may always be ours. I will wrap the rods in silk with great and exalted respect.

SECOND MAN

What misery ever to have been born, ever taken from my mother's womb, ever put to the breast! A snake's fangs have pierced me, and its venom has spread through me from my heel to my heart.

MOSES

Provided you sincerely believe that there is no God but one, He in whom it is man's duty to believe, you will recover from your foot to your head, healed by the power of the three rods as soon as you touch them with your lips.

SECOND MAN

I believe in God the Father, and I beg you, in charity, Moses, as you are a good man, make me whole through your compassion.

MOSES

In the name of the Father of heaven, three persons in one God, kiss the rods without delay, and he will surely ease your suffering.

SECOND MAN

Happy is my lot, for God has made me whole. I say to myself, you owe him worship when he is so quick to hear your voice.

FIRST MAN

Alas, Moses, oh sad, sad! Sleeping on the moor, I have been wounded by a black toad; his poison bloats me. My whole groin is inflamed. For the love of God, help me!

MOSES

The Lord will hear your cry, but take care that at this moment you have faith in the Father who made the heavens, the land and the sea, and man of clay.

FIRST MAN

Truly, truly, I swear to you that if he will lessen my pain, I'll never worship any other God.

MOSES

Then kiss the rods, tokens of the blessed Father, and they will surely restore you to perfect health.

(Here God the Father comes down.)

SECOND MAN

Moses, if you're really a prophet, you've got to find us water to drink. If you don't, many of our people are certain to die of thirst, and that would mean disaster.

MOSES

Through his grace, the heavenly Father will grant you your desire because nowhere will those who serve him be found to lack his forgiveness.

SECOND MAN

That foul God of yours doesn't give us either thing—food or drink. So you have my word on it, I'm going to worship sacred Jupiter.

MOSES

What advice have you to offer me, dear Aaron, about the bickering and uproar of these depraved people? For if they don't get water, they're going to turn away from the faith and worship evil gods.

AARON

I say, brother, that we should go and pray to our precious Lord, begging him in the fullness of his mercy to provide the people with water somewhere, thus removing any and all basis for disbelief.

MOSES

Bless you, Aaron, for your excellent advice, and most important, I ask your help in speeding my prayer.

(Here he prays on the mountain.)

Amid your splendor, O God and Father, hear the call of this people.
Give them the water of life that they may be refreshed.

AARON

Do this, O holy Father, that they may be unable to find occasion to
murmur and cry out against you. Surely, when once their thirst is
fully quenched, they will discard their abominable gods.

GOD THE FATHER

Moses, stand with your brother Aaron before the transgressors,
take the rod and twice smite the rock. Unfailingly at your command,
a natural spring, plentiful as a river, will gush forth.

There will be water enough for all who wish to drink of it, men
and beasts alike, in order that the wicked may witness how frequently
I aid them.

MOSES

O God the Father, precious, sanctified, to worship you too much is
impossible, seeing that your deeds are always good and your compassion great.

As for you, you self-deceived doubters, your way is the way of evil.
You cannot believe with all your hearts that our Lord knows no
equal; not even when, through the grace of the heavenly Father, a
God by his works made true, the mere pair of us, my brother and I,
can bring water from a rough flint stone.

(And he shall strike the rock with his rod, and water shall come out.)

CALEB

Beyond question, Moses, I have sinned, and therefore I cry for
mercy to God our Father that he may forgive my sin.

GOD THE FATHER

Because my name was not honored and because of the children of

Israel, disbelievers, neither you nor your brother Aaron shall lead them into the promised land.

MOSES

Dear Lord, wise of heart, who will lead them then, if I don't and Aaron doesn't?

GOD THE FATHER

Furthermore, because they are disposed to worship false gods, and act in opposition to the faith, of all who are alive today not one shall ever reach the holy land except Caleb and Joshua.

(Here God ascends to heaven.)

MOSES

I know now that I'm not to live any longer, know it well. The end of my earthly life has come. I will go and plant the three rods in the ground, and woe to him who bends the knee to Jove, thereby angering God.

(Here Moses plants the rods on Mount Tabor.)

In homage to the Father of heaven, I plant you. Take root, grow again, and may you abide in his ordinance. Precious God and Master, incline your ear to the sound of my voice. Bring me to bliss and receive my spirit *in manus tuas, Domine.*

(And then Moses shall die.)

KING DAVID SHALL APPEAR AND WALK ABOUT

KING DAVID

After talk and work, it is a good custom to take food and drink, followed by rest. So, butler, hasten and fetch me some of your best wine. My head grows heavy, and I feel the need of sleep.

BUTLER

My dear lord, please don't become annoyed, for as quick as you can say the word, I'll come to you anywhere I'm required. I'm always on instant call. *Parlez, vous-êtes mon seigneur*[11]. . . .

Now, this is a spiced and honeyed wine of choice quality. No better vintage will ever pass your lips. Drink it, matchless lord. It's the equal of anything this country has to offer.

KING DAVID

A toast to your good fortune, butler. . . . The drink is clear and well mulled, by the Lord, and has made me so drowsy that now I truly crave sleep.

COUNSELOR

Go, my lord, and lay yourself down in order that we may cover you with such rich stuffs as become a king of your dignity.

GOD THE FATHER

Gabriel, make haste and go to King David in Jerusalem. Say to him that on Arabia's Mount Tabor[12] he will find the rods which Moses planted.

Let him bring them to Jerusalem against the time that in Bethlehem a child is born who shall redeem the world. A cross is to be made from those rods, on which Christ, my beloved son, will be crucified. Blessed are they who shall worship him.

GABRIEL

O Father, full of grace, your will is my command and my duty without exception of time or place and without urging.

(And then he shall come to King David, he being alone, and Gabriel says:)

You are to proceed immediately, David, to Mount Tabor in Arabia.

Take from there the three rods which were planted by Moses and bring them promptly home with you to Jerusalem.

There will come a day when they are needed to make a cross on which the Son of Man, none other, shall be humbled.

(Then the king, awakening, says in astonishment:)

KING DAVID

Benedicite dominus! In my dream I saw an angel before me, saw him clearly. He ordered me to bring the rods of grace from Mount Tabor that through them we might obtain salvation.

Messenger, fetch me my horse. All men of my house, nobles and commoners, come with me.

MESSENGER

By God's day, my lord, the pick of the steeds are ready and the tawny coursers; likewise the hackneys and the palfreys, a noble sight in their array. Mount, lord, at your pleasure.

KING DAVID

Blessings, messenger. I shall set off at once and ride swiftly toward the mountain. And in order that we may be led to our destination along the right path, let us pray to God the Father in the fullness of his mercy.

(Here let King David come down.)

In the name of God, the Father of heaven, I will mount, and may his spirit keep watch over my soul.[13]

(Then he shall ride.)

Hallowed be the moment in which the angel instructed me, for look about you, we have come unhindered to the mountain.

Let every man dismount and fasten his gaze upon the rods before us so greenly growing. With great homage to our mighty Lord, I cut from the ground the rods of grace.

COUNSELOR

These are indeed the rods of grace, since nowhere have you ever smelled a fragrance the like of this. Now I know that God is in this place, I am sure of it, because the odor of the rods is so sweet.

KING DAVID

Musicians, play! Tabors, trumpets, and three hundred harps; cythol, viol, crowd, and psaltery; citherns, nakers, shawms, organetti, drums; also cymbals, recorders, and the rest.[14]

(To the riders.)

And now, knights and squires, to horse, each and every one of you, and hasten toward home in the precious name of God the Father.

A BLIND MAN

Most esteemed lord, in some way help me with those rods of yours, for I am blind. Bless me with them at this very moment of my darkness.

A LAME MAN

Also give me, a cripple, the strength to walk like a normal man, and I will believe beyond a shadow of doubt that they are the rods of exceeding grace.

A DEAF MAN

As for me, great king, I will thank God just that much more if through the Lord's favor and the power of the rods my stone-deaf ears are aided.

KING DAVID

I am disposed to help all three of you, provided only that your faith in the merciful salvation of the rods is perfect. *In nomine patris et filii atque spiritus sancti salui modo eritis.*

BLIND MAN

Glory be to the Father! We are truly healed of our afflictions. Praise be to God, who has heard our voice. These are rods that have no equal.

(Here let King David alight from the horse.)

KING DAVID

Now let us dismount, but before we go into the castle, tell me, my followers, where should the rods be planted that we may show them the most honor and afford them the best opportunity to grow?

COUNSELOR

While we're considering the matter, we can leave the three of them at rest in some verdant spot and appoint guards to watch over them with diligence, making the penalty for carelessness very severe.

KING DAVID

Faith, that is good advice. Butler, I order you and your companion to guard the rods. You are to see to it that they are not moved elsewhere under any circumstances, lest you be disemboweled and hanged, both of you.

In the meantime, before I eat anything, I want to sleep for a while. I am tired from so much travel and wish to rest.

(King David goes up into a tent.)

MESSENGER

I'm going to guard them with such respect and care that the boldest man alive, a king or even an emperor, won't be able to budge them from right here.

BUTLER

Emperor, king, sultan, never mind how great he is, he's not about to move them. Damn his eyes, I'm the one who's keeping these rods of grace in Jerusalem from now on.

MESSENGER

All right, then, settle down to one side, friend, and keep your eyes peeled right and left as well as ahead, because if anybody sneaks up on us and makes off with the rods without our knowing it, all we'll get for our pains is disgrace.

BUTLER

By my stones,[15] such as they are for size, nobody steals those rods, I don't care how big he is or how huge his coillons! Go ahead, sleep on your spigot and rest yourself, and if you get to hankering for a girl, I'll fix you up with one in a hurry.

(Then the king, waking from sleep, shall go to the rods and say:)

KING DAVID

How soft my rest has been, how sweet is the sleep of morning! In his work, may God the Father be glorified forever. If I have his favor, I shall proceed to plant the rods with fullest honors in some beautiful and unsullied place.

SECOND MESSENGER

Dear lord of peerless wisdom, a wonderful thing has happened. Within the span of this night alone, the rods have put down their roots into the earth and while you've been elsewhere, the three stems have joined together to make one.

KING DAVID

I praise God and lift my prayer to heaven from a full heart, for he is omnipotent and his every work a marvel.

(He shall go to the rods.)

Since it is the Father himself who has planted them, they shall stand where they are. Woe to the man who disregards the divine will, great the sorrow that lies in wait for him.

In order that we may honor the tree and, at the same time, gauge its growth, I direct that its stem be girdled with a silver band.

BUTLER

Here is the band you ordered prepared, made of pure, solid silver. I will put it in place so that we can tell exactly how much the tree has grown a full year from now.

(King David speaks to Bathsheba, who is washing her dress in the stream.)

KING DAVID

Through your gracious favor, my lady, show a little love toward me, for my eyes have yet to fall upon a woman who pleases me more. In return, I give you every hall and chamber of my palace and will be your husband. We shall never part as long as we live.

BATHSHEBA

My admired and beloved lord, king of the earth, you must know the pleasure it would give me to do as you wish if only I might manage it without the fear and risk of being discovered. Were a certain villainous man ever to find out, he would kill me then and there.

(Let Bathsheba go home with King David.)

KING DAVID

For your sake, Bathsheba, my flower of all the world, I solemnly pledge that the knight Uriah shall die. You are and will always remain the sole desire of my heart. Therefore come to my bed that I may make you mine.

BATHSHEBA

Being utterly unable to say no to you, I'll give you everything you ask of me. But sweetest lord, kill him, since if he lives and ever learns of our delight, he'll somehow find a way to do me harm.

KING DAVID

Dear heart, whom God has made the choicest blossom of her sex, in return for your love the man dies and no mistake about it. . . .[16]
. . . Uriah, best of my knights, trusting in your devotion, I am asking you to assemble and lead a well-armed force into combat against a dangerous enemy of mine who seeks to dominate the kingdom. Because of illness, I shan't be able to ride with you.

URIAH

I am always ready, my dear lord, to do everything in my power to carry out your wishes without being urged, and as a knight worthy of trust I shall never retire from the field of battle until the contemptible aggressor has paid for his insolence.

KING DAVID

Upon my soul, most noble Uriah, your answer becomes you, and I love you for it. Take care, accordingly, that you station yourself in the forefront of the struggle, where a charge of cowardice cannot hold, and the claim that you are afraid of any man is idle.

URIAH

My lord, I swear by the orders I have received from you that no man shall prove me coward, for mine will be the first blow struck on this expedition and I will demonstrate my prowess.
So now it's good-bye to you, my lord of lords, for I shan't delay longer, except to beg your blessing before I go.

KING DAVID

My blessing on you always. Our messenger will accompany you and our butler also, both of them armed.

URIAH

I must be sure to speak to my wife before leaving home, for, if I were to go off without a word, it would break her heart.

(He speaks to Bathsheba.)

Bathsheba, my own sweet one, I've got to journey into battle, there's no choice. But there is this—it will soon be over.

(Here Uriah is equipped and armed.)

BATHSHEBA

On my soul, don't go, don't ever leave me! It breaks my heart to hear talk like that. I swear by my loyalty to you, lord and husband, that if you leave home, I'll not only stop eating, I'll hang myself.

URIAH

Our sovereign's will, my faithful Bathsheba, my wife, must be done. That's as inevitable as that I can't stay with you any longer. So here's a good-bye kiss, and you pray hard for me, very hard.

BATHSHEBA

Oh, how I wish I'd never been born, for now I'm in agony on account of you, my sweet husband! . . . Nevertheless, my prayer for you is that you will never return, since that would be the better thing.

(Here Gabriel comes down.)

URIAH

Now, messenger, if you're in hopes of being rewarded, pray carry my banner properly, and you, butler, be as eager and aggressive as a well-armed knight.

(Here he mounts a horse.)

SECOND MESSENGER

Don't worry about me, Uriah, I tell you. My life on it, you're not going to have the slightest cause.

(And then they shall ride out of the platea, and afterward the messenger comes and says to King David:)

I wish you joy, my lord. As you see, I have come home again, but the knight Uriah has been killed and your butler as well. I grieve for them.

KING DAVID

Ah, so Uriah is dead! Mindful of your duty to the Crown, tell me the circumstances of his death and how he came to lose his life, seeing that he was both proud and valiant and regarded himself as a very formidable man.

SECOND MESSENGER

Nevertheless, he is dead, by God's day. Wanting to throw the enemy into disorder, he laid about him with fury, but a certain horseman gave him his fatal wound, brought him speedily to the ground, and there hacked him to pieces.

(Then the angel shall come to King David and ask him a question, saying:)

GABRIEL

Answer me this, mighty king: there was a man who had a hundred sheep while his neighbor had only one; if that man stole his neighbor's one sheep, what would be his fit punishment? Let me have the plain truth.

KING DAVID

I will answer at once and without equivocation. Beyond doubt, the only just sentence for such a man would be execution. Anyone who behaves like that merits death.

GABRIEL

You, David, are such a man. Although you could have availed yourself of any number of other women, you took from Uriah the only woman he had, his wife. Your own judgment be upon you.

KING DAVID

The Lord grant forgiveness to my soul. Great is the misery I brought upon myself when I sinned with the body of that evil woman. *Deus mei miserere*[17] in the light of your grace and pity, that I may be spared the torment which has no end.

(And then under the sacred tree he begins the Psalter, i.e., "Blessed is the man. . .")[18]

My esteemed advisor, I beg you to spell out a penance for my sins. What shall I do, seeing that I have angered God, my precious Lord and Father?

COUNSELOR

As an atonement for those sins, order the building of a temple, great in all its dimensions and lustrous throughout. Gather an ample roster of stoneworkers and notify the entire population of the city.

KING DAVID

May God favor you since surely, as it seems to me, your counsel is good counsel. I shall therefore act on it unfailingly from this time forward.

(King David goes up.)

Messenger, my worthy liegeman, come to me as fast as my words fly, so that you can carry out my wishes.

SECOND MESSENGER

By God the Father, my dear lord, at all times and in all places I am on the alert to serve you.

KING DAVID

Go then, messenger, and command all the city's masons, on pain of hanging and drawing, to report tomorrow morning in order to make a wall of selected stone bound with lime, its location here at the center of town. On this site, I desire to erect a temple in God's honor.

SECOND MESSENGER

Lord, I will dutifully execute your orders to the limit of my ability. So good-bye for the moment, best of masters. I shan't linger another moment, wanting as I do to hurry on my way.

KING DAVID

Good luck to you, messenger, for I know you as an agent who won't get into trouble and as a man in whom no fault has been found. But before you go, have a drink of something, wine, mead, since with that to fortify you, it strikes me you ought to set out on your errand the more nimbly.

(Here God the Father descends.)

SECOND MESSENGER

Now hear this! Attention all masons of the city. Under penalty of hanging and drawing, and I do not lie, you are to see to it that tomorrow finds you in midtown, ready to go to work on a temple.

(And again he shall come to the king, and he says to him:)

May it please you, my lord, all the masons from the most important to the least important have been notified, and every one of them has assured me that he will be on the job and ready to go to work in the morning.

KING DAVID

I shall reward you for your services, messenger. Assume for yourself the charter rights to Carnsew and Trehembis.[19]

SECOND MESSENGER

Thank you very much indeed, lord of outstanding worth, your gifts are never otherwise than good. In making a gift like this, you show yourself to be the most generous of men. . . .

FIRST MASON

You, boy, prepare the lime and clay and fetch me building stones, sledgehammers, and wedges, so I can hurry and begin to erect the walls.

SECOND MASON

Seeing that I raised a scaffold and began on them hours ago, the rest of you had better get a move on, or you'll be in for a nasty beating. . . .

KING DAVID

I suggest that we go at once, counselor, and have a look at how the workmen are doing. If they're not working well, they're about to smart for it.

(Here he comes down.)

COUNSELOR

These men who are laboring for you, most gracious lord and sire, are the best to be found in the entire kingdom.

(Let God be in the platea.)

GOD THE FATHER

David, because you are a murderer, you shall never complete for me the building of a house of worship. In very truth, you have destroyed a likeness of my face, namely, Uriah, a knight ever faithful.

KING DAVID

Who, then, Lord, will fully raise your temple?

GOD THE FATHER

It is Solomon, your most dear son, who shall fully raise it. Such is the fact.

(Here God goes up.)

KING DAVID

Now I know that my time has come, the term of my life having been long.

(David shall go to the tents.)

I entreat you, my lords, to crown my son, Solomon, king in my stead, and as your sovereign honor him as long as you live.

Esteem him even as you have esteemed me, for it is God who has revealed him to you, and the throne is his by the will of heaven.

SECOND MESSENGER

Regardless of what the future may bring, my lord, any wish of yours is both command and obligation in my eyes. Yet, God willing, the time would never come when I desired a king other than you.

KING DAVID

It is contrary to the will of the Father, hallowed be his name, that I remain longer among you. O God, my soul is in your hands. May they preserve it from the terrors of the hereafter.

(And then King David shall die.)

COUNSELOR

Deep, deep is our sorrow that our matchless lord is dead. Let us go and lay his body in the grave. Let us pray for his soul, that God in the fullness of his pity may take David unto himself and to heaven's eternal feast.

(And he shall bury him, carrying the body under one of the tents, and shall go to Solomon; and the messenger says:)

SECOND MESSENGER

Let us go and fetch Solomon and place him on his throne, king designate in his royal chair, that he may be crowned as was enjoined upon us by his father before he died.

HERE SOLOMON SHALL MAKE HIS APPEARANCE

COUNSELOR

May felicity be yours, Solomon, and do not delay in coming with us to the throne of your father, David. You have been chosen as our king, your coronation a certainty within a short time.

KING SOLOMON

I will come with you very gladly, lords, and for the honor you are prepared to do me, my heartfelt thanks. By my head, if a year from this day finds me still alive, I shall have repaid my debt to you, no matter who may attempt to object.

(Here Solomon goes down.)

SECOND MESSENGER

Proceed to enter your palace now, Solomon, for you are to rule, once having received the crown. Likewise take your seat upon the throne of David, your father, inasmuch as he has bequeathed it to you.

(Here he shall enter.)

KING SOLOMON

To you also, sirs, my profound thanks. If I live, you will hold top rank in my bodyguard, and, because I received the crown at your hands, I shall bestow upon you Bosvannah, Lostwithiel, and Lanner.[20]

(King Solomon shall walk about here, and afterward says:)

Messenger, my highborn, devoted, and trustworthy envoy and servant, come forward.

SECOND MESSENGER

In spite of any labor or pain it might cost me, my dear lord Solomon, I will never fail you.

KING SOLOMON

Go then and command the city's workers to assemble here under penalty of death: that is to say, the masons and carpenters, the stone-cutters and roofers, to the end that the building of the temple may be completed.

SECOND MESSENGER

By Saint Gylmyn, sire, I shall carry out your orders to the last detail and will put all your craftsmen on notice to appear before you tomorrow.

(Here he shall enter.)

Hear ye, hear ye, nobles and commoners! The king commands all carpenters, masons, and roofers into his presence tomorrow morning, his purpose to complete the temple which his father left unfinished.

(Let him return to his station.)

My dear lord, I have been in the city where I firmly instructed the craftsmen to come to you tomorrow without fail.

KING SOLOMON

I am indebted to you, Griffin,[21] for dehydrating yourself in your zeal. If mead or wine is not forthcoming, repair to the fountain.[22] For my part, I want to have a look at my workmen as soon as possible and charge them from the outset to produce results of high, individual quality.

(Here let King Solomon go down.)

FIRST CARPENTER

My God, what a beautiful tree for rafters! Big, well-rounded butt and a nicely tapered trunk, and from the top and branches I can cut me first-rate small stuff like laths and corbels.

KING SOLOMON

Heaven prosper your labors, men! It seems to me you work very steadily and carefully. Blend your lime and clay into good walls with a strong top on them.

FIRST MASON

Permit me to advise your majesty that the walls are now fully raised and are exactly plumb. Faith, I can vouch for them at this time, confident that nobody is going to find a single fault in any of them.

KING SOLOMON

Very well said, my good fellow. I find your work most satisfactory; in fact, both of you are excellent men. And as a reward for your fine work, I am giving you the parish of Budock, plus Seal Rock with all its land.[23]

SECOND MASON

Ah, such generosity! Many thanks, many thanks! We can really make merry over a gift like that. Now we see, comrades, that there are no true master craftsmen in this kingdom, except us masons.

SECOND CARPENTER

Mate, let's you and me check the rafters to make sure they're accurate for the walls so that we can go on to the bracing and then the roofing-in and wind up with a job that'll be a pleasure to look at.

FIRST CARPENTER

It won't do any harm to try. Ho, lads, lend a hand with getting the timbering up and fixed. At the ridge of the roof,[24] though, we'll need a firm support or else the whole thing will be weak.

SECOND CARPENTER

By God's fast, these rafters have been well set! They're exactly measured and accurate for the walls. All you roofers, hurry it up and get the temple under cover before rain can wet the rafters.

KING SOLOMON

Definitely, my men, you and you only are to do the roofing because you're clever in every branch of your craft. But let me have a responsible answer to this question: where will you find a timber straight as a spear-shank for the ridgetree?

FIRST CARPENTER

Upon my word, the truth is that in all your forests taken together there isn't a piece of standing timber good for anything when it comes to a center-beam and that goes for the rest of the kingdom as well, except the one tree which has those bands of silver around it.

KING SOLOMON

As heaven is my witness, I am very reluctant to have that tree cut down, but since no other is obtainable, go at once and fell it in honor of God, praised be his name, and then measure it with utmost care.

(Solomon returns to his station.)

SECOND CARPENTER

I will measure it carefully enough, God knows, have no fear on that score, my noble lord. I'll use a true square and a measuring stick so that the timber will come out neither longer nor shorter than my markings in any direction.

FIRST CARPENTER

Here we have it before us, measured so expertly that nobody on earth could do a better job of it. This is the point at which I'll make bold to cut it, and you keep it steady with all your strength.

SECOND CARPENTER

Damn your eyes, you held your line so true before cutting that now the thing is a good foot and a half too short.

FIRST CARPENTER

All I ask you to do is lower it to the ground, and it'll be fixed right away. There's no call to get mad at me, as I'll join an extra piece onto it. . . . Now it's bound to be the right length. Let's hurry up and adjust it to its place.

SECOND CARPENTER

The devil fit you into his gut, he can't fit this beam into its place. This time it's too long by a foot and a half. Cut it in the exact middle of the joint, and if that doesn't make it right, I don't know what to say.

FIRST CARPENTER

We'll handle it your way: I mean, cut it through the middle of the joint, the middle as figured, I swear, by every mark there is! I'm cutting it here, dead between the two ends of the joint, and absolutely for the last time ever, by the Lord God!

SECOND CARPENTER

So let's raise it. . . . Oh, for God's sake, now the fact is it's too short by at least a foot and a half! What an infernal nuisance! Let's go to the king and lay it on the line that this timber can't be cut to measure. . . .

FIRST CARPENTER

My lord King Solomon, this particular timber is a miracle-worker many times over. The truth is that no matter how carefully and patiently you measure it, it comes out too long one time, too short the next.

KING SOLOMON

Since that is the situation, I order it placed immediately and with full honors in the temple, there to lie and to be scrupulously venerated by all on pain of death.

And I direct you, respected carpenters, to locate in my forests another tree suitable for a main beam, a timber free from knotholes or blemishes. Do it yourselves and without trickery.

SECOND CARPENTER

If only it's the right length for us, I know where there's a timber already cut and cleanly shaped.

FIRST CARPENTER

Then in God's name let's get out of here and bring it into town where we can measure it for certain. . . .

SECOND CARPENTER

There it is, lying on the ground, and I've already measured it twice for this same job.

FIRST CARPENTER

We'll carry it to town on our backs and set it in its place, seeing it fills the bill so well. . . .

SECOND CARPENTER

Let's put the beam where it belongs. The sweet God grant that it settles in here for good and all!

FIRST CARPENTER

I'm ready to swear we couldn't have found a straighter tree any place or for this spot a better one, not if we'd searched forever.

SECOND CARPENTER

Then let's go right to our lord Solomon and tell him that the building of the temple is finished. . . .

(To King Solomon)

Greetings to you, my lord, on your throne! With quiet efficiency the temple has been brought to completion. We ask from you our wages.

KING SOLOMON

May you have the Father's blessing, and as for your wages, those you shall surely have, by God's foe. I give you forthwith the following: the entire field of Bohelland[25] and all of Penryn wood,[26] plus the whole of Gwarder, Enys, and Arwennack, Tregenver and Kergilliack.[27] Assume them for yourselves as a joint freehold.

FIRST CARPENTER

Our thanks, matchless lord. We can be justly proud, for never, by my cap, have a pair of artisans received gifts as good as these.

KING SOLOMON

I desire at this time to ordain the clerk of my privy seal[28] as overseer in the temple, who shall maintain the law and intone the service to God. I propose to consecrate him without delay.

(The Counselor becomes bishop, and he says:)

COUNSELOR

Sire and lord, may God reward you in your purpose of conferring upon me so great an honor. It is only fit and right that I should serve

you faithfully as, for advancing the legitimate interests of your subjects, this world does not contain your equal.

(Here the Counselor puts on clerical vestments.)

KING SOLOMON

In truth I have been contemplating for some time your preferment
to the first benefice I might have. Accordingly, I now consecrate you
bishop. Take your mitre, and in your service be faithful.

(Here he gives the mitre to the bishop.)

BISHOP

Since it is your wish, I will receive the mitre in the name and to
the glory of our heavenly Father and, God willing it for the best, will
immediately say a service to him in the temple.

(Here the bishop goes down and shall cross to the Temple.)

On the instant I direct that all present shall raise their voices in
praise and honor to God the Father. And after that let each of us
partake of a draught of wine to the comfort of his heart.

*(And then they shall pray and speak low as if saying prayers; Maxi-
milla shall come into the Temple and sit on the timber and her clothes
catch fire from the timber, and she cries out, saying:)*

MAXIMILLA

O Father God, in mercy send me help for the pain that pierces me.
Oh! Oh! Oh! I'm in fearful trouble, my clothes have caught fire from
the tree of Christ. I'm sure of it.

My dear Lord Christ Jesus, God of heaven, put out the fierce flames,
even as by your body Adam and Eve shall be redeemed and brought
to heaven with song.

BISHOP

What's that? Punishment awaits you, you blockhead! Where have
you ever heard God called by such a name as Christ by any man

alive? I have in my possession the Law of Moses, and I declare that nowhere in all its pages does that name appear.

Furthermore, we do not acknowledge the existence of any God save the Father of heaven above, yet you, a wench of doubtful reputation at best, have the audacity to fabricate a God for yourself alone. May I be pilloried like a naughty woman[29] if I let you get away before you make abject amends for your blasphemy and completely forswear every word you have uttered.

MAXIMILLA

Foolish bishop, I will not recant, for the truth is that those three rods which were planted by David and which grew into the one tree are a token, clear and beyond doubt, of the Three Persons in the Trinity.

(Here the bishop goes up to his tent.)

One is the Father of heaven; another is Christ, his only Son, who will be born of a virgin mother; and the third is the Holy Ghost; three and one, in single Godhead dwelling. That is my faith.

BISHOP

I denounce you, O most vile imposter, manifest and potent witch! However great your pride, you shall pay for it, base creature. By God's blood I swear it and in the near madness of my vexation. You there, boy, be a man and give me counsel.

CROSIER-BEARER

Without splitting hairs—what I'm about to say is no fable—my advice to you is that, if you want to destroy this woman, order your men to stone her and don't allow them to stop until she is dead for sure.

BISHOP

By the Lord's fast, well spoken. You're a good lad, so help me God, and when it comes to giving counsel, a prudent man. All torturers of every rank, come forward now in response to my need of you.

FIRST TORTURER

I salute you, my lord, ever powerful and magnificent! As sure as day follows night, I'm sweaty-headed from hurrying to reach you. So please tell me straight off what it is you want me to do. If I can, I will, my life on it.

BISHOP

Go, drag from our temple the hateful wretch of a woman who is conjuring up false gods and strike her down with stones. Take no rest until her soul leaves her body.

SECOND TORTURER

We shan't dawdle, by God's spirit, for we intend to strike and strike hard until we're exhausted. . . . You've drunk your last, woman, you're going to be very dead.

THIRD TORTURER

Look out! Give me room to let fly a real crusher on the nasty trollop's head with this mallet, so she'll never eat again but instead will rot and stink like whale oil or the mud of a marsh.

FOURTH TORTURER

I'll bludgeon her throat so hard it'll set a record for mashing skin and flesh into one festering bruise.

FIRST TORTURER

Square on the chest in front is my target, huge belts with plenty behind them until she drops, hammered down to bits no bigger than malt-sprouts.

MAXIMILLA

Lord Jesus Christ of heaven, take mercy on my soul while for your sake I am in torment! Because I called on your name that once, I shall surely perish. Lord, forgive my sins.

SECOND TORTURER

Do you hear, comrades, how the filthy whore cries out to a thing that isn't? Earlier she wanted to pull the wool over the bishop's eyes and trick him into worshipping some newfangled god.

THIRD TORTURER

Just for that, I want to pound her face, shatter her arms and legs. Foul, lowdown slut that you are, you're done for, completely and absolutely, in spite of your god or his power.

FOURTH TORTURER

I don't give a fart for his power, and I defy both his father and his mother. The jade dies. As of now, woman, your luck runs out. With my blow, every last bone in your body gets itself broken.

(Here Maximilla dies.)

FIRST TORTURER

Suppose we call it a day, boys, seeing that the tart was finished off quite awhile back by the treatment I gave her, making the heart-blood gush all over the place. Let's go to the bishop and tell him the job is done.

SECOND TORTURER

Ah! Do me a favor and shut up, chum. If they gave me the world, I wouldn't believe the drab is dead. Before ever I leave, I'm going to give her a good-bye pat with a nice big chunk of rock.

THIRD TORTURER

Again greetings, reverend sir and bishop. At this moment the girl lies stretched at full length, dead. Even so, though she died, she did not recant, either in the beginning or at the end.

BISHOP

There is no cause for worry on that account. Her reward has gone with her, and her punishment fits her crime. For your services you shall have Bohelland and Bosaneth.[30] Proceed at once to take possession of them before nightfall. I give you these places and all the Canonry of the Close[31] in addition.

FOURTH TORTURER

Aha! A generous gift, noble bishop. Let's all shout together: a generous gift! a generous gift! A man is always right to do his best for a bishop like this, a real highborn gentleman, as anyone can see.

BISHOP

You, Gebal, stir yourself and carry the tree out of the Temple. Put some drive into the task and let Amalek help you with it. Throw the tree, every inch of it, into the pool of Bethsaida,[32] an appropriately filthy resting place for a troublemaker.

(Here Gebal carries the wood to Bethsaida.)

GEBAL

The job will be done promptly. Hang you, Amalek, keep a grip on your end!

AMALEK

Let's get going right now and run with the thing, run hard and toss it into the water. . . .

(A messenger comes to the bishop.)

MESSENGER

My dear lord, it's only too evident that your disposal of the tree has accomplished nothing except to place you in a bad light. People keep saying that, from the time it went into the pool, the tree has been healing the sick, and, as a result, you are being very severely blamed because you had it removed from the Temple despite the great magic it possesses.

BISHOP

That doesn't matter in the least. I still have a good plan in reserve, I swear it! Since there is no bridge over Cedron, I will order my men to drag it there, where it can be trod underfoot and its virtue unfailingly lessened by the defilement.

Amalek and Gebal, convey the tree to Cedron forthwith that it may serve as a bridge over the stream.

AMALEK

The big stretch to your neck too, Gebal, unless you buckle down and lug one end to the river while I give the other a hefty boost. . . . This job depresses him so, he looks fit to choke on it.

(Here the wood shall be carried from Bethsaida and made a bridge over the water of Cedron.)

GEBAL

It's no wonder I'm blue, toting this log here, there, and everywhere and nothing in it for us, not a thing. So we keep on carrying it, confound you, until our arms and legs turn to lead, and we're clean worn out.

KING SOLOMON

Good people, you have seen how God the Father created the heavens and the earth, shaping them in accordance with his intent. After that, through his grace, he willed into being Adam and Eve and made them in his own likeness, indeed. He gave them and the children who should come after them the whole world as their dwelling place forever.

The fullness of God's blessing be upon you, men and women both. The play is ended, but, in order to see the Passion which Christ suffered for us, return tomorrow in good time. And now let us all go home. Play, good musicians, in honor of the Father on high.

II   CHRIST'S PASSION

Principal Characters

in

Order of Appearance

Jesus	First Doctor
Peter	Second Doctor
Andrew	Herod
Satan	Jailor
John	Jailor's Boy
Bartholomew	Lucifer
God the Father	Beelzebub
Michael	Dismas
Gabriel	Mary
James the Greater	Mary Jacobi
Matthew	Mary Salome
Caiaphas	Smith
Pilate	Smith's Wife
Simon the Leper	Jesmas
Judas Iscariot	Centurion
Mary Magdalene	Longius
Prince Annas	Nicodemus
Thomas	Joseph of Arimathea

Here Commences the Drama

of the

PASSION OF OUR LORD JESUS CHRIST

(Jesus stands on the Mount of the Forty Days' Fast, namely, in the desert between Jericho and Jerusalem.)

JESUS

My disciples, these are my words to you: pray forthwith, your voices as one voice, that almighty God on high will shed his grace upon you in this world in order that you may be saved in the world to come; that with the radiant angels of heaven your souls shall dwell forever, free from pain and in the joy that knows no end.

Pray that God the Father will preserve us from the Evil One, who at all times and in all places very cunningly tempts us to choose the bad and reject the good. Of this I speak truth.

The Evil One labors unceasingly to bring upon mankind not salvation but the pains of the damned. That is his whole desire.

And though both young and old find themselves deceived by his witchery, let them implore forgiveness since thus the Evil One's power will soon be lessened. Mercy is a shield to him who prays for it, regardless of who he may be. Prayer from a full heart banishes temptation and secures peace of soul.

(Here let all come down from the mountain.)

And for your sake I beseech my Father to grant you salvation through the fullness of his grace, taking you unto himself and his kingdom, where there is neither trouble nor strife but only joy, sure and everlasting in the company of the angels.

Heart cannot conceive the bliss that shall be yours through all eternity.

81

PETER

May our love and devotion be yours, dear Master, in return for the wisdom and beauty of the words by which you teach us, the lettered and unlettered alike, how deeply we desire to pray for God's mercy.

ANDREW

All of us, regardless of age, will ceaselessly implore God's favor upon our cause, that we may be shielded from the Evil One and attain salvation through time without end.

JESUS

It is also necessary to mortify the flesh through penance if the destructive power of the Devil is to be weakened, even as I, having fasted for forty days and forty nights, now know what it is to be hungry.

SATAN

If he longs for food, I am sure beyond the possibility of doubt that he is not God. I'll go and tempt him to eat, on the chance that I can induce him to commit gluttony.

Yet in spite of all my power, it's as good as certain that I shan't ever manage to entrap him in sin's net since he is the one man who shall redeem all men. But for his work and his teaching, mankind would perish.

(Here Satan comes down and says to Jesus:)

I say to you, if you are really the son of God above, command this heap of stones to become bread. Then I'll know for sure the nature and extent of your power.

JESUS

The fullness of man's life is not contained in bread alone but in the saving words that come from the Trinity.

(To the disciples:)

Through this, my disciples, you can perceive how the word of God sustains the man who is able to receive it.

JOHN

O dear and beloved Master, in accordance with your teaching, I believe that our souls will be fed by God's word, and I believe, as it is written in the Scriptures, that we shall be brought to the everlasting light and joy of heaven, the spirits of evil overcome.

SATAN

If you are the Lord of bright heaven, show me a miracle so I may see it for myself. Mount the pinnacle of the Temple and seat yourself there, not that it's a particularly comfortable location for you.

JESUS

I will ascend to the pinnacle alone and take my seat, withdrawn for a little while in meditation.

(Then the Devil shall tempt Jesus, saying:)

SATAN

You're seated high and precariously, i'faith! It's written in Scripture that angels are guarding you for fear you'll topple and fall, dashing your foot against a stone. If, however, you are the great and only son of God, just descend to the ground.

JESUS

It is also written in the Scriptures that you shall not tempt the Lord your God but rather shall yield him universal worship.

(Jesus descends.)

Let us leave this place, companions, and go into the hills, there to walk and pray to my most precious Father, whose name be glorified, that through his will you likewise may be kept safe from downfall.

ANDREW

As long as I live, dear Lord, I will follow your wishes in everything and with fasting and praise call upon God in all his strength
and goodness to send us his grace.

BARTHOLOMEW

The entire world owes you its homage, dear Master, in return for
the transcendent worth of your message. Fortunate is the man who
abides in your service ever free from sorrow.

(Again the Devil shall tempt Jesus, saying:)

SATAN

Before us is a high mountain from whose summit I will show you
an immense prospect. The whole world shall be yours, my solemn
word on it, if you will listen to what I have to say.

Feast your eyes upon the joys of all the world: rich cities, valuable
towns, great and lofty castles. On the instant that you kneel to me in
worship, you shall have them all.

JESUS

Satan, devil accursed, it is written in the Scriptures that you shall
worship the name of the Lord your God alone. Depart from me,
accursed one, into wilderness and darkness, your power over men's
souls forever destroyed.

SATAN

To have approached him was a calamity, since during this one day
I have been defeated by him not once but three times and through
him have completely lost the great power that was mine, my only
song, "Alas, alas!"

(Satan retires.)

GOD THE FATHER

Angels, arise! Leave our presence and go hence to serve my most treasured Son, who this day has thrice overcome the false fiend. Happy he who worships him with a full heart.

MICHAEL

O Father God, Almighty, our obedience to your command is ever sure. In reverence and high respect I will serve your dear and only Son, Jesus Christ, and Mary, his mother.

(Here let the angels descend.)

GABRIEL

Jesus the Christ, king in heaven and earth and Lord most powerful, we wish you joy! Your dear Father, his name be praised, has sent us to serve you and to bear witness that you are very pleasing in his sight.

JESUS

For so greatly honoring me, in that he has sent his archangels to be my servants, I render my devout thanksgiving to God, my most merciful Father.

(Then sending two disciples to a village to seek for an ass and foal, Jesus says:)

JESUS

My disciples, I desire that two of you go at once into the village that now lies before us. There you will find an ass and a foal tied together. Bring them directly to me.

And if anyone says anything in opposition to you, you are to answer him, saying, "The Lord has a purpose for them." They will be given over into your hands.

JAMES THE GREATER

I will unfailingly carry out your instructions, dear Lord, exactly as you have delivered them. Let's be on our way, sweet brother. I'll talk to the man so agreeably that he won't object to what we're doing.

(James and Matthew go for the ass and foal.)

MATTHEW

I'll go with you gladly, and we'll bring the two beasts back with us. Lead on then, I beg you, in the Lord's name.

JAMES THE GREATER

The sum of my prayer is that God the Father, who made all things, will allow us to do well with this day's work, Amen. Look, there's the ass, and the foal is tied with it. As you are a Christian, lend me a hand.

KEEPER

Tell me now, you two fellows, why are you leading my animals away?

MATTHEW

I'll give you the answer: the Lord God, by your leave, has a certain purpose in mind for them.

KEEPER

Since that is his wish, let him take them and use them entirely as he pleases. I'd be only too glad if they turned out to be worth a thousand pounds of good gold to him.

JAMES THE GREATER

That he is the Lord is true, and his work proves it. In my opinion, whoever fails to worship him as he should is not a wise man.

(And then he shall come with the ass and foal to Jesus. Matthew and James kiss Jesus, and Matthew says:)

MATTHEW

May your heart be gladdened, sweet Master! See, I have for you the ass and foal. I'll spread layers of cloth on the grown one's back to make you more comfortable as you ride. If the time has come, I suggest you mount.

JESUS

I pray that my Father in his splendour will ever help you, each and all of you, to resist the temptation of the Evil One, to the end that when I have passed from this life, your souls may inherit the joy of heaven. You are the chosen, the faithful twelve.

(Then the Hebrew children come, and let them bear palms and flowers toward Jesus, and the first boy says:)

FIRST BOY

They say that Jesus, the holy man, is coming here to the city. I want to go and meet him and see him. They say he's God and very, very good and kind.

SECOND BOY

We'll all go to meet him and show our respect. He must be everybody's God of kindness.

THIRD BOY

Boys, let's hurry up and make it a procession of us Jewish children and go to meet Jesus, the real God coming to town.

FOURTH BOY

We'll do it, and when we find olive branches we'll lay them on the ground in front of him and honor him the best we can, all of us on our knees singing a worship song.

FIFTH BOY

If I can't find any good branches, I'm going to take off clothes and lay them under his feet and sing to our Messiah, "Blessed is the Son of Grace who comes in the name of the Lord."

SIXTH BOY

I'll do the same: take off my best clothes and throw them down before him. Besides that, I've got beautiful flowers in honor of the good Lord and will scatter them in his path.

SEVENTH BOY

I've got palm and bays and ripe box. Lord of heaven, guard me from all evil.

(Now Jesus shall mount upon the ass with its foal and shall ride to the Temple, and he says:)

JESUS

My blessing be upon all of you for gathering to do me honor with branches and with flowers. The day will surely come when I shall repay you in equal measure, honor for honor.

FIRST BOY

Son of David,[1] joy to you! I beg you to save us and bring us to heaven. Blessed is he who comes in the name of God. Praise him, the King of Israel, the mighty Lord!

SECOND BOY

Joy to you, Son of David! Son of Man you are also, and Son of God. Because you come in the name of the Lord, I believe you blessed.

THIRD BOY

Blessed indeed are you! Happy the man who is worthy to worship you faithfully. I truly believe that through you we shall be saved. O Son of God, joy to you!

FOURTH BOY

Joy to you, Lord of heaven and earth! Grant me the grace to dwell with you among the angels.

FIFTH BOY

Joy indeed to him who is both true God and man! Through him we shall all be saved.

SIXTH BOY

Merciful Jesus, Son and Father, full of compassion, we pray that unfailing joy be yours.

SEVENTH BOY

Sweet Jesus of Nazareth, may your joy be unhindered and your honor great! I truly believe you are the world's salvation. Have mercy on me.

JESUS

My eternal blessing upon all of you, my children. Your wish shall be heard, and you shall be well rewarded, in very truth, for the honor you have done me this day.

(Then let Jesus dismount and go into the Temple, and Jesus says:)

I will dismount and go into the Temple that I may see for myself the nature and extent of that so-called fair. If there are buyers and sellers of goods in the house of God, I will drive them out, to the last man, and overturn their wares.

(Here Bishop Caiaphas shall parade.)

CAIAPHAS

Tell me, companions, who is that fellow who rode into the city on the back of an ass with a foal, taking the route to the Temple? It's my thought that he will have taken another way yet, before he dies.

CLOTH DEALER

He is the prophet Jesus, who says he is the son of the God of heaven above. Actually, he hails from Nazareth, a town in the Kingdom of Galilee.

(The cloth dealer shall go to the Temple. Caiaphas goes up to the tent.)

JESUS

Out, all you traders, get out! You are making a mockery of God and his holy church when you turn my house of prayer into a bazaar, into a den for loathsome thieves.

TRADER

Say now, you there, Jesus, what token have you got for exhibiting all this muscle, giving us the back of your hand, scattering our stock hither and yon and ruining the fair?

JESUS

Indeed I will show you what token: if this temple were to be leveled to the ground, not a stone left standing, within three days I would build it again, making it more beautiful than it was before.

CLOTH DEALER

That's just a sneering joke, pure and simple. It took forty-six years to build the Temple, yet this man is going to raise it in three days even though it had been reduced to rubble.

(Here Pilate parades.)

PILATE

I shall proceed to the Temple[2] for worship and for prayer to Jove, convinced that that fellow Jesus is overreaching himself. In his arrogance, he seeks to destroy the fair.

(Having gone down, let Pilate cross over to the Temple of Jerusalem, and the trader says to Caiaphas:)

TRADER

Greetings, Caiaphas, lord and bishop, I beg you to help me! That haughty fellow, Jesus, has been blustering much too much here in town, claiming that though the Temple were demolished he would raise it up again in three days.

CAIAPHAS

The rascal lies. Unless he retracts his nonsense, by sacred Jove, he shall pay for it! Here comes the magistrate. Suppose we let him deal with the fellow as he sees fit, once he hears what the man has been saying.

(Then Pilate shall come to Caiaphas, the chief priest, and says:)

PILATE

Felicitations, Lord Caiaphas. What goings-on we're having in the Temple at the hands of that faker and vagabond Jesus! He's wrecked the market and is making a big thing of it because he's hungry for prestige.

CAIAPHAS

Welcome, Pilate, and well met! The man has caused a great deal of disorder, on top of which, out of sheer egotism, he has proclaimed that though the Temple were leveled to the ground he would rebuild it, not only completely but better than ever, within three days.

PILATE

He's just boasting. Everybody knows that no man in the world could rebuild it in three days' time under any conceivable circumstances. I'll question him. If he can make his claim good, we ought all to worship him on land and sea alike.

(Then all go to the Temple, and the blind man says:)

BLIND MAN

Jesus, gracious Lord, since you are the Messiah, I implore you in charity to heal my eyes. Never yet, come good times or bad, have I had a moment's sight with them.

LAME MAN

And I, a cripple, fervently beseech you for the sake of the hallowed Father to enable me to walk by virtue of your grace, and from this day on I will believe that you are the virgin-born Son of God, our Redeemer.

JESUS

It gladdens me to make you whole, *in nomine patris et filii et spiritus sancti. Amen. Transite a me sani.*

BLIND MAN

O sweet Jesus, of infinite mercy, with these eyes I now can see . . . can see! Most truly and with all my strength I believe you Lord of heaven and earth.

LAME MAN

O precious Lord, I am straight and comely, cured of all disease! Blessed be your name above all names.

FIRST BOY

Son of David, blessed beyond all, joy to you! When I am dead, write my soul in your book, I pray.

SECOND BOY

Joy to you, son of David, blessed beyond all! Son of God and man are you, come in the name of the Lord.

THIRD BOY

Jesus, King of Israel, I ask that joy be yours! And when I pass from the world, let an angel bring my soul to you.

PILATE

What do you have to say, Jesus, about the children's singing? Youth is often very vocal and opinionated.

JESUS

Scripture records that it is in the mouths of innocent children and those still put to the breast that praise achieves perfection.

(Pilate says to Caiaphas:)

PILATE

This is getting us nowhere, Caiaphas, it's a dead end. Everybody is lining up behind the man.

CAIAPHAS

To put it bluntly, you don't know what you're saying or even what you're trying to say. Take my word for it, it's better for one man to die than for all the faithful to be lost.

PILATE

By Jupiter, the ruler of the world, we'll deal with the stubborn and repulsive fellow as you suggest. I'll trap him in his own words, to which nobody should pay serious attention.

(And then all shall go to their tents and Simon the Leper shall come to Jesus, and he says to him:)

SIMON THE LEPER

Lord, provided you are willing, I beg you and your disciples to eat a meal with me. Food has been prepared for you and them at a place close by.

JESUS

We will be glad to accept your invitation. Peter, Andrew, and John, Simon, Jude, let us be on our way. . . .

(Here Mary Magdalene shall come to Jesus in the house of Simon the Leper.)

JUDE

It was good to have accepted this invitation, Lord. Invariably you know what's best for you to do. And the counsel you give, you, the source of all things, is the wisest in the world.

MARY MAGDALENE

I will go and anoint my Lord's hands and feet with precious ointment and pour it upon his head, that it may salve his hurts and banish all weariness.

Joy to you, sweet Master! If you will let me, I want to kiss your feet, unworthy though I am. There, my tears have wet them, but they are tears of honest love, and I will wipe them away with my hair.

I want to break the costly box that holds the ointment and pour it upon your head and your feet.

SIMON THE LEPER

Were he an ordained prophet, surely he'd know that the woman is a sinner. He wouldn't allow her to anoint him.

JESUS

Simon, I have something I wish to say to you. Let me have your attention.

SIMON THE LEPER

Speak your full mind, Master, without delay, I shan't raise a single objection.

JESUS

Somewhere on the face of the earth, there were once three men, comprising two debtors to the one creditor. I believe the first debtor owed the creditor five hundred dinars, while the second owed him fifty dinars. He canceled both debts in their entirety because neither man had anything with which to meet his obligation.

Answer me this in brief: which of the two men was bound to love this same creditor the more?

SIMON THE LEPER

There's no need to be slow with my reply. He to whom most is forgiven will love the most, any time, any place.

JESUS

Your decision is doubtless sound. Now observe this woman. Since I entered your house, you have issued no order for the washing of my feet, yet the woman has indeed washed them, with her tears moreover, and with her hair she has dried them.

You have given me no kiss, but this woman has never ceased, since I came to you in your house, to kiss my feet and anoint my head.

Surely, therefore, the full sum of her sins is forgiven because her love for me has been so great. I say to you, woman, go in peace, your faith has made you clean.

JUDAS ISCARIOT

Why was it necessary to waste the precious ointment? It could have been sold for three hundred dinars or more and the money given to the poor of the world.

(Here all shall rise and walk about.)

JESUS

Do not harbor resentment in your hearts against her who anointed me, for the time of suffering draws near when I may no longer remain among you. Unlike me, the poor you have always with you, calling upon you for that charity which you are free to bestow at will.

Contrariwise, the balm which the woman poured upon me was for my burial and was a deed of love. Wherever the good report of what she has done may hereafter be read, her name shall be held in imperishable honor.

(The sequence continues with Caiaphas.)

CAIAPHAS

Clerk, bring Prince Annas to me that I may hear the best advice on what strategy to adopt against the traitor to whom so many of our men and women are turning with such alacrity.

CROSIER-BEARER

I will, sir, without fail. Bless you and goodbye for the moment. It would be gratifying to have destroyed this false prophet before the Sabbath comes around again.

(And then he shall go to Prince Annas, and as Annas makes his appearance he says to him:)

Good day to you, brilliant and princely sir! Lord Caiaphas sends his greetings by me, *par foi,* and begs you to come to him at his home to give him, if agreeable to you, the benefit of your advice as to what shall be done about this Jesus.

PRINCE ANNAS

I shall be glad to join my father-in-law, to the end that we may eliminate the villain if his utterances prove illegal.

(And then he shall go to the bishop.)

Greetings, Caiaphas, powerful lord and bishop, the best to you a thousand times over!

CAIAPHAS

Welcome, by the blood of Mohammed! Come close and sit with me.

(Annas goes up.)

There's a certain unbelievably arrogant fellow who's in the process of subverting the entire city, I swear it on my hood, from the faith of the Prophet and undermining our doctrines.

PRINCE ANNAS

Send men to ferret him out, in case he's to be found in some house, and let them tie him up, hand and foot, and bring him to us.

(Here Annas and Caiaphas wait, and Judas shall come to them, and he says:)

JUDAS ISCARIOT

Tell me what you're prepared to give me if I make it possible for you to capture Christ without trouble or delay.

CAIAPHAS

On my honor, dear friend, you can have all you want. In fact, don't hesitate for a moment to name us your price.

JUDAS ISCARIOT

Make it thirty pieces of silver money. The truth is I won't accept less, and in addition you must furnish help to go with me and take him secretly at night.

CAIAPHAS

All your demands will be met in full and for certain. As you see, I have the money on hand right here, so now, my good fellow, at what time should the men be dispatched to seize him? And mind that we're not disappointed.

(Here Judas shall take the purse with the money.)

JUDAS ISCARIOT

Once he has sat down to supper, I will come and alert you. But make sure that the men are armed with swords and clubs and are supplied with lighted lanterns so that we won't lose our way in the dark.

CAIAPHAS

Faith, Judas, you've proved yourself a true friend; I will reward you for your services.

(And then Judas Iscariot shall come to Jesus and the Apostles.)

And now we have plenty of weapons and enough strong men to make quick work of seizing the fellow.

(Now let Jesus send disciples to prepare the Lord's Supper.)

JESUS

Go into the town, some of you, and order the Passover food for us. Peter and John, you two go, so that we can have it prepared as soon as possible.

PETER

Only tell us, dear Lord, where in town you'd like to have the meal ordered, and I'll see to it that we're able to eat under fitting circumstances and offer our sacrifice to God the Father.

JESUS

Soon after you are within the city limits, you will meet a servant carrying a pitcher of pure water. Follow him into whatever house he enters and be sure to say to the head of the house that your master has sent you to inquire where he may eat, he and all his disciples, and the man will promptly show you a large room. Ready sufficient food there for our supper.

JOHN

Dearly valued Lord, we will do exactly what you have directed us to do. Friend Peter, let's move on and do our errand carefully.

PETER

Let's do that, as the Master has ordered, and if we find the servant carrying water, we'll follow him indoors.

HEAD OF THE HOUSE

Go to the fountain, trusted servant, and fetch us clear water for cooking the supper which is customary on Maundy Thursday.

SERVANT

I'll fetch it right away. As you see, I have the pitcher with me.

(And then he shall go and fill it.)

I'll double-time it home on my shoulder.

JOHN

Look, Peter, I see a man hustling along with a pitcher of water. The words of our unequaled Master, man and God both, are of necessity coming true.

(And then he shall go to the master of the house, and Peter says to him:)

PETER

God's peace be upon this house. Jesus, our worthy Master, has sent me to inquire about a place hereabouts where he may eat the Passover meal.

HEAD OF THE HOUSE

Come with me. I will show you an accommodation for your Master's supper so roomy that every mother's son—he and all his disciples—can take his ease without crowding.

Here we have a really nice room, spacious as a barn, plenty of straw on the floor. I wouldn't mind having this place inspected by anybody, whether cleric or layman.

JOHN

I'm well pleased with the house. May the great Father of heaven above receive you and your wife into his keeping when you die.

(And then they shall prepare the supper.)

PETER

Suppose you help me get a fire going, John, since it's certain there's enough food on hand here for supper once it's all cooked. Please hurry now so that things can be gotten ready fast.

JOHN

You can see for yourself that the fire has caught. Let them come whenever they have a mind to, their food will be ready. It's still too early for supper, yet this big fire is overbrowning the lamb on the outside before it has a chance to roast tender on the inside.

(Now Jesus arises and shall go to the supper.)

JESUS

Let us be on our way, for Peter and John have prepared the evening meal. By the time we join them, the hour to sup will have arrived.

And now, dear Simon, my blessing be upon you and remain with you.

(And then Jesus withdraws from Simon and shall come to Peter and John, and kissing them, he says:)

JESUS

May the peace of God inhabit this dwelling and my blessing be also upon each of you. Is the Paschal Lamb ready for us that we may go in to supper? Even as my affection for you is great and constant, tell me the fact of it, Peter.

PETER

Beloved Lord, it is ready, and God grant that I and all my brethren are found worthy to be your faithful servants. Sit down quietly, everybody; you'll be served at once.

(And then all sit at supper, and Jesus says:)

JESUS

I speak only the truth when I tell you how great has been my wish to share the Paschal meal with you this night, my last ere I am delivered over to cruel torment and to death before tomorrow midday.

Take up your wine and drink, for I shall not again partake of it with you until the final day; until I, and you with me, enter into my Father's kingdom and mine, there to dwell forever in joy that has no end.

JOHN

Dear Master, I, for one, will gladly do what you ask. As long as you are in the world with us, we'll never be anything but happy unless, seeing trouble come to you, our God and our leader, it comes to us as well.

JESUS

Again the truth. I say that one of you, this very night, has sold me to my enemies. One who is eating with me at this moment will surely betray me and will, indeed, send me to my death.

JUDAS ISCARIOT

If, Lord, I am the one, you must tell me so that no other man can be falsely accused.

JESUS

Eating with me at this very table and from my dish is the man who has already sold me. The Son of God shall pass from the world, as it is written of him at more than one place in the Scriptures, but woe to that man by whom I am betrayed! It were a thousand times better for him, by my Father, had he never been born.

JUDAS ISCARIOT

In the name of your Father, dear Master, tell me without delay, am I the one who has betrayed you to your death at the hands of the Jews?

JESUS

I have told you before and will tell you again: you have said it, Judas—the truth, by my faith.

(Here Jesus gives the Host to the Apostles.)

Each of you take now a portion of this bread and eat it. As I have taught you, it is the offering of my body betrayed and stretched in death upon the tree of the cross. Through it you and all my people, both men and women, shall be redeemed. . . .

ANDREW

O my precious, consecrated Lord, I wonder and wonder which of us the betrayer could possibly be.[3] . . .

JAMES THE LESS

Who is regarded as the foremost man among us, your disciples, Master? Let whoever knows, answer, no matter how stubborn and grudging he may be at heart.

JAMES THE GREATER

The man who holds the highest rank will be called the greatest. Everybody knows that.

SIMON

Then come out with it at once, James, seeing that you are considered wise among present company. Who is it, pray?

JESUS

Hitherto, certainly, kings have always held dominion over their subjects, and those in power have invariably been accounted great by young and old alike.

May it never be thus with you, however. Let him who is the most important among you and has the greatest power be like the least of you, while he who heads the table ranks himself with him who serves it.

So give me a thoughtful answer to this question: which of these two is the greater in your opinion—he who serves the food or he who is served?

SIMON

Isn't it the one who eats? It seems to me that's surely right. A lord is greater than a butler.

JESUS

I have taken my place in your midst as a servant serving, and you have lived through all my temptations with me. I have ordained for you the kingdom of heaven, that you may abide there in joy, even as my Father ordained it for me, and likewise blissfully eat and drink at my table on high. On Judgment Day, you shall sit as judges over all mankind, rendering justice to each and every man in accordance with his deserts.

BARTHOLOMEW

May you be blessed, Master, for your flawless teachings which are ever at our disposal. No man can dispute what you say because it is so soundly and compellingly reasoned.

(Here Jesus gives wine to the Apostles.)

JESUS

Now let all drink of the wine, for this is my blood in fee, which shall be shed for you as an atonement for sins. Unfailingly remember me whenever you partake of it.

PHILIP

I pray that God the Father, of his grace, will make us worthy to receive your precious blood this day as you have decreed.

(Here water is got ready for washing the Apostles' feet; also a towel.)

JESUS

Let someone heat water at the fire, for after supper I will wash the feet of all of you and with a clean linen towel wipe away the last traces of grime and mire.

(Then John the Apostle comes with warm water and a foot tub, and John says:)

JOHN

Lord, there's enough warm water for everyone to have his feet washed.

JESUS

Pour it into the basin, and I will straightway wash them spotlessly clean.

(And meanwhile Jesus, girt with a towel, shall begin to wash the disciples' feet, and when he comes to Peter, Peter says to him:)

PETER

Lord, if you wash my feet, I'm surely going to be ashamed for the rest of my life.

JESUS

You do not yet understand what it is I do, but in the end, after my departure, you will understand.

PETER

I swear by my father that even if they never get washed, you shan't wash them in any case. My mind is made up!

JESUS

Hush, Peter, hush. I say again, you do not at present grasp the meaning of my action. If by my grace you are not made clean, heaven will never become your home.

PETER

Then, Lord, leave no part of my head or my feet unwashed.

JESUS

He whose spiritual body has been cleansed by baptism has no need of further washing, except his feet that they may not remain dry with dust, for he is already clean.

You are purified from all taint of sin, and yet, indeed, not all of you are pure, since there is one among your number who is much defiled.

JOHN

O dear Master and Lord of heaven, I am utterly persuaded that the ultimate wretchedness for that man is that he ever came into this world!

JESUS

You call me Master and Lord; such is the fact. Therefore, since I washed your feet and wiped them, let each of you, following my example, wash the feet of another.

And, my loved ones, be on your guard against Satan, who, I am convinced, is determined to sift you like corn in a winnowing sheet; precisely as in your case, dear Peter, for whom I have often prayed that your conscience will not be perverted by fear for your life.

PETER

Precious Lord, I am ready to go to prison with you and to be put to death.

JESUS

Before a single night has passed, you will find yourselves, every mother's son of you, bitterly defamed for my sake. When the shepherd is struck down, the sheep run far away, and the flock is scattered. Nevertheless, after my resurrection, I shall, without fail, meet you in Galilee, the whole group reunited there.

PETER

Though the others were estranged to the last man, I will never turn from you, not even in the face of death.

JESUS

Peter, I say to you that before cockcrow, you will deny me thrice.

PETER

Though I were tortured to death through the cruelest of agonies, I would never deny you! And no matter how dreadfully I was threatened, I would not disclaim our peerless Lord, I swear it!

JESUS

Answer me this, my disciples: did you feel the lack of anything essential when I used to send you out, night or day, without staff or purse?

ANDREW

No, dear Lord, we never wanted for anything. Everything was ready for us whenever we needed it.

JESUS

Then let him who has a staff lay his purse aside, and let him who has neither sell his cloak and use the money to buy himself a sword, that the Scriptures may be fulfilled.

(Here two swords are made ready, and let Peter bear one.)

PETER

We are ready armed with a pair of swords,[4] both of them hard-edged and keen.

JESUS

My blessing be ever upon you! Past doubt two such weapons are enough to control the world. . . .

(Then Judas Iscariot shall go to the chief priests, and he says to them:)

JUDAS ISCARIOT

Greetings, my lord bishop, who sits vested in his cope, and greetings, Prince Annas, may good health and prosperity be always yours.

CAIAPHAS

Welcome, Judas, by my faith! By the creed of Mohammed, welcome to my hall and that a thousand times! Is it time to send the soldiers with you to bring in that low rascal?

JUDAS ISCARIOT

It is, sir, in the Devil's name, only let every man make sure that he carries a club or a good sword while you quickly dispatch serving girls with lighted lanterns to show the way.

(Judas Iscariot waits where he is.)

CAIAPHAS

May Mohammed's blessing always be yours, for you have certainly proved loyal, trustworthy, and steadfast in your promises.
All torturers, whatever your rank, come here to me at once. I have need of you.

FIRST TORTURER

Salutations, most honored sir! Awesome was the thunder of your summons. Tell me in confidence what you desire, and I will surely do it.

CAIAPHAS

Torturers, you are to go with Judas to fetch the lunatic who is pretending to be the Son of God. Nothing is more certain than the deep trouble in store for him when I set eyes on him.

PRINCE ANNAS

Inform us, Judas, good friend that you are, how we're to recognize the tricky rogue among his men, since there are no doubt more than a few of his followers who resemble him so closely that we shan't be able to identify the prophet himself.[5]

JUDAS ISCARIOT

I'll give you a reliable sign. As soon as I approach him, I'll greet him and, stepping forward immediately, will kiss him. Faith, that will be your man. Seize him without delay.

(Judas stands and waits with Prince Annas.)

CAIAPHAS

And now, Annas, my dear son-in-law,[6] here is your opportunity to demonstrate that you are prince of princes when it comes to destroying Christians. Bring right here to me this rascally knave who says he's King of the Jews.

PRINCE ANNAS

There's no need to doubt that I shall do just that, because I have a nice bit of strategy for nabbing him. As soon as he's kissed, he's caught, without a chance of lying his way out of it, the faking soothsayer!

CAIAPHAS

Then hurry, sweet son, and mind the rogue doesn't slip through your fingers. If I mean anything to you at all, handle him roughly once you've got a grip on him.

SECOND TORTURER

Let me take prompt care of that, by Mohammed the peerless, and in spite of anything the rogue can do. Let's go, mates. I'll fetch him home to you, my lord, in line with your instructions.

JUDAS ISCARIOT

It's important that you be cautious. The man is very sharp, no doubt of it, and knows a lot of tricks. Sneak up on him, feeling your way, for if he catches no more than a glimpse of you, he'll decamp and hide in a twinkling.

PRINCE ANNAS

What you say makes good sense. Furthermore, when you kiss him, grip him by the throat and squeeze so hard that he can't talk himself free no matter how he tries.

(Then Jesus shall go to the Mount of Olives to pray and shall take with him Peter, James the Greater, and John.)

JESUS

Seat yourselves here, my disciples, and take your rest while I am at prayer; all of you except Peter and James and John, who must come with me.

(Here Peter, James the Greater, and John depart with Jesus.)

THOMAS

Master and Lord over all things, as long as I live, I shall ever do your will.

JESUS

Come with me, the three of you, for my soul is invaded by an exceeding, even a deathly sadness. Sacrifice your comfort, my beloved, and watch with me.

JAMES THE GREATER

Hearing your words, I grow sick at heart. Were I to see you in your agony, I would go down to death with you.

(Then Jesus withdraws from them, and he shall pray, and they shall sleep.)

JESUS

My Father, tender, good, and full of mercy, to whom all things are possible, I your Son, beseech you, if it might be so, to put this death from me that I may live. Yet not my will, Lord, but your will be done, now and forevermore.

(Jesus remains at prayer.)

GOD THE FATHER

Descend to the world, my gentle messenger, and offer to Jesus, my Son, the fairest and most joyous counsel that in you lies.

GABRIEL

O blessed Father, all my desire is to go to him who is my precious Lord.

(Then Gabriel goes down, and he says to the praying Jesus:)

Joy to you and worship! Your Father, in Glory, hallowed be his name, has charged me to bring comfort to your spirit.

JESUS

May my dear Father be praised, for his comfort ever awaits me.

(And then Jesus shall come to the three disciples and shall find them sleeping, and he says to them:)

Peter, could you not have watched with me one brief hour, before the time of my keen torment is upon me? Watch with me again for a little, you three, and in deep earnest pray to my Father that you be kept from weakness. The spirit is indeed willing, but the flesh, under the burden of exhaustion and grief, can be brought strangely low.

PETER

O treasured Master, if humanly possible, we will do as you ask. I fully realize that so far we haven't done well.

JOHN

Our eyes, Lord, are incredibly heavy from staying awake with you, though to watch was our one desire.

(And again Jesus withdraws from them into the garden to pray, and they shall sleep.)

JESUS

Father, if it may not be that death is turned away but rather that I must undergo it, your will be done, for holy Scripture is, of necessity, true.

(And again he shall come to the disciples and shall find them sleeping, and he says to them:)

Once more, my dear ones, awake and together pray for strength to overcome the failings of the flesh. Judas does not sleep a wink but eagerly hastens to hand me over to the erring Jews.

(Here Prince Annas, Judas, and the torturers shall come walking onto the platea.)

JUDAS ISCARIOT

Remember, friends, all of you, the signal I've already told you about. The one I'm going to kiss is your man, my word on it! Don't let anything hinder you from keeping a tight hold on him.

(Jesus shall pray again a third time, saying:)

JESUS

Yet again, most dear and gracious Father, if it is your will, grant that death may not come to me. Nevertheless, if it cannot be otherwise, ever to do your will in all things is the wish of my soul.

(And then he shall come to the disciples a third time, saying:)

Sleep on now, my loved ones, and take your rest. My petition to the Father is complete, and the moment draws near in which the Son of God shall be delivered to deceiving Jews.

(And Judas shall appear again and shall confront them.)

Let us rise and leave this place at once, for the betrayer, Judas, who has sold me, is at hand.

(Here Peter, James, and John depart with Jesus.)

JUDAS ISCARIOT

May happiness be everywhere yours, O dear Master!

(And he kisses Jesus.)

JESUS

Shall I tell you, my good friend, why you kissed me? For a certainty, you have come to kiss me in order to sell me to outright traitors.

(Here Jesus says to Prince Annas and the other Jews:)

For whom are you Hebrews looking? Enlighten me.

PRINCE ANNAS

None other, *par Dieu,* than Jesus of Nazareth, the Christian trickster.

(Then they shall retreat and fall to the ground, and again Jesus shall ask them, saying:)

JESUS

At this moment, then, direct your gaze to me. I am Jesus of Nazareth. However, since you are so eager, again tell us whom you seek.

PRINCE ANNAS

By my faith, Jesus of Nazareth, and for him there will be no pardon.

JESUS

I have already told you that I am he, the very same. Hence, if I and I alone am the object of your search, permit these my followers to go free, for such is my Father's will.

PRINCE ANNAS

So go, and bad luck to you, you rascals! As for the rogue himself, clap hands on him who claims he is the Son of God, and let us give him a most rapid escort to the Lord Bishop Caiaphas, no worse a fate than he deserves.

THIRD TORTURER

I'll put a plenty tight hold on him, my grip so hard he won't be feeling too good.

(And then they shall seize Jesus.)

To the bishop with him, fast, and just so there won't be any time lost on the road, let's get moving right now.

(Then Peter cuts off the ear of a torturer named Malchus and says:)

PETER

Tell me quickly, Master, if it agrees with your judgment and the will of the Father that I use my sword on these people who are holding you, the ugly disbelievers!

FOURTH TORTURER, MALCHUS

Oh! Help, comrades! Look at it, my ear, cut clean off my head by one of his people! Feels like the miserable pain is going right through my heart.

(Here Jesus shall take the ear of Malchus and shall heal him.)

JESUS

Control yourselves, you fools! I will restore the ear forthwith.

(The ear of Malchus is healed.)

In the sacred name of my Father, let it cleave to its place and wholly resume its former condition.

And, Peter, put up your sword, return it to its scabbard again. It is written, "He who lives by the sword shall surely perish by the sword," and the truth of the Scripture is certain.

What is more, do you doubt that I could pray to my Father and he would presently send me from heaven in the one gift twelve legions of angels? Were I to ask it of him, he would not refuse me.

Nevertheless, it is destined, as one may read in many places, that the Son of Man shall suffer on earth before he enters into his beatitude.

(Jesus says to the Jews:)

You have come to me with weapons, with clubs and swords, as though I were the veriest thief in the land. Yet when I taught in your houses of worship, no man laid a hand on me.

(Then all the disciples shall take to flight, except John, who is wrapped in a piece of linen; and Peter follows Jesus at a distance.)

FIRST TORTURER

Son of a no-good, are we ever eager to get you, you monstrous traitor you! Tie his arms together so he can't get away by some nasty trick. He's going to catch it on the jaw, and don't anybody be the least bit afraid.

(Then the second torturer shall lay hold on John the Apostle, and he, abandoning the linen cloth, shall flee naked.)

SECOND TORTURER

Why, you little bastard! What's a kid like you doing with this Jesus fellow? Leave your shirt as a deposit and I'll have it as my tip, while you, by God, will hang!

THIRD TORTURER

By the King of Hell, I don't care how big your arms are, I'll tie them together the way we do for the best of thieves and will take you to Caiaphas because, damn your eyes, you've been such a fool.

FOURTH TORTURER

You tow the scum and I'll drive him with my whip and that ought to give him the staggers for fair. Get a move on there, blast you! By God's face, I think the punk has farted!

(And then they shall come to the bishop with Jesus and shall say to him:)

PRINCE ANNAS

Greetings and salutations, Bishop Caiaphas! Here's our man come with us right into your hall. We're much indebted to Judas, the fact being he led us straight to the rascal.

(Here let Thomas be present and ready to act.)

CAIAPHAS

You're a very welcome sight in this house. But first, let us have a good fire, for the weather has turned extremely cold, and then I shall immediately examine the man and his followers and his doctrine. Why, indeed, don't they declare themselves?

(Here Bishop Caiaphas goes down.)

FIRST TORTURER

It would certainly be a good thing for us to make a fire, my lord bishop. My hands and feet are shaking off me and have set my teeth to chattering.

(Here a fire is got ready in the hall.)

SECOND TORTURER

Fetch some wood, comrades, and I'll blow hard so that the fire will kindle in a hurry. For I'm that frozen, faith, I don't even feel the cold in my feet. I'm numb.

(Here let the portress be ready to act, and Thomas shall lead Peter to her and say:)

THOMAS

Provided you're kind enough to allow it, portress, I'm asking your permission to bring my friend inside, and if you'll let him in, speaking for your ear alone, by God who made me, I'll do a lot for you.

PORTRESS

Faith, whatever you'll do for me, friend, I'll do more for you. Name of Jove, come on in!

(The portress says to Peter:)

Let me ask you, mister, are you one of the men with this Jesus?

(Here Peter shall deny Christ for the first time, and Peter says:)

PETER

I'll answer you on the spot. I was never one of his men nor, I swear, have I ever seen hide or hair of him before.

THIRD TORTURER

I've got enough wood on hand. Now let everybody blow with a will, and anyone who doesn't blow can stand up to the hearth and fan with his dingle-dangle.[7]

(Here Caiaphas says to Jesus:)

CAIAPHAS

I demand an immediate answer to this question: what has become of your disciples and why are they not present? Further, I require that you disclose to me a sample of the reasoning by which you support your doctrines. Let us have this demonstration here and now that we may inform ourselves concerning you.

JESUS

My presentations to the Jews were always made openly. I preached to them by the light of day, not under cover of darkness, and I did not whisper my message in someone's ear but delivered all of it in the synagogues where it was heard by many. By the same token, the instruction of my disciples was carried on in full view at the Temple.

Hence, rather than questioning me, you should question those who have heard me. They can furnish you with the substance of all that

I said to them, and it therefore obviously follows that you ought not to be conducting this nocturnal inquisition.

FOURTH TORTURER

Why, you bigmouth, is that any way to answer a bishop? I'd say you definitely need a going-over. Seeing as you've given him a cheeky answer, I'm giving you a healthy smack. Take that, God plague you!

(And then he shall give Christ a slap in the face.)

JESUS

If what I said was false, you can bear witness to that effect. But if I spoke the truth, why do you strike me? As it stands, you have merely rewarded truthfulness with brutality.

(Here the torturers withdraw from Jesus, and the maidservant who keeps the door tests Peter, saying:)

PORTRESS

Upon my soul, I could swear that this man has been traveling around with Jesus of Nazareth.

(Here let the cloth dealer and the hireling be ready to act.)

He oughtn't to deny it because he's from Galilee, and is his man, always with him at table.

PETER

Don't talk drivel, woman. I've never worked for the man, my life on it! Fact is I've never as much as laid eyes on him or any of his people and couldn't recognize a single face among that crowd, his or his followers.

(Caiaphas speaks to Jesus.)

CAIAPHAS

Tell me for both our sakes, my dear Jesus, why are you being so foolish? It's really too bad, by Jupiter, that you refuse to modify your stand in a way we can accept.

JESUS

I have never wronged you but rather have always sought your good, rendering help in time of need. Yet surely it was not a return of good for good to send armed bullies like these to seize me.

CAIAPHAS

For all my actions, I accept full responsibility and will produce witnesses to testify that you have made unlawful statements.

(He addresses the cloth dealer.)

Speak up now, traders, inasmuch as you are regarded as fairminded men. What did this man say?

CLOTH DEALER

I am certain I heard him say several times that he would demolish the Temple and then rebuild it in three days exactly as good as it had ever been. To this I am a witness.

HIRELING

And I can testify to the fact that I heard him declaring that, within three days after destroying it, he would build it again.

CAIAPHAS

Have you no reply to make to these trustworthy witnesses against you? It appears to me that your silence implies an intent to deceive. In the name of God, therefore, I urge you as strongly as I can to tell me whether you are or are not the son of the Lord Almighty on high.

JESUS

It is as you have said, and I say to you that in time to come you shall behold the Son of God sitting on the right hand of the Lord and Father of Heaven, may his name be glorified.

And on the Day of Judgment, he will come to you and you will see him in the sky as he judges you and all men on earth, the exalted and the humble alike.

(And then the bishop in his vexation shall tear his clothes, and he says:)

CAIAPHAS

This impostor has merely been trifling with us. There is no need for anyone's testimony since you have heard for yourselves his lying devil's talk.

(He speaks to Prince Annas.)

In your opinion, what had better be done with him? Tell me, please.

PRINCE ANNAS

A just verdict would call for his execution, a thing he amply deserves.

CAIAPHAS

Well and truly spoken, by my faith! He shall surely receive in full what is coming to him for his blasphemy. Torturers, all of you, come out here, in the Devil's name, or it will go exceedingly hard with you!

FIRST TORTURER

Here we are, exalted sir! You have only to instruct each and every one of us at your pleasure, dauntless bishop, as to what we are to do, and I and the rest will do it, by my skull, whatever it is, with no if's or but's.

CAIAPHAS

Good lads, without horn-blowing[8] or other racket, fetch Jesus in to us and proceed to punish him severely about the ears, laying it on hard with your hands.

(Here a piece of cloth is made ready for blindfolding Jesus.)

FIRST TORTURER

By Saint Jove, Lord Caiaphas, I'll be tickled to death to do as bid! Well met, stubborn mule, both sides of your face are due for a good hard workout.

SECOND TORTURER

Wait now, comrades. I'll cover his eyes with this cloth, and then one of you hit him. After he's had it, let him guess who did it. Put him in the middle and hold him there.

(Here Jesus is blindfolded.)

THIRD TORTURER

By Jehovah, that's a good game! I'll blindfold him quick, and somebody belt him one, and if he really is the God of Mercy's son, he'll know who it was that smacked him to larboard.

FOURTH TORTURER

Here, you good-for-nothing, sample this!

(He slaps Jesus.)

So guess, guess, you cocky dog, if you're Christ and son of the Most High, who gave you that love-pat. And if you're right, I swear I'll blindfold him!

FIRST TORTURER

Even though he won't play along, let's keep on with the game, dusting him good with hands and switches about the ears, on account of all those lies he's been telling around.

SECOND TORTURER

I'll just take off his blindfold and by way of letting him know what

I think of him, spit in his face—his eyes, too, while I'm about it.

(Here let him spit in Jesus' face.)

And the rest of you do the same. I say keep after the fellow and give him hell.

THIRD TORTURER

I'm making sure to launch a whopping gob of spit square in his eyes, enough to flood half his face. He earned his hard time, every last bit of it, when he gave Caiaphas that snotty answer.

FOURTH TORTURER

(He addresses Peter.)

You're the bloke who was hooked up with Jesus, working for him, and don't try to deny it because the way you talk proves you're from Galilee plainly enough to everybody here.

PETER

No, by God the Father, no, I never worked with him! Before this minute, I had only the vaguest idea of what he even looked like. With you to witness, may I be damned to hell if I was ever one of his followers!

(And then Jesus shall look back upon Peter, and Peter says:)

Oh, the wretchedness of it and the shame, oh, the shame! To think that I could deny my Lord, who loved me. He foretold that I would deny him and in my anger I swore it could never be.

It is right that I mourn and am the most unfortunate man in all the world, my heart so fearfully weighed down with the sickness of grief it cannot be lifted. What utter misery ever to have done such a thing!

In my shame I shan't dare to show myself among the brethren or say anything to them, not a single word. Woeful creature that I am, what can I do? Ah, the anguish of that denial!

Sweet Jesus, my precious Lord, remember me still and forgive my wicked act. I was overcome by folly yet will trust in your mercy, fallen as I am into the depths of sorrow.

I committed a grave, a dreadful sin when I denied him, the God of heaven, and all his work as well. How sad and terrible to have done it! From the fullness of my heart, Lord Jesus, I implore you to forgive me this once.

CAIAPHAS

Again, my dear Annas, what do you consider the best plan for us to adopt in dealing with the traitor?

PRINCE ANNAS

Without hesitation I suggest that we go together and re-examine him, the repulsive dodger.

CAIAPHAS

Upon my word, that's a good plan, and I'll follow it. Let's go to him immediately. I have here a crosier-bearer, a capable fellow, who's well up on the law and is a shrewd, crafty debater.

CROSIER-BEARER

Whether he's the Son of God or of the Devil, I couldn't care less. By Satan, I'll take him on, whichever he is, and shut him up in a hurry!

(He goes down.)

CAIAPHAS

Bring the prophet in, for I intend to question him privately this once more. If he tells further lies, I swear on my honor he's going to pay for it before he's through.

FIRST TORTURER

I will bring him to you, sirs. Come out here to take your medicine,

God plague you! As for us, no matter what we do to him, by Satan, he won't talk!

(And then they shall lead Jesus into a corner among them on the platea.)

CAIAPHAS

Tell us the truth without fantasy or subterfuge. Are you Christ, the son of David, ranking first among the prophets?

JESUS

Though I speak truth, none of you will believe it. If I ask anything, you cannot answer me. Hereafter, nonetheless, you will behold the Son of God seated at the right hand of God the Father in bliss.

CAIAPHAS

Going by that, are we not correct in assuming that you name yourself the veritable Son of God in all his majesty and grace?

JESUS

You have said that I am, and I am truly what you have said of me. On the Day of Judgment, you shall acknowledge it and find it proved.

CAIAPHAS

What need is there to delay or produce other witnesses since you have admitted it yourself? He is condemned out of his own mouth.

PRINCE ANNAS

In view of his guilt, I move that we take him to Pilate, our magistrate, that he may receive sentence and be put to death before the Sabbath.

JUDAS ISCARIOT

I committed a wickedly perverse, a monstrous act when I sold the very blood of God. It is therefore best to give back all the money that was paid.

CAIAPHAS

What is that to us, seeing you were the one who wanted to sell him? You know perfectly well nobody forced you into it.

JUDAS ISCARIOT

Since there is no other way, I leave the silver, every last coin of it, on the floor.

(Here he throws the money on the ground.)

And I will go and hang myself, for in selling the Anointed to you, my sin was past belief.

(A tree is made ready and a halter for hanging Judas prepared.)

So great, yes, so very great was my transgression, in that I sold Christ himself in all his grace to the Jews and to certain death, the enormity of it surpasses God's mercy, and I am left no path to salvation.

I will make a running knot, thus assuring that the loop tightens around my throat at once and strangles me quickly. My end is hideous, my sorrow eternal.

(Here he hangs himself.)

SATAN

I'm anxious to get my hands on you and take you with us to damnation. But your soul, you loathsome wretch, won't come through your mouth because you have kissed the Christ.

CAIAPHAS

(Here Caiaphas shall take the money.)

I shall take this money and keep the sum intact for the time being. Yet it certainly should not be put into the treasury because it bought the death of a noble man.

PRINCE ANNAS

My advice would be that you use it to buy a parcel of undeveloped land somewhere as a burial place for Christians in order to avoid their rotting and stinking aboveground. A stench such as that might infect and kill a large number of Jews.

CAIAPHAS

Upon my soul, your idea appeals to me. I'll acquire the land where-ever we chance to find it.

CROSIER-BEARER

It just so happens I have a good-sized piece of open land I'll sell you right now for thirty sterling.

CAIAPHAS

And I'll buy it from you. Here's the money to pay for it.

(He shows the purse with the money.)

All dignitaries present can witness that I'm handing it over to you forthwith.

CROSIER-BEARER

I'm happy to accept it, and in return hereby convey the land to you in perpetuity for the purpose of burying Christians that their excessive stink may not linger among the Jews.

(Then Caiaphas pays the money to the Crosier-Bearer and afterwards shall go with Jesus to Pilate.)

CAIAPHAS

Respectful greetings and best wishes, Pilate. I bring before you as a prisoner in bonds, a certain Jesus, having found him perverting our people from the faith on a daily basis and in numerous communities.

PRINCE ANNAS

I have personally heard him forbid the giving of any tribute money to Caesar under any circumstances and boasting that he is none other than Christ, the true and only son of God on high, and has no equal in this world.

(Here the torturers shall go to their station and let all go up except Jesus, who shall stand before Pilate's tent.)

PILATE

You are truly welcome in my hall, Caiaphas, on my honor; you and all your companions.

(He speaks to Jesus.)

And I require of you, Jesus, that you declare yourself forthwith. If you are indeed the King of the Jews, speak out strongly and affirm the same.

JESUS

Pilate, your words and the reality are one. Let this day witness that you have spoken of me the absolute truth.

PILATE

Thus far I can seen no reasonable grounds whatever to support the contention that this man deserves the death penalty. It would be preferable to let him live.

PRINCE ANNAS

Yet the fact remains that he is corrupting the entire Kingdom of Judaea from Galilee to us, here in Jerusalem, ceaselessly teaching everybody to believe in him and worship him as God.

PILATE

Tell me then, at once, is he a Galilean and a subject of King Herod? If such is the case, I shall certainly send him to his master, Herod, and promptly.

PRINCE ANNAS

It is an established fact, sir, that the man was born in Bethlehem, Judaea, and nowhere else. In my opinion, therefore, it would be well were he sent to King Herod since he is our sovereign.

PILATE

He shall go to him, my word on it, and there will be no further delay. Horsemen, I ask that you take the accused to King Herod forthwith. Say that I am sending him to the King for such action as His Majesty deems appropriate.

(Here Pilate goes down, and Caiaphas shall go to his tent.)

FIRST SOLDIER

I'll take him to Herod, I will, by my soul! If I don't take him, may a thousand devils break every bone in his back so that he'll never sit up and take nourishment again. Come out, I have a little device that's sure to turn your blood to ice.

PRINCE ANNAS

So help me, Caiaphas, I'm convinced it would be all to the good if we were to go with the prisoner to Herod, thus affording ourselves an opportunity to accuse him in person, meanwhile sending for our doctors of law that they may uphold our dignity and support our case by arguing against the man.

CAIAPHAS

By Satan, that makes good sense, my dear Annas, or else may the Lord God bring down the weight of his hand on you! Now hear me, good messenger. Have the kindness to go to the two doctors and request them to present themselves for a debate with Jesus.

FIRST MESSENGER

It shall be done at once; otherwise may the Devil take you home with him to hell.[9] Unless I fetch your doctors to Jerusalem quick as an arrow off the string, God's vengeance on all of you!

(Now the bishop and the prince and all the soldiers move off with Jesus and walk to and fro in the platea.)

CAIAPHAS

A happy journey to you, messenger. Speed the word, and you shall be rewarded, on my honor, before the month is out.

(Here the doctors shall parade, and here Caiaphas, Prince Annas, and the soldiers cross over with Jesus to Herod.)

FIRST MESSENGER

Respectful greetings, doctors and master scholars! My lord Caiaphas asks you to come to Jerusalem to debate with one Jesus, a man born in Bethlehem who says he is the Son of God.

FIRST DOCTOR

We are more than ready, both of us, to respond promptly and without fail to your lord's bidding and will so thoroughly silence this headstrong fellow, who presumes to assert he is our God, that he will find no more to say than might a blind horse.

SECOND DOCTOR

I will refute him with ease; he won't know how to make any reply whatever to my argument. It's clear that the man must be uncommonly foolhardy if he seeks to debate with us. *Vraiment!*

SECOND MESSENGER

His words are bold, and he proudly tells everyone that he is, beyond a doubt, the Son of God, who will appear in the sky on Judgment Day to judge us all, and his name is Christ Jesus.

(Then the doctors shall come and go over to Herod after the others.)

SECOND SOLDIER

Get along there, Jesus, you dog! You'd better know a lot of Scripture today, that's for sure, if you don't want to be flattened when the doctors bear down on you.

(Here Herod shall parade if he wishes.)

HEROD

From this day forward, I shall no longer indulge myself in the bad habit of self-praise. For, by my father, no man will honor me the more, however much I seek to flatter my own image.

(Here Bishop Caiaphas speaks to Herod and the princes, saluting Herod.)

CAIAPHAS

Hail, sire and emperor! Now hail, king of kings the flower, fair, sweet, and dazzling to look, and the ruler of the whole earth! With due respect, Pilate sends to you a malefactor.

(Jesus here walks before the tent of Herod briefly.)

HEROD

Welcome, Caiaphas, by Jupiter, and Cousin Annas and all your company. And now let me hear, though at no great length, who this evil-doer may be.

PRINCE ANNAS

This is that same Jesus who says he is the Son of God while also being the son of old Joseph, a fellow who works with his hands.[10] He likewise maintains that he could, if he chose, demolish the Temple and then rebuild it within three days so that it would be better than ever, what's more.

HEROD

If he is *the* Jesus, I am happy to receive him, by the Lord God! I've been very much wanting to see him, and to Pilate goes my warm and permanent gratitude for sending him.

FIRST DOCTOR

Hail, sire and imperator! Jove grant that you be a virtuous man and rule your kingdom justly. Hail, Lord Caiaphas! Hail, Prince Annas! And hail to you, Jesus, the peripatetic pretender!

HEROD

Consider yourselves welcome to my palace, my dear sirs, and may Jupiter bestow much honor upon each of you in your lifetime. But kindly do not delay in assuming your places, worthies, for I wish to try conclusions with Jesus, the Nazarene.

(Herod addresses Jesus.)

And now let me ask you this: are you Christ, the Son of David, Son of the true God and yet also a man? Answer forthwith and of your own free will.

CAIAPHAS

He has said that he is, and I have heard him say it on too many occasions for him to retract it at this point. He declares himself to be, at one and the same time, Son of very God, born of an untouched virgin, and a man like ourselves; a combination which, were it true, would be indeed a great wonder.

SECOND DOCTOR

I will prove that claim false. The nature of God and the nature of man are completely antithetic concepts. God is a disembodied spirit;

man is a creature of flesh with arms and legs. Therefore, this Jesus cannot be both God and man.

HEROD

Let us now have your reply to the learned doctor, my good Jesus, out of devotion to your sovereign. To have you speak wisely would please me very much and, if you are God, reveal it to us.

FIRST DOCTOR

I shall answer my colleague. The man might well be half human and half divine. A mermaid,[11] for example, is some fifty percent human, being a woman from the head to the belly. Jesus is similar.

SECOND DOCTOR

He has also said, however, that after three days in the grave he would rise from it alive again. Whereas the truth is that, once a man is dead, his spirit never returns to his body.

FIRST DOCTOR

Here is my candid rejoinder to you on that. At no time has he asserted that his resurrection would involve the body as well as the soul. True, he will rise again at the end of three days after death but in the spirit only, we may be certain.

HEROD

Why is it, Jesus, that you fail to answer? If nothing else, tell me whether you actually said that though the Temple were utterly destroyed you would restore it to better than its original condition within three days.

SECOND DOCTOR

If you ever said such a thing, you are an offspring of the Devil. No man under the sun, unless it were through sorcery, could in three days rebuild the Temple, and by rights all sorcerers should be burned alive.

(Jesus shall continue to remain silent.)

HEROD

Assuming that you are none other than the Son of the merciful God, show us some great feat in order that we may believe in you; in which event, I will adjudge you a holy man and pay you homage from this day forward.

(And Jesus shall still be silent, answering not a word.)

What, then, is the meaning of this continued silence? Obviously, the rascal is afraid that if he once opens his mouth, his tongue will be tied for him. Since, therefore, he has proved himself neither more nor less than a dunce, he shall not leave us before he is appropriately decked in white.

(Here a white garment is made ready for Jesus and is handed to Herod's counselor.)

As a token that he is a fool and that all his pronouncements have been such mischievous nonsense that he does not now dare to acknowledge them, fetch hither a satin surcoat which I shall bestow upon him in return for the vexation he has caused me.

COUNSELOR

It is here, Sire, and ready, as you can see. He could put it on and wrap it around himself this minute if he wanted to. It gleams as white as crystal. What a pity to give a piece of goods like that to a tramp!

HEROD

A promise is a promise. Bishop, Prince, doctors, and servants, I ask that you return with the man to Pilate in his capacity as magistrate. For my own part, I find in the man's behavior no grounds which would make it my duty to have him executed.

CAIAPHAS

Sire, we shall take him home to Pilate immediately and let him determine the truth of the issue. We bid you goodbye, Majesty, and will take our departure. Finding you so full of wisdom, I call down my blessing upon your house.

HEROD

Farewell, noble Caiaphas, and Cousin Annas. Be constant in advising Jesus to quit his foolishness and return to good sense, lest he find himself in serious trouble.

PRINCE ANNAS

If I've advised him once I've advised him a thousand times, but nothing can persuade him to abandon his heresy. Yet even so, I'd be prepared to forgive him his every offense if only he'd ask for pardon.

(And then they shall proceed with Jesus on their way to Pilate, and the First Soldier says:)

FIRST SOLDIER

You, Jesus, step lively there, you low-down scum, the noose will choke you yet! How crafty the fellow was when he played dumb before the lords and wouldn't answer the great doctors, not him!

FIRST DOCTOR

So it's goodbye, sirs, and good luck. We shall take our leave of you now since we have completely dispatched this bit of business, my life on it! And one thing remains sure, namely, that although the man has kept silent, under the law he merits a bad end.

CAIAPHAS

But until that bad end is accomplished, learned sirs, you must continue the journey with us because the rascal can, in all conscience, speak most glibly. I tell you, by my faith, he doesn't know the meaning of shame!

SECOND DOCTOR

Provided we can be of additional service, we shall be glad to accompany you to the place of your choice, there seeing to it, moreover, that the fellow finds not a word to use against us in argument.

(And they shall come to Pilate, and the soldier says:)

SECOND SOLDIER

Greetings, my lord magistrate, in your palace. With all proper respect, King Herod returns Jesus to you, having dressed him in white, and conveys to you his lasting thanks and kindest regards.

PILATE

May sacred Jove favor him and honor him above all men, as well he might.

(Here Pilate descends.)

And now, Prince, learned doctors, and last but not least, Bishop Caiaphas, you have again brought this man before me, alleging that he has alienated the people from the God of Heaven. Yet, by Satan, when I question him, I find no fault in him and neither does his puissant Majesty, King Herod.

The king himself found the man blameless when he was denounced by you and has now recommitted him to us. If he would but mend his ways, it would be preferable to set him free without our having done him injury.

(He speaks to the jailor.)

Ho, there, jailor! In Jupiter's name, you and Lashbutt, that lad of yours, come out at once, both of you.

JAILOR

We come at your command, my dear lord, Johnny-on-the-spot without hitch or grumble.

PILATE

Open the door of your prison and admit Jesus at once in order that he may rest for a while. And while you're about it, bring in a girl for him.

BOY

My noble and wise lord, the truth is the prison is already open, I swear it to you on my word of honor. But nobody there, by night or by day, gets any peace.

(Pilate and all the Jews shall move on to the tent of Caiaphas.)

JAILOR

Now, boy, keep a tight hold on the prisoner, for he knows many a trick to fool you with. He's a very crafty type, very ingenious. We must take care to hog-tie him so he can't escape, now or later.

BOY

I'll tie him around his middle in such a way that before he's through he'll be on his knees, begging forgiveness, and I'll tame him to where he won't have the strength to get away, not never! After all, he's only a tramp.

JAILOR

In with you, then, like a good fellow. And incidentally, if it should happen to suit your mood, try asking Jove for mercy, quit talking so much hot air, and right off you're sure to start pleasing the quality, no lie.

BOY

And if you do that, you can say goodbye to disgrace or being ashamed. Instead you'll be real happy and people will look up to you from here on out and everybody'll love you a lot and mean it.

(Here Lucifer shall parade if he wishes.)

LUCIFER

Oh, it was bad, bad to have gone so far with things! As a result, the Christ will inevitably weaken our power. Although for the moment I don't know what would be the best course to pursue, I do know that as of now we all thoroughly realize that Jesus is the Son of God Almighty.

SATAN

It's our misfortune, alas, that we failed hitherto to recognize in him the true Godhead. But what's to be done about it, seeing that he's bound to rob us of everyone who doesn't worship Jove and will involve us in a grim tug-of-war?

BEELZEBUB

I think we should speedily inform the wife of Pilate, the proconsul, that a severe reprisal will be visited upon her husband and also her children should Jesus Christ, the genuine prophet, be put to death.

LUCIFER

Bless you, Beelzebub! As prince, archduke of the realm, and the wisest head among your peers, you are the one who, losing no time, shall go to the woman and counsel her.

BEELZEBUB

My journey will be prompt, my errand discharged with diligence, expedition, and certainty.

(And then Beelzebub shall go to Pilate's wife, sleeping in the tent, and he says to her:)

Greetings and salutations, great lady! To be brief, send a messenger to Pilate, warning him that if the innocent prisoner is destroyed, unsparing vengeance will be exacted from you and from your children, as will shortly become only too clear.

PILATE'S WIFE

Is this the truth you're telling me? I wouldn't want that to happen for anything on earth. If I should ever see my children harmed or in pain, my heart would surely break.

BEELZEBUB

I speak nothing but the truth when I say that if the man is put to death, both your husband and your children will be punished accordingly. He is the Christ, the holy Son of God, sent from heaven into the world.

PILATE'S WIFE

Since that is who he is, I will send a messenger in all haste to warn my husband.

(Beelzebub retires.)

Messenger, you are to go to my lord and say to him that he must not condemn Jesus of Nazareth, for in my sleep I have seen how, were Jesus slain, a fearful death would come to my lord, by sacred Jove, and to our children also, as would soon be revealed.

SECOND MESSENGER

I will speed your message, dear lady, and will warn him at once, lest my failure bring shame upon you.

PILATE

Since you want to do away with the man, tell me again what accusation you are lodging against Jesus of Nazareth.

CAIAPHAS

I hasten to answer you with the exact truth. If he weren't a criminal, we would not have brought him before you.

PILATE

Then I urge that you take him and according to your law and conscience sentence him to death if that is the right of the matter.

PRINCE ANNAS

We must never, on the other hand, execute any person anywhere, regardless of his crime, without a trial and a judge's verdict.

(Then Pilate shall go to the prison alone and say:)

PILATE

Jailor, open the door, because I wish to confer with Jesus yet again. For him not to give up his folly and madness would, in his case, be indeed a pity.

JAILOR

I'm opening it as fast as I can, and I'll say this: you should be the one to get the credit if ever you brought him around to a different way of thinking. Meantime, he's brought hundreds and hundreds of folks around to where they've quit their way and taken up his.

(And then Pilate shall enter the prison, and he says to Jesus:)

PILATE

Tell me, now, and without hesitation, are you the King of the Jews as has been charged against you?

JESUS

Are you speaking for yourself or have you been coached by others?

PILATE

Are you calling me a Jew? Obviously, it's your own people, including the priests, who brought you here to me. What have you done to provoke them? Answer me in terms that cannot be mis-construed.

JESUS

I will do so. My kingdom is not of this world, for if it were, my subjects would never have abandoned me for sale to the Jews. Truly, my realm is a thing apart.

PILATE

Then, Jesus, since you have spoken of a kingdom which belongs to you, it follows that you are indeed a monarch of a kind.

JESUS

What you have said is true. I stand possessed of a throne and of a dominion which are my birthright. It is for their sake that I came into the world, ceaselessly bearing witness to the truth and serving it.

Whoever embraces that truth shall hear my voice on earth, whether he be Saracen or Semite.

PILATE

Since you speak of it so much, answer me this in good faith: what is the truth?

(And Jesus does not answer him, and Pilate goes out and says to the assembled Jews:)

I hereby put you all on notice that I find in the man no cause for which I ought to condemn him. It has long been a custom among you that at the Passover I should release a prisoner and place him at your disposal.

For this Passover, have I your assent to release Jesus, King of the Jews?

CAIAPHAS

No, my lord magistrate, we will not assent to it but ask instead for Barabbas now bound in prison.

(Then Caiaphas shall go to his station with Annas, and Pilate turns to Jesus in the doorway to the courtyard and says to him:)

PILATE

Ah, Jesus, how foolish you are! For you, suffering and ruin lie close at hand. Torturers, in the devil's name hurry up, hang you! Every man equip himself with a good quality whip or expect the consequences.

(Here whips are got ready for the torturers, and a pillar for the binding of Jesus with a cord and chain, and a crown of thorns prepared.)

FIRST TORTURER

We salute you, lord magistrate, and ask that you take note of how we are assembling at the first call. Please let us have direct word of your wishes, that no time may be lost in idle rumors.

PILATE

Torturers, you are directed to beat this man Jesus, front and back, laying it on with stout whips and scourges, having first bound him to the nearest pillar by means of a rope and cold chains.

And if he refuses to retract his lies, cry for mercy, and amend his treasonous behavior, you are to cap him with a crown of thorns as a suitable token of the rascal's pretense that he is King of the Jews.

(And then Pilate goes up into his tent.)

SECOND TORTURER

By my foot, that's exactly what I'll do! I've been itching to get at him and do him in for good. You're going to be tied to a post, you damned rogue, and take your medicine!

THIRD TORTURER

God's face, I'll tie him and get rid of that big coat he's inside of.

(Jesus is deprived of the white garment, and a purple one is got ready.)

If we're going to give him some real hell and get some system into it, I say we fix anybody who tries to ease off and spoil the game.

(Here Jesus is bound to the pillar.)

FOURTH TORTURER

I'll truss him up good so everybody can get their cuts in where they want. All hands now, lay into him like he's got it coming. Warm his sides for him proper.

FIRST TORTURER

I'm for thrashing him until he's one sorry fellow and we see his back is broke. Have that, you filthy dog! I must be slipping—the man won't make a sound and don't beg for mercy.

SECOND TORTURER

I'll whale him without let-up till just the sight of his carcass will set 'em shuddering. Before I quit, his whole hide will bleed, hairy rump and all.

THIRD TORTURER

Damn me if I don't wreck you, you filthy brute! Hanging's too good for you. I'm gonna slash your face till you see stars and your eyes cross.

FOURTH TORTURER

You whip him like a sissy, better at blowing big farts than delivering big blows! But with my lash, whistle—wham! I'll face you down, Jesus, oh, you rascal! and make you a present of a wicked hiding.

FIRST TORTURER

You dirty-mouthed boasters ought to be ashamed of yourselves. For all your bragging and noise, a mere beating can't finish him. No matter how much damage we do him, this rascally slave for an idiot master won't just curl up and die for us.

SECOND TORTURER

All right, since he won't oblige, I'll crown him King of the Jews. Take a look at these thorns I've got here. The barbs are long enough and sharp enough to reach a man's brains.

THIRD TORTURER

I vote we decorate him in rich purple like a newly crowned king is supposed to wear.

(Jesus is released from the pillar.)

Hail, King of the Jews! We salute you for nothing.

(Third Torturer genuflects.)

FOURTH TORTURER

I've the very thing we need. See, purple cloth, no less, a regular pall to wrap him in.

(Here they put the purple on him.)

By my jaw, it's an awful pity that a devil's spawn should get to wear it. But here, take it anyway, damn you!

FIRST TORTURER

Now he has his robe, the next thing is to set the crown on his head, king-style.

(Here Jesus is crowned, and they put a white rod in his hand, and one of their number strikes Jesus on the head.)

Everybody, now, drag down on it really hard so's the thorns will punch through to gray matter.

SECOND TORTURER

I'm giving it everything I've got to force the tough spikes through scalp and bone to scatter the brains. Hail, King of the Jews! Let's see you rescue yourself from this painful fix.

(Here Caiaphas and Annas come down.)

PILATE

Bless you for a job well done, torturers. Rest yourselves for a while. Go home and get some sleep. In the meantime, I shall question the prisoner.

(The torturers go to their station, and Pilate shall approach Jesus where he stands in the court.)

Come with me now, Jesus, for I am determined to set you free if I can; truly I am.

(Then Pilate shall come out to Caiaphas and Annas, leading Jesus by the hand.)

Good day to you, sirs. You see who is with me, witnessing in complete seriousness that where he is concerned I do not find sufficient cause to justify punishment by death. On the contrary, I hold that his unconditional release would be by all odds the best policy.

PRINCE ANNAS

I say put him to death forthwith! Stretch him on the tree of the cross and nail him to it, bound hand and foot.

PILATE

Here he is. You take him and crucify him as soon as convenient. Speaking for myself, I declare on my honor that I find absolutely no cause or reason to kill him.

CAIAPHAS

We have a law under which he unquestionably merits death because of his repeated assertion that he is the Son of God on high. He has proved himself a traitor to the faith, a renegade and an apostate.

PILATE

In the light of this renewed charge against the man, I will again interrogate him privately.

(And then Pilate fears the more and returns with Jesus into the hearing room and says to him, "From where do you come?" and Jesus shall remain silent. Whereupon Pilate repeats himself, saying:)

I appeal to you, Jesus, as a friendly and reasonable man, to tell me the truth about your origin. . . . You don't answer, I suppose, because you are unaware of how much power of choice I have with respect to you at this time. I can crucify you, or I can set you free, whichever I please.

JESUS

You would have no power over me at all were it not granted to you from the Lord of Lords. Hence, by that much more has he who sold me sinned against me and, in sinning, incurred a dire fate.

(Then Pilate shall go out, and a messenger shall meet him, saying to him:)

SECOND MESSENGER

Best wishes to your lordship. My lady has ordered me to entreat you, in her name, not to execute the prophet of Nazareth under any circumstances. For if he should die, immediate and manifest vengeance, as sharp as it is certain, would fall upon you and your children also. All that I have said was revealed to her by an angel this very night while she lay awake in her bed.

PILATE

I conjure you in the spirit of your loyalty to me, messenger, is what you have just said the truth?

SECOND MESSENGER

It is, sir, upon my soul, and you will have visible proof of it.

PILATE

Insofar as I am able to afford him protection, he shall never be put to death, never. I will exonerate him as fully and as promptly as any man could.

(And then Pilate says to Bishop Caiaphas and Prince Annas and the doctors:)

Lords, on my honor, I find no fault in Jesus, none whatsoever, and no reason for having him killed.

(Here a chair is got ready for Pilate and stools for the others.)

It is my duty, therefore, to release him without further punishment.

CAIAPHAS

If you let him go, it will be obvious that you're no friend of Caesar who is, after all, our sovereign. Anyone who presumes to name himself king speaks against Caesar, and to kill a person of that stripe is merely routine.

PILATE

Arrange for the seating of a tribunal, and I shall render a verdict on this man since necessity leaves me no choice.

FIRST SOLDIER

I'll arrange it at once with plenty of chairs and forms. Be seated, my lord magistrate.

(And then Pilate shall go and sit before the tribunal, and he says to the jailor:)

PILATE

Bring out all the prisoners immediately—Dismas, Jesmas, and Barabbas—in order that they may be judged. Ho, jailor, come out, in the devil's name, and that boy of yours with you!

JAILOR

Right away, Judge, sir. We'll get a tremendous move on, we will.

(Here they shall all sit before the tribunal, i.e., Pilate, Caiaphas, Prince Annas, and the doctors.)

Now, Lashbutt, I'm begging you, as you love me, to get on your feet. Pilate is furious and baying like a hound!

BOY

I don't care if he busts his gut. If it's you who's scared of a beating, trot right off to him as fast as you can.

PILATE

Bad luck to you, jailor, you rascal! When that worthless pair begin to squabble, they pay no attention to my shouts. The prisoners, the prisoners, bring them before me for judgment. All of them, I say!

JAILOR

Faith, now, Pilate's really worked up. In Satan's name, bring the thieves out!

BOY

It's time I gave it to you straight. You owe me back pay. I quit.

JAILOR

You're under contract, boy, so you'll do your job whether you like it or not.

BOY

I've never seen my wages. Never gotten a half-penny out of you, not to date I haven't.

JAILOR

I'll slap a warrant on you, I will, by God! and cart you off to jail.

BOY

I don't give a windy stink for what you'll do, day or night. You can't touch me.

JAILOR

It's a real stubborn lad we've got here, who goes in for mighty big talk, he does, answering me back all-fired strong.

BOY

I couldn't find a worse master than you between here and Tregear.[12] I swear I couldn't.

JAILOR

Don't talk through your hat and quit trying to be a smart aleck! Instead, bring out the prisoners, or we're in for serious trouble.

BOY

Oh, shut your face! I'm not running any more errands for you. Fetch the jailbirds yourself if you want them.

JAILOR

That's exactly what a bad worker always says when he's done a poor job. Do it yourself, he says, if you think you can do it better.

BOY

If I'm that kind, honestly now, I say go ahead and beat my ears back for me good and plenty.

(Here two swords are got ready.)

JAILOR

Let's just get moving with those prisoners. You go bring them out so we can be on our way.

BOY

All right, only I'm telling you this: somebody could grab them off us enroute.

JAILOR

Then on the chance they might jump us anytime, and we wouldn't be able to hang onto the prisoners, I think we'd better take along a sword apiece.

BOY

Now you're talking, but before we go we'd better pick a spot and give ourselves a tryout with the swords. That way we'll know for certain whether we can put up a decent defense.

JAILOR

So watch yourself, boy, because I'm about to run a little test on you to see what sort of stuff you're made of. Mind your elbow, mind it good, for that's where I'm aiming to pink you anytime now.

BOY

It's me as is running that little test on you and watching you take to your heels any second.

JAILOR

You're not man enough to make me run, not yet you aren't, that's for sure.

PILATE

Ho, there, jailor, hurry up! Bring in the prisoners. He doesn't hear a thing. Damn you, you two dogs, your only idea of fun is to mix it with each other. I'll separate you and crack your skulls for you, depend on it! Get a move on, knotheads, and bring those prisoners before me—now!

JAILOR

Mercy, oh, mercy, dear master! I'll bring them to you anything but gently.

BOY

We won't stall any longer. I'll take them out and get them underway in a jiffy before it grows dark. Dismas, Jesmas, come up, and you too, Jesus and Barabbas, you're to be sentenced. Pilate sits in judgment, and that's where you're headed on the double-quick, by Malan.

JAILOR

Hail, Pilate, brave and exalted magistrate! Hail, my lord Caiaphas, bishop of proud estate! Hail, Prince Annas! Hail, doctors and masters! Soldiers, hail! And to all present, of whatever rank, greetings! Behold Barabbas and Jesus, with vigor and dispatch, Dismas and Jesmas, in one sweep of the eye, produced for you.

PILATE

They are a welcome sight, by the Lord God! You see before you King Jesus, standing there at your pleasure.

PRINCE ANNAS

Kill him, my lord magistrate, kill him! To the cross with him, as he so surely deserves.

PILATE

It is, then, your solemn, your final wish that your king, Jesus Christ of Nazareth, be crucified?

CAIAPHAS

We have no king but Caesar. Such is my conviction, and I swear to it on my soul.

PILATE

Nonetheless, I am firmly convinced it would be the wiser course to hang Barabbas and set the prophet free.

PRINCE ANNAS

Whereas, my lord magistrate, I urge that as a Passover observance you release Barabbas without shedding his blood.

PILATE

Then suppose you tell me what, having freed Barabbas, we are to do with Jesus.

CAIAPHAS

Let him be placed on the cross, bound hand and foot, and pierced through the heart.

PILATE

Such being your wish, may we hear a legal justification for putting him to death in this manner?

SECOND DOCTOR

My associate and I will fully undertake that responsibility with all deliberate speed. Colleague, will you kindly lead off?

FIRST DOCTOR

A legal basis for this man's condemnation does not appear nor will it ever appear. When he was accused, he made no reply, and even if in so doing he acted like a fool, the fact remains that whoever preserves silence before a judge in this country shall not be judged. Hence, for good and sufficient reason, the man should not be crucified.

SECOND DOCTOR

I disagree with you completely and am astonished to hear you speak in such terms—you, a doctor of law, blindly defending so stupid and repellent a person. Beyond the possibility of successful contradiction, he has presumed through lying tales to represent himself as both God and man. As a result and regardless of whether he denies it or not, I swear by my jaw he deserves the death penalty.

FIRST DOCTOR

Your contention has no substance, doctor, nor is it susceptible of any, that a man should perish because, of all things, his utterances are enlightened and virtuous. Redirect your attention to the mermaid, who is half fish, half human, clearly a dual nature to which we nevertheless give credence. Let us entertain an analogous belief in Jesus as both God and man.

SECOND DOCTOR

Learned sir, I say to you that the man deserves to die. The late fair in the Temple, for instance, was undertaken by upright men and was conducted in an orderly manner, as was witnessed by many people. Yet this man not only broke it up, he threw the merchandise into the street.

FIRST DOCTOR

You amaze me. To think that you, with your knowledge of the Scriptures, should now be bent upon straying from the paths of righteousness. A market in the house of God is not seemly under any circumstances, but rather worship and thanksgiving to him who is Lord over land and sea.

SECOND DOCTOR

That he has availed himself of every opportunity to oppose our law and has led astray multitudes of the faithful are thoroughly established facts. In consequence, he should be executed without further delay. All the world's savants taken together cannot save him.

FIRST DOCTOR

Your enmity toward him is as clear to me as is the further consideration that it is not just to deprive an innocent person of his life. Nor have I heard that he has ever committed a single crime of any description whatsoever. It would be a sad thing indeed to destroy a blameless man through error.

SECOND DOCTOR

Allow me to inform you, then, of his often repeated boast that he could level the Temple to the ground, thereafter rebuilding it as good as it ever was: an act he cannot accomplish, whether now or in the future. There is no saving him from immediate execution.

FIRST DOCTOR

What this case needs is an infusion of truth and good faith, for the one follows the other. Assuredly an argument carried forward in the light of these principles could at no time result in death for the accused.

Your wish to have him executed is, it seems to me, a personal matter with you, and I say woe to him who is responsible for such an act. The accused has wronged no man. Hence, the retribution which follows upon the shedding of his blood will be poignant, dreadful because, to tell you the truth, this man is the Son of God.

SECOND DOCTOR

I will now tell *you* the truth. It is far better that the man die than that the people be led astray and condemned to wander in error's endless night. There is no point in further argument or talk. Let the magistrate make his finding while all the commoners support it.

Lord Pilate, the moment has come to deliver judgment upon Jesus Christ. We call upon you to sentence him as we cry with one voice, "Crucify!"

(And all the Jews say "Crucify.")

CAIAPHAS

Raise high your voices and shout aloud that Jesus, the smithy's son,[13] be crucified and Barabbas set free. This thing is the right thing, proved before all the world!

("Crucify him.")

PRINCE ANNAS

In the devil's name, my lord magistrate, we beg you to consent and let us have Barabbas and crucify this false Jesus along with Dismas and Jesmas. Surely that is how it ought to be.

(And all say "Crucify him.")

PILATE

Since that is law, the three shall go to their deaths, and Barabbas shall be set at liberty.

DISMAS

Oh, have mercy, my lord magistrate, and allow me to answer my accusers before I am condemned to die.

PILATE

Forasmuch as judgment has been pronounced once, I will not pronounce it a second time. But as a token that I am innocent of the blood of Jesus of Nazareth, I now wash my hands in the sight of all present.

(And then he shall wash his hands.)

CAIAPHAS

If any vengeance for that blood is to come, let it fall upon us and upon our children, each and all!

PILATE

My sentence is that Dismas, Jesmas, and Jesus be crucified.

(And then sitting, he calls for the torturers and says to them:)

Torturers, all of you!

(Here the torturers shall come.)

FIRST TORTURER

Greetings, my lord magistrate! The fact is I was wrestling, on my soul, I was, to where I got myself practically fagged out and just couldn't run fast, what with panting and sweating all over.

PILATE

Torturers, you are to put Jesus on the cross at once, nailing him to it firmly through the hands and feet. Place Dismas on the right, securely bound to his cross with rope, and Jesmas on the left in the same fashion. Off with you and no fooling around!

SECOND TORTURER

Within minutes, sir, bless me, they'll be sticking to their posts until they're dead, no matter what they try to do about it.

(He lays hold of Jesus and says in derision, "Hail, King of the Jews!")

Hold my hand there, Jesus, and come along. Hail, King of the Jews, you're in for a bad, bad time!

THIRD TORTURER

Let's get that fancy robe off him right now and leave the bastard in his own hide again.

(Here the torturer strips Jesus of his purple costume, and he stands naked.)

But look here, chums, where are we going to find the wood to crucify him on? You could kill me, and I still wouldn't know.

FOURTH TORTURER

Sweet Saint Jove, me neither, leastways not something halfway decent. I mean straight and strong enough for the job. Everybody'd better use their heads and maybe somebody can figure out where there's the right sort of tree.

FIRST TORTURER

I've got it! There's a likely bit of timber lying at Cedron, bedad, and it's got a curse on it besides, because so far nobody's been able to use it for anything worth a damn.

SECOND TORTURER

Thanks no end. That'll make a pip of a cross on account of how, with the wood being cursed and this Christ the same, it's no more than right that the blasted pair should get together.

THIRD TORTURER

Let's go fetch it, men, so we can get him on the cross before the Sabbath.

(They go to Cedron for the wood of the cross.)

Now, here it is and not a better piece of timber in the kingdom. Let's make it into a cross fast.

FOURTH TORTURER

We've got to cut it in two to get the transom, then peg it to the upright. I'll just take my axe and whack her through in a hurry, paying no attention to a little thing like trouble.

FIRST TORTURER

I'll be owing you from here on out, for the tree's well cut. Nobody could have done it better. I'll soon finish boring the holes and with the pegs made already, the timbers can be stuck together neat and proper.

(Here two crosses are made ready for the thieves.)

SECOND TORTURER

All right, seeing the holes are bored, suppose we drive the pegs through and that does it. Yeah, but where are we going to find the extra crosses for the thieves, lads? Tell me that.

THIRD TORTURER

I know where there are a couple of extras, built to order and waiting for those two fellows, my life on it. So now heave up on the tree-cross we've made, lay it on Christ, and let him pack it into town.

(Here they put the cross on the shoulder of Jesus.)

FOURTH TORTURER

Get your back under the thing, you dirty lout, and keep it there. The load should be about right for you, and you're gonna sweat it every foot of the way. All you rogues get moving, God plague you!

(Mary passes by another way because of the multitude of people.)

MARY

Oh, son, dear son, that I should have to see you in such pain, my Christ! Why doesn't the pity of it draw me fainting to the ground? Who is to say what I, his mother, endure for my son and with him? I bless him now and always, yet I no longer know where on the face of the earth I can find a place to call my own. Fate seeks, if it can, to destroy me amid my sorrows.

(Here Mary shall meet Jesus at the gate of the city.)

Grief, oh, grief, grief and woe, that wicked men should treat my son so inhumanly before my very eyes! Son, the sight of your shame is death to me, my tears blind me. I don't know what I'm to do. Unbearable thoughts sicken me to the heart, my knees fail, I sink under the weight of my anguish.

(And then Jesus falls to the ground, and they shall meet Simon the Leper and shall say to him:)

FIRST TORTURER

You there, numbskull, make yourself useful. Hoist the cross on your back and lug it, because Jesus here has gotten real tired out. He's down, weak as water, so you take up where he left off and no stalling.

SIMON THE LEPER

To spare him suffering, I'll carry it gladly, very gladly. Lay it on my shoulder. God, but you're a miserable lot, killing an innocent man without cause! Vengeance hasn't caught up with you yet, but it will.

MARY, MOTHER OF JAMES

It's sad, oh, unspeakably sad, to witness the shame, the villainous wrong they heap on you, dear Jesus. I pray that the Father in heaven will bring down the dreadful hand of his punishment upon them, all of them, before they eat their next meal.

SALOME

Jesus, it twists my heart within me to see you undergo such evil treatment; you, who always did so much for anyone in need. Your plight shakes me to the depths of my soul.

(Then Jesus turns to them, and he says:)

JESUS

Daughters of Jerusalem, do not weep for me nor make lament. It is rather for yourselves and your children that you will have cause to shed tears in aftertime.

For the day shall surely come when you will bless those whose wombs are barren and whose breasts are dry, accounting them the fortunate ones.

At that time, you will beg the mountains to fall upon you, out of sheer horror you will beg them, and beseech the hills to hide you, so stark will be the terror of that hour.

SECOND TORTURER

Now look, blockhead, you aren't about to do yourself the least bit of good with these yarns of yours, believe me. Your finish is too near.

(To Simon.)

Drop the cross on the ground and let it lay right there.

THIRD TORTURER

Hey, can any of you lads tell me quick-like if you know where there are nails we can use to pin him to the cross? Somebody get moving and go ask the smith in Market Jew.[14]

(And then Fourth Torturer shall go to the smith, and he says to him:)

FOURTH TORTURER

Good day to you, smith, how goes it? Say, would you have on hand as many as three big spikes of the kind for fastening a fake prophet, name of Jesus, to the wood of a cross? If you haven't, you've got to make 'em right away.

SMITH

I can't make any nails for you, and that's the honest truth, because my hands are so sore I can't hold the tools.

(Then his wife, scolding him, says:)

THE SMITH'S WIFE

That's a flat lie! When you got up this morning, there was absolutely nothing the matter with them. Take them out from under your coat and show them. I swear by the sun you ought to be hanged!

SMITH

I'm willing to show them. There's not an inch of skin on either one that isn't split and peeled.

(He holds out his hands.)

Look at them if you won't believe me. You can see for yourselves they're just like I said.

THE SMITH'S WIFE

God give you what for, you dizzy ass! Somehow you must have found time to bend the knee to that false rascal of a prophet, giving him a chance to work his black magic on your hands, because they were normal enough earlier today, my faith on that! Still there's one thing sure: sore or not sore, those two hands of yours will never be without nails.[15] So come straight over here and work the bellows, and I'll begin making the spikes this minute.

(The smith withdraws from them; his hands are healed.)

SMITH

May your name, O Jesus, be worshipped and glorified, for now I know past doubt that you are both human and divine. Happy is the man who believes in you, since your help is ever prepared for those who serve you in this world.

FIRST TORTURER

I'll blow for you like a good operator should. Fact is, there's no one in the county who blows better. I've never heard of a smith in all Cornwall who works his bellows any better.

THE SMITH'S WIFE

You blow like a dirty operator, that's what you do. Take it easy, damn your guts, or not a spark will stay in the forge! All right, stop blowing, Useless, and beat the iron with me stroke for stroke. You'll be hung up if you don't![16]

FIRST TORTURER

I'll stroke it, God catch my soul, real, real careful so's to make it stretch out for you one hundred percent! There's not a son of a smith in the country who can equal me at stroking. Ask anybody.

THE SMITH'S WIFE

Then do it in the right place, bad cess to you, you punk! If your aim's wrong and meanwhile it cools off, it won't come out straight. Oh, well, so what if they do show hammer-dents? They'll just feel that much worse to the prophet-toad who'll get them all rough in his hands. Look how you're stroking there, you lowdown good-for-nothing, every which-way! Make it steady and even or the hell with you!

FIRST TORTURER

My job will get by. As you say, if the spikes are kinda rough, so much the worse for the blighter. . . .
Mark a pair of holes for nailing his hands, men, and one for his feet. Let's get on with it.

SECOND TORTURER

I'll bore the hole for one hand, seeing there's not a man west of Hayle[17] who'll bore it better. Bring a spike, faith, and I'll pin down his left hand with all I've got.

THIRD TORTURER

I'll do the same for his other hand. We'll tame the loon easy as pie. Come on, nobody's boy, stretch that arm of yours along the timber. Oh, my God, it don't reach the hole!

FOURTH TORTURER

It don't reach?

THIRD TORTURER

No, chum, it don't, by my noodle. I can see plain as day it's short ten, twelve inches.

FOURTH TORTURER

Reach or not, we're makin' no more holes for him. We'll just stretch the arm until it's long enough.

(Here cords are got ready to drag the arms of Jesus.)

FIRST TORTURER

Let me make this nice length of rope fast to the dog's wrist, and you three pull together until the hand comes flush with the hole. Then somebody drive in the spike like mad.

SECOND TORTURER

God's fast, I'm for pulling so's it'll line up with the hole in a hurry. Heave, everybody, heave! Pop his joints for sure. There . . . now nail the hand to the wood. Nail it!

JESUS

O sweet Father! forgive them for they know not what they do, whether evil or good. And if they did know, surely they would not destroy me. Therefore, precious Father, forgive.

THIRD TORTURER

I don't care a fart's worth for your old man's forgiveness, and in spite of your mother's son, who's supposed to be yourself, I'm gonna drive this spike through both your feet, which won't feel any too good. You men bind the two crooks to their crosses before it's time to eat.

(Here the two thieves are tied to the cross.)

FOURTH TORTURER

Here's the rope to tie one of them. I'll make quick work of it.

FIRST TORTURER

And I'll take care of the other one before getting out of here.

PILATE

Sirs, I have set down your reason for putting Jesus to death. Let it be nailed above his head.

(Here he writes the title of the death judgment against Jesus.)

As you see, I have it in my possession, fully prepared. It names him Jesus of Nazareth, King of the Jews.

CAIAPHAS

Do not write king of the Jews but rather that the villain said he was king of the Jews. I'm ready to prove the point by everyone's testimony.

PILATE

To that I give you my candid answer: what I have written I have written, nor will I ever alter it even though I should be threatened with death.

PRINCE ANNAS

Then give it to me so I can tack it securely over his head where all may read it, men and women alike.

SECOND TORTURER

Name of Satan, raise the cross up and put it in place!

(They raise the cross.)

Hey, everybody haul, and let's leave her drop into the socket with a bang, for hell's sakes!

THIRD TORTURER

This oughta cure him of what ails him. Leastways his carcass sure gets a good rattling out of it. Come on now, all heave up on the other two crosses, God plague you!

FOURTH TORTURER

Me and my crew will make sure Dismas is up, let's bear a hand here; and you raise the other, so both these rascals will croak as soon as possible.

FIRST TORTURER

I'm your man, willing and able. Haul, haul her as high as she'll go . . . . And now if there's time, what say we leave the jailbirds on display while we kowtow to the great king himself.

(They kneel, mocking Jesus.)

CAIAPHAS

Hail, King of the Jews enthroned, and joy to you! You are indeed elegantly seated. Would you like to have a wench? If you would, I'll fetch you a beauty, on my soul I will.

(Here the garments of Jesus are divided by lot.)

SECOND TORTURER

Here's where we divvy up his clothes between us, and I'll guarantee to make the split exactly even, bedad!

THIRD TORTURER

It bothers me to think of chopping the rogue's coat into pieces. A better idea would be to draw lots, winner take all, because what good is a piece of a coat?

(Here let Third Torturer be blindfolded, and he shall hand out lots on Jesus' coat.)[18]

FOURTH TORTURER

I'll take the third.

FIRST TORTURER

And I the fourth.

SECOND TORTURER

All right, here's mine, so get the blindfold off and say which lot wins the Nazarene's coat.

THIRD TORTURER

Sure and you all know which one. It's number three.

FOURTH TORTURER

Jove, it's mine then! Let's each grab his own share to take home.

(Here the chief priests and scribes begin to salute Jesus, kneeling before him and deriding him.)

CAIAPHAS

Shame on you, Jesus, with your mouthings about how you could destroy the Temple of God and yet raise it again better than before inside of three days. If you truly are the Son of God on high, delay no longer, save yourself from this plight!

PRINCE ANNAS

If you are the Son of God Almighty, come down from the cross and give us a sample of what you can do. Then, perhaps, we will believe your claims and yield you our permanent devotion.

CAIAPHAS

In how many places have I heard him say that he was definitely able to save the lives of other people, yet when it comes to saving himself, he's powerless.

PRINCE ANNAS

If he is the king of Israel, he has only to descend from the cross and we will hail him as our sovereign. Let him do that, and we will believe in him, accepting him as a holy prophet.

CAIAPHAS

He put his trust in a God of his own, now let his God, assuming he is so minded, rescue him from harm. Time and time again he boasted that he was the Son of God. Praise him, lord of the fools!

(And then Pilate, Caiaphas, and Prince Annas go to their stations, and the thief on the left, railing at Jesus, says:)

JESMAS

If you be Christ, Son of the Great God, hurry and save yourself before you're dead, and save us along with you so we won't have to face this miserable, grisly end.

(Then the thief on the right, rebuking his fellow, says to him:)

DISMAS

Shut your mouth, windbag! You're not making sense when you don't fear the Father of Mercy, and you condemned to die! Me and you, we're crucified the same as he is, only we deserve what's done to us on account of a bad record in the past.

But this man has never hurt anybody, anywhere, nor he hasn't made any kind of mistake at all. Lord Christ, I'm begging you to remember me when you come into your kingdom.

JESUS

I say to you truly that before the evening of this day you shall be with me in Paradise, your faith rewarded. . . .

FOURTH TORTURER

Double blast him to hell, the foul sack of guts won't kick off for nothing or nobody! Let's get ahold of that blind fella Longius, and have him run a spear through the animal's heart, no softy stuff allowed.

FIRST TORTURER

I'll get right on it, as I swear I can't think of a better way to take care of the filthy idiot. Once there's a spear in old blindy's hands. I'll talk him into driving it straight for the heart.

JESUS

Woman, can you recognize your child in him who hangs here, served a thousand times worse than a badger at the mercy of a hound?[19] And, John, turn your eyes to the mother you are to receive as your own and cherish as long as you live.

MARY

Oh, son, son, the heart within me weeps when I see my Jesus crowned, alas, with thorns, and he a king of kings and Son of God Almighty! His feet are nailed fast and his wide-flung hands are pierced with iron! On the day of judgment, he who sold the Lord shall feel in his very flesh and blood an immensity of punishment.

The anguish and, ah, the sorrow that are mine for my son, as I look upon his piteous state in this blackest of hours. How atrocious that I still live, that I, too, don't die now, now, before there comes an end to my son's life on earth.

JOHN

Dear Mother, be comforted. I will always provide for you well. Such is your son's wish for you, as it is also his intent that not a single soul shall be lost from the company of the righteous since the creation of Adam.

JESUS

Father! *Eli, Eli, lama sabacthani?* Why have you forsaken me even for this moment, O my God and my treasure?

FIRST TORTURER

He's calling for Elijah. We'd better watch close to see if the prophet really does come to the rescue. If he does, by any chance, it will be up to us to start believing in this Jesus and worshipping him from then on.

(Here a sponge is made ready with gall and vinegar, and the Centurion, standing in his tent, says:)

CENTURION

I'm going to see how things are with that dear man, Jesus. It would be a disgrace to have abused a good man with so much scorn and insolence. Whereas if he were evil, he couldn't possibly have had all that power for saving people by no more than a word.

(The Centurion goes down.)

SECOND TORTURER

He wasn't calling for Elijah, he's just thirsty, sure, and finds himself in a bad way for a drink.

(He holds out a sponge.)

This here is a mixture of gall and vinegar. See? Makes an elegant toast—if you're thirsty enough!

JESUS

I thirst.

THIRD TORTURER

Look, here's a swig for you. Why don't you take it? Seeing as how you used to pass miracles for us, come on down from the cross now, and we'll fall on our faces to you.

JESUS

Father, into your hands I commend my spirit. As by your will you sent it into the world, take it to yourself again.

(Then Jesus shall die, and the sun is darkened.)

FOURTH TORTURER

Merciful Jupiter, it's dark! How can we ever make it to the city? What with the sun losing brightness like this, I'm thinking we could have done a mighty bad day's work when we killed the Nazarene.

(Here occurs an earthquake.)

FIRST TORTURER

The ground is heaving so, I can't keep my feet. Don't see how I'm to get to town. Ever to have put him to death was a sad, sad mistake!

(Here the graves open.)

SECOND TORTURER

And the graves are opening! On my soul, I see them. Seems like if we stay here any longer, we gonna be sorry. . . .

THIRD TORTURER

Longius, you've got to stick with us for another minute or two and do a job of work. Magistrate's orders.

(And he leads Longius to the crosses and puts a lance into his hand.)

LONGIUS

I'm glad to go along with you if I can be of service.

FOURTH TORTURER

There *is* a small assignment for you. Take a grip on that spear in your hand and drive it upwards. Put muscle behind it.

LONGIUS

I'll thrust it the best I can, but don't blame me if I fail since I'm stone blind.

(Here he pierces the heart of Jesus.)

FIRST TORTURER

Bless you, Longius, and sweet Saint Jove love you! That stab of yours exactly fills the bill. Our man is now completely done for.

(Then let the blood flow upon the lance down to the hands of the soldier Longius, and he shall wipe his eyes and shall see, and he says:)

LONGIUS

Lord, on my knees I pray for your forgiveness. I was ignorant of what I did because I could not see. Had I seen, though I were to perish, I would never have done it, for I know you to be the true and only Son of God the Father, brought into this world by a mother pure and virgin. And I implore that you also, O Father on high, will forgive me my great, dark deed through the power of your goodness.

(The torturers shall leave the platea.)

LUCIFER

It was clumsy of me, oh, clumsy! and a prime example of what comes of rushing into things headlong, when I caused Pilate to put Christ to death. As a result, he will now proceed to get Adam away from us, wrongfully, of course, and Eve and many another legitimate prize as well.

Therefore, Satan and Beelzebub, let us move quickly to bar our gates, for if once he reaches the threshold, he'll break down the doors and liberate the entire group.

BEELZEBUB

His banner, my dear lord Lucifer, streams in triumph from the head of his cross, a sight so terrible that the wicked will shudder at it.

SATAN

All the same, I shall block the door of the gateway so completely he won't be able to carry off even one of our inmates despite the big front he's putting on. Though admittedly, if he ever gets inside the walls, he'll take our people from us, every last soul.

LUCIFER

Dear Beelzebub, sound your trumpet, blast it into each nook and cranny and summon every devil we have that we may see whether Christ's invasion of our house can be stopped at the doors.

BEELZEBUB

Such will be the might of the blast I blow, there'll not be one devil in hell who won't hear it clearly, since were the Christ to penetrate beyond the gate, he'd do us a bad turn, my word on that.

(He blows the horn.)

SATAN

Reinforce the gate with timbers and put your shoulders to it as well, for if Christ enters, I swear he'll set our rascals free to the last man.

LUCIFER

Push, O riffraff, strain, blast your tripes! or else you'll get it hot and heavy since the plain truth is, he robs us of our power each passing instant and will leave us, I am convinced, without the strength even to break wind.

CENTURION

Surely this man was the Son of God on high, his death a monstrous evil. Had it been only a human being who lost his life, the sun would not have dwindled, the dead would not have risen nor the earth have shook.

When the veil of the Temple was rent, that was a witness of his divinity, and this day of his so sudden taking-off afflicts my spirit. Oh, God, they are indeed accursed who gave the order for his execution, inescapably condemned to the fires of hell in all its horror!

I mourn the slaying of him who never turned aside from doing good. How wicked the return they made for his loving kindness, in that they slew him without pity!

(Then come Joseph of Arimathea and Nicodemus, and Joseph shall beg for the body of Jesus.)[20]

NICODEMUS

Joseph, go to Pilate, the magistrate, and ask him for the body of Mary's Son, which hangs in death upon the cross. It is fitting that we should give burial to the Son of God, who was sent to us.

JOSEPH

If the Jesus we loved is dead, my happiness dies with him as I remember all his kindness to the poor and how he healed the sick, no matter what their malady, provided they lived in a state of grace.

(And then let him go to Pilate.)

Respectful greetings, my Lord Justice! I petition you to allow me to take the body of Jesus, he who has perished on the cross, in order that, with your permission, he may be laid in a rock tomb.

PILATE

I find it impossible to believe that Jesus is dead. Centurion, I call on you to give me the full truth of this matter.

CENTURION

Sir, the man yielded up his soul at the ninth hour and is indeed dead, the event having been marked by a dimming of the sun itself when Jesus of Nazareth passed from the world.

PILATE

It was my wish to spare his life, yet I could not find a way to do so. The universal cry was for his crucifixion, that and nothing else. But now I am glad to give you irrevocable permission to claim him and bury him in a sepulchre of stone since that is your desire.

JOSEPH

My Lord Justice, I thank you. He will rest where no man has lain before, in a burial place intended for me, cut from alabaster white as milk.[21]

(A sepulchre is prepared, and a stone put upon it.)[22]

NICODEMUS

The precious body, Joseph, could you get permission to bury it? If you did, let us go and take it down from the cross. As you see, I have all this myrrh, no less than a hundred pounds of it, which is much.

(Here Nicodemus shall have a pair of pincers.)

JOSEPH

Nicodemus, good friend, they were happy to give me permission for his burial. Let's go to him at once. Do you have pincers for drawing the nails out of the wood?

NICODEMUS

Here they are, a good pair. . . . I'll start pulling the spikes out of his hands and feet while, dear man, you ease him toward you and wrap him in the clean linen.

(Joseph shall receive Jesus in his arms and carry him in the linen.)

JOSEPH

Gladly, by the Lord God, and how much more gladly were he alive! Lower him into my arms; the linen is spread for his shroud. Huge the guilt of his slayer!

MARY

Kind gentlemen, bring my dearest one to me, and let me hold him.

(Mary shall receive Jesus.)

Ah, I sorrow for his sorrow and yearn to have died in his stead if only he had been willing to have it so.

The pity, the pity of it. O Son, King enthroned! How can I look upon you—heart pierced, feet torn, hands nailed through, each joint wrenched from its socket—look, and still live!

To see you is to burn with longing I cannot hold back, and little wonder . . . your body flayed, speared, broken—the bones of God's Son, of God himself laid bare!

Jesus, oh, my son, the grief and shame of it, all your dear flesh ravaged by wicked men. My heart swells to bursting in its agony.

What can I know save anguish at the vision of my son so foully used, the very Lord in the fullness of his grace? Grief on grief is mine for you, my Jesus. Yet, O Lord, happiness too, happiness too, that I am able this once more to hold in my arms and in my faith the Son of God.

NICODEMUS

Permit me now to embalm him before we wind him in his shroud. Aloes and myrrh shall preserve his body from slightest taint though it lie in the earth a thousand years.

(Here the body shall be anointed. Mary shall anoint the head; Mary Magdalene shall anoint the feet; the other Mary shall anoint the heart.)

Neither shall his skin ever come to further harm. He is truly well embalmed. And so, let us wrap him in the linen.

JOSEPH

I will wrap him without lingering, i'faith. . . . Let us, then, lay him in the tomb and set the stone over it.[23]

(Jesus is buried.)

It remains our duty to pay homage to Jesus, for the angels who were sent to him, themselves did no less.

(Here John and the others approach the sepulchre on their knees, and they give thanks to the Father and retire.)

NICODEMUS

I will adjust the stone; you are witnesses to the care I take. And now let us turn homeward, and may God the Father, author and finisher of all things, grant to every man that he end his days in righteousness.

Hear me, good people! The blessing of Jesus, full of grace, be upon you, men and women. You have seen in its entirety how Christ was martyred for the sake of the human race.

Go, reflect on his passion, each of you in his heart, keeping that heart steadfast and true. It was not for his own sake that he suffered, assuredly not, but out of his love for mankind.

Therefore, show like love to him, lifting your souls in worship day and night, and when you pass from the world, may you dwell with Christ in his kingdom.

I ever pray that the blessing of Jesus will descend upon you and remain with you, always. Depart for your homes; the play is ended. But I ask that you return early tomorrow that you may see how Christ rose, radiant and gentle, from the grave.

III   RESURRECTION OF OUR LORD

Principal Characters

in

Order of Appearance

Pilate	Four Soldiers
Joseph of Arimathea	Mary
Nicodemus	Jesus
Jailor	Jailor's Boy
Spirit of Christ	Mary Magdalene
Lucifer	Mary Jacobi
Beelzebub	Mary Salome
Tulfric	The Eleven Apostles
Adam	Cleophas
Eve	Companion of Cleophas
Enoch	Emperor Tiberius
Elijah	Messenger
Dismas	Veronica
Satan	Four Torturers
God the Father	Nine Angels

Here Begins the Drama of

THE RESURRECTION OF OUR LORD JESUS CHRIST

PILATE

That same Jesus who received burial at the hands of Joseph and others and was placed in a rock-hewn tomb is also known to have declared that on the third day, absolutely and without fail, he would rise from the dead.

Should he actually return to life and rise from the grave, multitudes will believe him to be none other than the God of heaven; all Judea will fall into chaos and Rome's authority be swept away. These are consequences which I am prepared to demonstrate by solid logic.

Therefore, counselor, let me have your best advice concerning the matter, and promptly too. What do you recommend? Upon my soul, I am deeply concerned, keenly apprehensive.

COUNSELOR

Your lordship, my greatest worry and fear are concentrated upon one thing: the body which was buried today. Suppose Joseph of Arimathea were to steal the corpse of Mary's son and then give out that the man has risen.

PILATE

So what do you advise me to do? Let us have it now, and you can count on a reward within the week.

COUNSELOR

Put Joseph and Nicodemus under no less than nine locks and keys, thus making sure they can't secretly steal the body from its grave through some deceitful trick or other.

179

(Here Joseph and Nicodemus shall come to Pilate.)

JOSEPH

Best wishes to you, my lord Pilate. The body of Christ, which you entrusted to me, has been laid in the tomb.

NICODEMUS

What a crime you have committed, sir! Such an end for such a man was so grievous a sight it very nearly struck us blind.

PILATE

It was the boast of him you have entombed that he would surely rise again after three days. Where is the body at this time? Unless you improve on the answer you have already given, you will find yourselves prisoners in bonds.

JOSEPH

We have left the body in the grave where we laid it. Through him we buried, there will be joy forever in Christ's heavenly kingdom! On the third day he will return to the world, and with our own eyes we shall see that return.

PILATE

Deceiving rascal, barefaced liar that you are, you shall be deprived of your liberty and imprisoned. Moreover, I am taking measures to prevent you from stealing the body and from saying one word to the effect that the man will return from the dead.

NICODEMUS

Nevertheless, as surely as he has redeemed this world with his flesh and blood, so will he rise again. I tell you the truth as it is set down in the writings of many a prophet.

PILATE

And you likewise shall go along with Joseph here, secured by nine locks and keys and confined in a lightless dungeon for an entire year.

JOSEPH

We wouldn't care though you were to sentence us to rot away in prison for the rest of our natural lives, since Jesus, in the fullness of his mercy, would bring us without fail to that joy which never knows decay.

PILATE

In the devil's name, open your doors now, filthy jailor! Put these two under close arrest and when they are thoroughly locked in, give me your keys while sparing me your tongue.

JAILOR

So, traitors, good-for-nothings, in with you on the double! Great god, what fools you are!

(He says to Pilate:)

Without ceremony, my lord magistrate, take personal possession of all nine keys of your jail, that there may be no fear of trickery.

(Here he shall give him the keys.)

PILATE

Because you are such a trustworthy jailor, I bestow upon you the manor of Kennall in its entirety, plus Carminow and Merthen[1] as well.

JAILOR

Many, many thanks, my lord magistrate. I am permanently obliged to you.

(Here the Spirit of Christ comes to the gates of hell.)

SPIRIT OF CHRIST

Open your gates, devil princes, and if you do not, certain will be your woe before I pass onward. For the everlasting gates shall, in their turn, be flung wide that the King of Glory may come in.

LUCIFER

It will do you no good to trifle with me. Rather tell me at once, who is this king of glory?

SPIRIT

A lord strong and mighty, marvelous in battle. Open, therefore, on the instant, princes all!

LUCIFER

It is idle to contend with me. Hence, tell me again, who is this king of glory? As for you, go your way at once since you shall never enter these gates.

SPIRIT

A lord strong and mighty, against whose entry the gates of hell shall not prevail nor withstand the power of his grace. Princes, he is the King of Glory, mighty in battle!

(The gates of hell are broken as challenge and response are exchanged a third time. Then Jesus shall enter hell, and Lucifer says:)

LUCIFER

Ah, out upon it! Help, oh, help! Thieves! The gates are smashed to pieces, their supports a rubble. Beelzebub, Leviathan, release the lightning and thunder that they may consume him utterly.

BEELZEBUB

For us there is no help since even a thousand thousand devils would prove feeble against this spirit. Let's just hide in some hole until the heaven-bound people have quit our domain.

TULFRIC

Ah, Leviathan, my pig, you and I are in for it even while we stoke the fire under the cauldron where I was simmering more than a million souls into a first-class broth.

(Here the Spirit extends his hand.)

ADAM

I see the hand that made me; an odor sweeter than honey envelops me. Through my sin I was lost to you, and by your blood I am redeemed. I pray mercy.

EVE

Now do we owe honor in the highest to Christ Our Lord, who has delivered us from hell. The time is blessed when he was born of woman, of Mary precious and virgin.

(Here the Spirit, accompanied by all, comes onto the platea.)

SPIRIT

All of you, O souls, who have done the will of my Father, come with me rejoicing. As for those who have not done his will, let them remain behind, dwelling forever in joyless torment.

To you, Adam, and to each and every one of my children who are loyal, peace. Come, then, to my sanctuary in Paradise, you for whose redemption I gave my heart's blood.

(Here the Spirit leads them.)

ADAM

Lord, our thankfulness is great since we knew no joy where we were but rather scorching and burning and, like dogs, we reeked and stank.

EVE

Jesus, King of Heaven, you have heard our cry from the depths. Woe, oh, woe to the unbeliever, in hell's agony doomed to remain even to the end of the world.

SPIRIT

Go now into Paradise, those whom I redeemed with so great a measure of suffering, and tarry there until I ascend to heaven. At that time, I desire to take a number of you with me.

Michael, lead them on their way to that exceeding happiness which was formerly lost to them through sin, and when I rise to heaven, I shall have about me not only angels but, in addition, saints.

(The Spirit goes to the sepulchre with a company of angels. Then Adam, when he sees Enoch and Elijah present, asks in amazement:)

ADAM

You flesh-born creatures who were not among us in hell, how is it that you are here? I am most eager to learn the truth concerning you. Tell me who you are.

ENOCH

My name is Enoch. I was brought to this place a natural man, destined to return to the world in order that I may undergo death before the day of judgment.

ADAM

Alas, how will you fare in the world where suffering and grief are ever present? It saddens me to think that you, who have tasted pure joy, should again endure a mortal's crushing load of anguish.

Let me tell you the truth about myself. I lived long in the world, a life of labor and sorrow. I also disobeyed God's command and for that was condemned to hell through all eternity.

Yet in his mercy, my Lord Christ saved me from damnation by the sacrifice of his body and blood. He brought my soul and those of certain others from that pain and darkness into this light. So I say to you in all honesty, do not seek to return to the earth.

ENOCH

It is my obligation to enter the lists and do battle against the Antichrist, in that struggle forfeiting my life. After some three days, my risen spirit shall take its place in heaven on high with Christ, the transcendent king.

(Adam speaks to Elijah.)

ADAM

I cannot comprehend how you, a mortal, are here in the flesh. I beg you, also, to give me your name, seeing that doomsday is yet to come.

ELIJAH

I am Elijah, who was brought to this place in a chariot of fire. I wait for the day of Antichrist when I shall go to encounter him on earth.

ADAM

Why is it that you undertake this thing? Christ, whose suffering redeemed us, brought you here from the world, that harsh abode of toil, sweat, and trouble by night as by day.

ELIJAH

Everywhere he journeys, Antichrist will turn men from God. We revisit the world to meet him and overcome his wicked tongue through Christ's grace.

Antichrist will order us to be killed because he is unable to vanquish us with words, and surely you will know that before we may enter into rest we must submit ourselves to death and the grave.

(And then let Adam turn to the thief, and he says to him:)

ADAM

How did you, one of the blessed and not with us in hell, come to peace? Tell me who you are since your presence in this region is beyond my ken.

THE THIEF DISMAS

I am the thief who was sentenced with Jesus Christ and raised beside him on the cross. I cried out to him when in his agony he had nowhere to rest his head.

I hailed him as the Son of God, making sure that he would remember me when he came into his kingdom. This was his unhesitating answer: "Before the night is come, you shall stand in Paradise."

ADAM

Ah, God, how fortunate you are! Although you underwent the earthly suffering of crucifixion, you will never have felt the anguish of the evil of hell, nor what it is to be in that baneful furnace, roasting in the perpetual torment of fire and smoke.

THE THIEF DISMAS

Christ is the Lord of Mercy. Whoever will believe and pray to him will surely be saved. And when such a man has passed from the world, he goes to heaven.

(Tulfric speaks in hell.)

TULFRIC

By the Infernal, if only I had him by the wing this minute, I'd toss him right into the middle of the fire! What a shame that I didn't let go from my backside a flash of lightning and a thunderclap to blast him.

BEELZEBUB

Sad to say, it's no use our trying to burn him with lightning and thunder. And the worst thing of all, as far as I'm concerned, is the fact of so many souls going from us to heaven.

SATAN

Our greatest misfortune was simply in our being devils! The light almost blinded us when that fellow appeared, while all those souls have escaped from pain and darkness. Bad, bad!

(Then Joseph speaks from his prison.)

JOSEPH OF ARIMATHEA

God the Father, Maker of all the world and Creator of man from clay, and Jesus our Savior, Son of Grace, come to us and help us!

NICODEMUS

Amen to that, and send your angels to rescue us, O King of Kings— we, who laid you in the tomb.

GOD THE FATHER

Go, angels, to my faithful servants who are in prison and free them without opening a door or breaking down a wall.

MICHAEL

Instantly and with whole heart, precious Lord, we will do your will as at all times and in all places is befitting.

(Here let the angels go down, and they shall pass to Joseph and Nicodemus in prison.)

GABRIEL

You have been summoned and are released, having no need for a breach in the wall or for a key, because you have honored the tomb of the Lord of Lords.

JOSEPH

Thanks be to Jesus, full of grace and mercy. Through solid walls he comes to us nor heeds the barrier of doors.

NICODEMUS

I have always believed him to be our mighty Lord, who shed his blood for the salvation of all men willing to accept it.

(Here four soldiers come to Pilate, and the first soldier says to him:)

FIRST SOLDIER

Sir, it would be my advice that you appoint a guard to protect the tomb of that dead traitor. Many's the time he boasted how he would come to life again on the third day even though he was so roughly and thoroughly killed.

SECOND SOLDIER

And if his body isn't guarded, his followers will secretly steal it from its grave and go around everywhere saying that he has come back from the dead and gone to another country.

THIRD SOLDIER

If that should happen, the end of the affair would be ten hundred times worse, I swear by Saint Jove, than the beginning. So put a heavily armed guard on him before it's too late.

FOURTH SOLDIER

Unless there's a watch, his people are sure to make away with the body, smuggling it from the tomb and sending it to some foreign place, while to a man they'll claim that he has risen from the grave and doubtless gone with his angels to the bright lights of heaven.

PILATE

Go quickly, then, my soldiers, to the tomb, bearing yourselves like the strong men you are. Under penalty for failure, make sure that Christ, King of the Jews, is not stolen by the Christians.

FIRST SOLDIER

Pilate, matchless lord, we are duty bound to guard the corpse. If any man tries to snatch it, upon my soul he'll pay for the attempt with his life.

PILATE

As faithful soldiers, therefore, be alert and diligent since everybody knows what the man claimed he would do. Provided you succeed, you shall have a good reward, consisting of Dansotha Down and Crukheyth.[2] Should he slip through your fingers, you will forfeit your lives.

SECOND SOLDIER

I'll hang on to him even though he comes alive again, and nobody is going to get him away from us, never fear. Once I get my hands on him, he won't escape a thrashing though he might like to.

THIRD SOLDIER

I'm not a bit afraid of him, not me, and even if it just might happen that he rises up, I'll hit him so hard it'll ram him right back into his shroud. Rocked in like he is, I'll guard him day and night, no matter his lousy disciples or how softly they creep up on me.

FOURTH SOLDIER

Let's go, comrades! I'd love to see him try to rise. If he so much as moves, I'll knock his head off, regardless of how high he talks.

(And then they shall go to the sepulchre.)

FIRST SOLDIER

I've checked on the tomb. There's a big stone on top of it. We can sleep easy because even if he comes to, he can't budge it from its place.

SECOND SOLDIER

Stop making with your mouth, friend. By my father, that kind of jabber is no good, and that's a fact. We've got to set up a regular watch, each man relieving his mate by turns. Who'll be first?

THIRD SOLDIER

Whoever wants it, let him have it. Me, I've got to catch some sleep, by Saint Jove. Of one thing I don't need to be any surer than I am already: a dead man don't come to life again until the Last Day.

FOURTH SOLDIER

Let's station ourselves on all sides of him. I'll sleep opposite his head.

FIRST SOLDIER

Nobody could lay out a better plan than that, not ever.

(Here let the soldiers sleep.)

(Then Jesus rises from the dead, and he shall go wherever he pleases, and the angels sing "Christus resurgens," and afterwards Mary says:)

MARY

O dear Father on high, you who created both heaven and earth and are as gracious as you are powerful, you know in all its fullness how my son was slain; how they put his sweet body on the cross, how they hung him there between two thieves.

When I saw them plunge a spear through his heart, I fainted dead away. From that instant, I saw no more.

But now how dearly I would love to see my Jesus again and speak to him. If he should never come to comfort me, my mourning will be desolate indeed.

I buried him and laid him in a tomb of stone. If it be your will, grant my wish for a sight of him, and O Father, sustained by your abounding grace, I do entreat you not to tarry now, for my cause is just.

Dear son, with all my heart I beg you to make haste and come to me, for you promised me that you would surely return to life on the third day. Nevertheless, my beloved one, do only what seems best to you.

JESUS

I salute you, O beloved and saintly Mother, ever cherished through nature and reason alike. When your earthly life is ended, you shall ascend to my throne on high, exalted above the saints and the angels by your motherhood alone.

MARY

Are you my son Jesus, and have you come to comfort me? Today is the third day since he went away from me, yet in all that time I could not learn how it was with him. I have so yearned for a glimpse of him if only it were his wish.

JESUS

Dearest Mother, I am Jesus, the son you loved, come to bring you comfort and make an end of your distress. I am risen from the dead, do not doubt me, dear Mother, but rather heed my words in perfect trust, for each and all are true.

(Mary embraces and kisses him.)

MARY

Joy to you, my precious Son and Savior of this world! That you have risen from the grave, I wholly believe and, believing, am greatly strengthened. No anguish afflicts me. Blessed be the time when I bore you in my womb.

But you, do you still have pain, do you still suffer? Are your nail and spear wounds healed, those I saw tear and defile your dear flesh? Tell me now, Beloved; give me word of how it is with you.

(Jesus kneels.)

JESUS

May honor, reverence, and blissful happiness be yours, treasured Mother. No pain touches me nor can I ever again be harmed by it. I have overcome sorrow, anguish, and death and am made whole in the perfection of well-being.

MARY

My heart is eased now that I have heard from your own lips that your ordeal is over. I give thanks to you, O heavenly Father enthroned, who were willing to send your Son of Grace to comfort me.

(They kiss and separate.)

FIRST SOLDIER

Faith but I've slept heavy and 've had me a nasty jolt. In my sleep it seemed like I saw that dead one in the tomb come to life again with a crowd of angels singing.

SECOND SOLDIER

The fact is I was dreaming too, and I felt his foot on my back as he came out of his grave. If he's gotten away, we're in trouble! because as of now I see the big stone sitting mighty high[3] on the edge of the tomb.

THIRD SOLDIER

You two must really have been pounding your ear for fair. Now me, I was wide awake and saw him pass by, and I know in what style. He had a banner with a cross on it, which right away he unfurled.

FOURTH SOLDIER

With my own eyes I saw him rise up, I'm positive I did. Fierce and monstrous huge he was as he came out of the tomb. I was too scared of him to hold my head up, and that's the truth. Besides, the light he gave off was awfully bright, I'm telling you.

FIRST SOLDIER

So get a move on. Find out if he's hiding in some bush or pitch-black nook. If we can discover him, I'll truss him up like a bale of hay till he can't put hand to mouth.

SECOND SOLDIER

By God's blood, I'll capture the rascal, never mind how wild he is or how tall he stands. For I'm not afraid of his ruddy banner and his cross, by my hood I'm not, or that we won't be able to bring him in to Pilate.

THIRD SOLDIER

Well, we're not going to find him, my life on it, though we run around forever searching in every hole there is. I saw him riding the air with many followers dressed all in white.

FOURTH SOLDIER

And I saw him too. There was a regular army in his train, so many you couldn't hope to count them. Surely it's useless to look for him any longer. Instead let's get together on what's best to do.

FIRST SOLDIER

Yeah, what's going to be our story, the four of us, when we face Pilate? The one thing we absolutely can't say is that our man just up and came to life and climbed out of his grave.

SECOND SOLDIER

I think we ought to claim as how an armed force jumped us and carried him off, making it sound like we were wounded and bewitched besides.

THIRD SOLDIER

No, now that's something we won't do. I'm simply going to say that he is risen from the dead because he really was the God of all grace and won the struggle through his banner of the cross.

FOURTH SOLDIER

I'm for that too—now—and agree it's the best way. I'm sure of it. And I'm not going to lie about it either, even if I am scared for my life. He has gone to bright heaven with the holy angels.

FIRST SOLDIER

Sure, but which of us is actually going to say that the fellow came alive again today, no less, and who has the nerve to go to Pilate with that? I swear I won't, being as I'm the timid type when it comes to getting myself killed.

SECOND SOLDIER

Don't be afraid. I'll go with you in case you need help and will explain how it happened.

THIRD SOLDIER

All the same, if he starts raving, we'll start lying our way out because everybody likes to live.

(And then let them go to Pilate, and the fourth soldier says:)

FOURTH SOLDIER

Good-day to you, my lord Pilate. Though there were four of us, we
couldn't guard the tomb. We were ready to strike him down, but he
pulled a trick on us and got away.

PILATE

Shame on you, paper soldiers! What is this gossip and rumor I hear
to be going the rounds in the province? If he really has been stolen
from the grave, I swear by Mohammed you four will die!

FIRST SOLDIER

Your words, my lord Pilate, are not good words. Woe to him who
fails to recognize Jesus as his Savior. Being greatly favored, with my
own eyes I saw him ascend from the tomb to heaven.

PILATE

Hold your tongue, scoundrel, and get out of my sight! And if, between you, you men don't find him, I give you my word you'll be
punished. When I set you to guard the tomb, you promised me that
no man would be able to steal the corpse.

SECOND SOLDIER

I've got this to say in our favor. You show us Nicodemus and
Joseph of Arimathea, and we'll show you the body you put in the
tomb, namely, that of Jesus, son of Mary.

PILATE

Ho, swine of a jailor, open the doors at once and bring out the prisoners. If you don't, seeing that here are the keys, by God's peace, I'll be the death of you.

JAILOR

The quicker I'm handed the keys, the sooner I'll open the doors, all nine of them. And so's you won't think there's been any dirty work going on, you'd better look in on the two lads yourself—in person.

(And then let Pilate go to the prison, and he shall not find the prisoners, and he says:)

PILATE

There is sense in what you say. . . . Where are you, Joseph, you good-for-nothing, and where is Nicodemus, that crony of yours?

(Pilate goes down.)

Ah, blast it, where the devil are they? If I don't find them before me within a matter of minutes, you people will need to do a lot of praying.

SERVANT

Oh, sir, don't blame us. Didn't you have all the keys and aren't the doors still in one piece?

PILATE

You speak the truth, my word on it. This is surely a miracle, for the doors are perfectly intact and the walls as well.

Soldiers, I find you blameless, holding that to punish you would be itself a crime. First it was the dead man who vanished and now the prisoners, who were under no less than nine keys yet did not break their way out.

THIRD SOLDIER

This is something we'll tell about everywhere we go: how, without a doubt, Jesus has come back from the dead and how, just as he was rising from the grave, we saw him ascending with many angels to heaven.

PILATE

For Lucifer's sake, keep your mouths shut! Say nothing about that affair, not a word, under any circumstances, and you shall have a handsome reward. I will make you a present of Penryn and Helston[4] as freehold gifts, both of them.

FOURTH SOLDIER

Since you are being so generous, we will do as you ask, the four of us ever remaining at your service from now on.

(And then shall come Mary Magdalene, Mary the mother of James, and Mary Salome, and Mary Magdalene says:)

MARY MAGDALENE

What future is left for me, alas, now that my Lord has gone to his grave? Nevertheless, since he so firmly assured me that he would rise again on the third day, which is today, I can do no less than go and see.

MARY JACOBI

I am determined to go and learn whether the body of him who suffered such agony for my redemption has indeed returned alive from its sepulchre. How great a comfort he was to us. Sad, oh, sad, that we saw him die!

MARY SALOME

This is the third day, when I must discover for myself whether

Christ is risen or no. For I cannot forget the suffering he endured nor for even a moment turn from my sorrow.

(Here Mary Magdalene shall meet the other Marys.)

MARY MAGDALENE

Greetings to you both, Mary Jacobi, and Salome. My spirit is heavy with grief, alas, as I keep asking myself, where will the body of the Lord ever be found if it should once disappear?

MARY JACOBI

Our torment for him, yours and mine, is one and the same. Unless, through his grace, he comes quickly to my aid, my heart will burst within me for sheer grief.

MARY SALOME

I share your burden. May the Lord ease my anxiety for him. Because he is King of Kings, I have faith that he will rise from the tomb this day.

MARY MAGDALENE

Ah, let us now make haste, for I see that the stone is raised from the sepulchre! How can I face the coming of night, Lord, if I do not know where you have gone, my Emperor?

MARY JACOBI

Oh, we are too late, too late! Past doubt, my Lord has left the tomb and gone away. My heart aches with grief, and I know nothing of when I shall ever again see him who is none other than God himself.

MARY SALOME

I have complete faith that he has risen this very day, yet what will happen to us now, since we have failed to find our Lord? Oh, the sadness, the terror of it, and the woe!

(They sing.)

> Alas, mourning I sing,
>   Mourning I call;
> Our Lord is dead
>   That bought us all.⁵

MARY MAGDALENE

Ever regretful is my sorrow. My sweet Lord, who was crucified, is dead.

(Mary Magdalene weeps at the tomb.)

Without a murmur, his dear flesh endured great pain for the world's sake.

MARY JACOBI

In my distress, I cannot as much as glimpse his form anywhere I look. What happiness would surely be mine were he to allow me to exchange a few words with him.

MARY SALOME

My spirit thirsts and mourns unceasingly. Alas, my Lord Jesus, so filled with power and in might supreme.

> Alas, mourning I sing,
>   Mourning I call;
> Our Lord is dead
>   That bought us all.

MARY MAGDALENE

Christ Jesus, oh hear our cry! Miserable is the man who believes not in you and forfeits salvation. When I think on Christ's passion, all joy deserts me, and, ah, how great my loss that I cannot now speak to you, Heavenly Lord.

MARY JACOBI

He has gone to another world, a host of angels in his train, while my only portion is, oh, grievous, the weight of unbearable thoughts. I beg you, Lord of grace, to send us a messenger, that we may know at least something of how you fare.

MARY SALOME

In the fullness of your pity, O my Jesus, remember us and hear our voices, that we may come into your kingdom. I grow faint with yearning; I sink to the ground. Lord on high, what is to become of me now?
>   Alas, mourning I sing,
>   Mourning I call;
>   Our Lord is dead
>   That bought us all.

FIRST ANGEL

I know that you seek Jesus. He is not here, for he is risen. He lives as surely as I tell you of it because he is worthy.

MARY MAGDALENE

Tell me then, Angel, where is he who is without equal? Since his loving kindness is great, may he allow these eyes of mine to see him once more.

SECOND ANGEL

Go at once, Mary, and say to his disciples and to Peter that even as he promised he will come to them in Galilee.

MARY JACOBI

Surely, then, he is risen! Jesus our Savior has gone out from the tomb! May he be forever glorified as King of Kings and Lord of heaven and earth.

MARY SALOME

Let us return to the city and spread abroad the news that Jesus has ascended from the grave to heaven.

MARY MAGDALENE

As for me, I will never return to the city unless I find my crucified Lord. O Jesus, gracious King, allow me sight of you this once more. Amen, amen.

MARY JACOBI

Mary, may you have the blessing of all women and of Jesus, Son of grace. And I most earnestly entreat him and God the Father in their mercy to grant us a life of good works from this day forward.

MARY MAGDALENE

My blessing upon you in turn. May Christ, who descended to the grave, bestow upon you from this moment the gift of well-doing, and may he graciously permit me to see his face again.

MARY SALOME

Amen. So be it that we seek the Christ who suffered and who redeemed us with his flesh and with his blood. Mighty king though he is, great was the agony he endured for love of the world.

(Here Mary, the mother of James, and Salome retire from the tomb and sit down a little way from it.)

MARY MAGDALENE

Since he who made heaven has gone to his grave, my yearning heart ever follows after him. Christ, hear my voice and my prayer that you will be with me at the hour of my death.

Lord Jesus, give me the grace to be worthy of being in your presence, of finding you somewhere this day so that I may see your face.

Creator of heaven and earth, our Redeemer forevermore, ah, Christ my Savior hear me, and if it is meet, grant my soul's desire and disclose yourself to me.

The thirsting of my spirit has exhausted me. I am weary to the marrow of my bones. Who knows, as evening falls, where the Lord may be? Oh, that I might yet find him—Christ in the fullness of his testament.

(She goes to the garden.)

CHRIST AS A GARDENER

My poor woman, where do you go, keening and praying in your sorrow? You need not weep nor lament, for you have already dried your tears from the feet of him you seek, dried them with the very hairs of your head.

MARY MAGDALENE

Good sir, if you have chanced to see Christ my Savior, can you tell me truly where he is? I would give all I have in the world for a glimpse of him. . . . Jesus, Son of grace, hear my wish!

GARDENER

Mary, knowing you to be one of his followers, let me ask you this: if you saw him before you, could you recognize him?

MARY MAGDALENE

I would recognize him easily, at a glance, as Mary's son, Jesus. Yet since I cannot discover him anywhere, why should I not, alas, give voice to my woe?

(And then he shall show his side to Mary Magdalene, and he says:)

GARDENER

Look, Mary, upon my five wounds, and believe that I have truly risen from the dead. Know also that I am thankful for your devotion, pledging to you the joy of my kingdom hereafter.

MARY MAGDALENE

O my dear Lord, who was crucified, although it is not fitting that my lips should touch your head, I beg you to allow me to kiss your feet.

GARDENER

Do not at present, my sorely burdened one, touch me[6] at all or seek to make a gesture which would not serve its rightful purpose. For the time is still to come when, having ascended to my Father, I shall return and speak to you.

MARY MAGDALENE

Christ, hear my words. Name the day when you will come from heaven to earth again and speak with us. Your disciples are deeply troubled, surrounded as they are by strong bands of Jews.

GARDENER

Tell them, Mary, that I shall go to Galilee even as I said. And, in addition, remember to deliver words of good comfort to Peter. He is much loved.

(Here Mary comes to the disciples in Galilee and says to them:)

MARY MAGDALENE

I am now able to give you, his disciples, news of him. I have seen Jesus risen from the tomb and have spoken to him. Also, I have viewed his wounds, a pitiful sight, though for the world they are tokens of healing.

THOMAS

Spare us your fables, woman, and let us have facts, I beg you. I will not believe that Christ, so cruelly done to death as he was, is alive. Waste no more words, as I don't like falsehood. Our Lord is dead. Sad to say, I speak the truth.

MARY MAGDALENE

Thomas, so do I, and I shall prove it before we part. I repeat, I just now saw him, the peerless Lord himself. By me he sends word to all of you, though mentioning only Peter's name, that he will come to you even as he said he would and without further warning.

THOMAS

I'm asking you to hold your tongue. Stop this idle talk, woman, and don't trifle with us. Keep it up and, stout though Castle Maudlin be, I'll crack your battlements[7] for you.

MARY MAGDALENE

Fear's not going to silence me. Instead I'll prove that what I say is true, yes, and before we separate. Even as he is King of Heaven, our Lord is with God the Father, enthroned at his right hand.

PETER

Ah, what happiness to hear that Jesus the Christ has risen from the grave! Well I know him to be not only Mary's son but likewise God himself.

THOMAS

Let us rather have nothing from you unless it makes sense, Peter. There's no point in the claim that he has risen. No man, once dead, can ever live again under any circumstances.

JAMES THE ELDER

On the contrary, it may well be possible for the Son of God, who can rise even from the dead if he so wills, since the Jesus who is Mary's son created heaven and earth from the formless void.

THOMAS

Your statement gets us nowhere because it is certain man lives but once. It's pure folly, James, not to leave off talking about the impossible and go on asserting a blank.

JOHN

Thomas, you're being a fool. We all believe that Jesus Christ, having died and been buried, would rise again on the third day.

THOMAS

Oh, don't be absurd. I'm very much surprised at you; you, John, indulging in nonsense! Sheer torture brought Christ to his death upon the cross, a death indeed. I curse those who are guilty of it.

BARTHOLOMEW

Before my hair turns gray with waiting, listen to me, Thomas, and believe. Mere men could never of themselves have had the power to take his life. He chose to die for us, descend into the grave, and rise from it in order to carry all who believe in him to heaven.

THOMAS

Either you're being stupid or have gone crazy. Without dying, the Lord could have saved everybody in the world.

MATTHEW

True enough! He could also have destroyed a second time everything that lives, sparing nothing. Nevertheless, God elected to go down to the grave on our behalf and return from it again.

THOMAS

Matthew, you're a dolt. If you've got any sense left, you'll hold your tongue and back off. No amount of talking will revive the one I saw hang lifeless on the cross.

PHILIP

It's pitiful to be so foolish, so muddleheaded that you won't believe the King of Kings when he said to us that after dying he would
rise from the tomb.

THOMAS

Just sit tight, will you, Philip! And save your breath, for you're
wrong about him, that's sure. Christ, whose arms and legs were
battered, whose whole body was a numberless mass of wounds, will
not rise, alas.

JAMES THE YOUNGER

Oh, never say that Jesus, the peerless Lord, cannot rise, since in all
truth he has risen. It's only too clear you aren't worthy to serve
him.

THOMAS

James, James, if he were alive, I would most joyfully serve him.
But cease your noise, he is not alive. The thorns penetrated his skull
and went on into his brain.

SIMON

Despite the thorns that pierced his head, the spear-thrust seen to
enter his heart, we are bound to have faith that Jesus Christ, who is
truly God, has risen.

THOMAS

Distress yourself no further with such talk, Simon. He has not
risen. Yet, ah, if he had, how greatly comforted we all would be.

JUDE

Surely it is so. Today he has come forth again from the sepulchre,
for, if not, Thomas, we shall never have the joy which knows no end.

THOMAS

Give up your belief, Jude, give it up. With these eyes I saw his heart sliced in two. Regardless of what any man may claim, that body, once and for all, stirs no more.

ANDREW

Hush, Thomas, and stop arguing. Assuredly our dear Lord has returned to life. Just as plainly, you have overdone this skepticism of yours, considering the fact that Mary spoke to him only hours ago.

THOMAS

She's made a fool of you. The girl has lied, Andrew, and don't think she hasn't. That he has risen from the dead is a thing I'll never believe as long as I live.

MARY MAGDALENE

When I said he showed me all his wounds, every word was the truth. I'm ready to swear to it at any time.

(Here let Thomas and Mary Magdalene go down.)

THOMAS

Regardless of the plausible air you give your report, I don't believe you; you can't make me believe you. No matter how much you work at it or how insistent you are, I shan't for a moment take you seriously.

MARY MAGDALENE

This is the truth: the angel at the tomb unmistakably said to us that Jesus had risen and gone up to the brightness of heaven in the company of many angels.

THOMAS

Stop trying to coax me, woman, and let's have no more from you.

Though I am very anxious about what has happened to the body of Jesus, I will not believe that it has gone to heaven.

MARY MAGDALENE

I'm positive Mary Jacobi and Mary Salome will bear me out, because they witnessed exactly what I did, which is neither more nor less than I'm telling you. Please believe that.

THOMAS

My spirit will never accept the idea that the body which hung dead before us came alive again. Whenever I think of the torment he endured, grief seizes me, and I am in misery for him.

MARY MAGDALENE

I wonder, then, how you can be so stonyhearted as not to believe. If you don't change, you'll never come to heaven's bliss.

THOMAS

For shame! Stop that kind of talk! You don't enjoy the Master's confidence, not by a long shot in my opinion. You've been a sinner, recognized, indeed, as the greatest in all the country round.

MARY MAGDALENE

I have sinned, yes, sinned very greatly. But I implored Jesus to forgive me my evil-doing, and he said to me: "Your sin is forgiven you. Through your faith you are saved. Go, and sin no more."

Thomas, you're being crazy stubborn in refusing to believe that the Lord rose again from the dead at dawn this spring morning. No unbeliever will be saved or ever dwell with God. Therefore I entreat you to have faith before it is too late.

THOMAS

You might as well stop your chatter right now because I can't and won't trust you. I saw his body nailed to the cross. I saw them drive a sharpened lance into his side so that it passed through his heart. I saw the blood streaming to the ground, and with it quickly went his life.

That body, woman, cannot live again, cannot rise, nor is there at this time anyone, anywhere, who can make me change my mind.

MARY MAGDALENE

It saddens me to realize, Thomas, that you are crazed, gone mad. I can only counsel you once more to have faith, for if you fail, your remorse will surely be agonizing.

THOMAS

Since it's impossible to have any peace and quiet as long as I'm with you, I shall take myself elsewhere. You are a parcel of dolts, all of you. So help me God, I hate lies!

(Then, although the doors are made fast, Jesus comes to the disciples in Galilee and kisses them, saying:)

JESUS

The peace of God be with you, O apostles! Fully believe that I am Christ, risen from the grave. All who believe and are baptized in the faith shall be saved.

PETER

Ah, dear Lord Jesus, how I am happy to be a witness of your resurrection, I who once denied you. Protect us, I beg, in the abundance of your compassion, from those Jews who surround us day and night, seeking to trap us.

Lord of heaven and earth and our Savior, forgive my trespass which has brought me such great sorrow. I repent my denial to the bottom of my soul, imploring your mercy from a full heart.

JESUS

You shall obtain forgiveness, Peter, through the power of the Holy Ghost, for your repentance is perfect. And even as I redeemed you at so great a price, do you fortify your brethren in the true faith.

JOHN

How great my joy, Lord, that you were willing to come to us here and lift our hearts, for it must be said that we have been sorely distraught because of our longing for your presence.

JESUS

From you I go hence to my kingdom, to the place which awaits me at the right hand of God the Father. But that your belief may be confirmed, I shall send to you the Holy Ghost, the giver of strength.

(Here Jesus departs from the apostles.)

JAMES THE ELDER

Ah, God, what a wondrous thing it was when Jesus, in all his strength, came to us, and though our doors were fast shut, looked on us and delivered his message of peace.

He is the Lord almighty who with his blood has redeemed mankind. Jesus Christ is risen! And there will come a day, a day of woe, for as many as do not believe it!

MATTHEW

Before they happened, he told us of all that he would do and suffer in this world: how he would die for our salvation and would rise again thereafter.

JOHN

He has spoken, as always, the absolute truth. He who created not only land and sea but everything else which exists, also for our sake was brought into the world by Mary, ever dear and virgin.

JAMES THE YOUNGER

May the spirit of Jesus permit us the bliss of never doubting that as the Christ, who redeemed us by his anguish, he came and spoke to us in answer to our prayers.

SIMON

Now let Thomas say that the Lord has not risen again! We will testify as one man how we saw him, Mary's son, standing before us and heard him speaking to us.

JUDE

To my way of thinking, Thomas doesn't believe even yet that Jesus Christ has returned from the grave by virtue of his exceeding grace. I fear he cannot be considered as within the fold unless he does believe it.

ANDREW

He will come to it in the end, since from the early days he was much loved by our Lord whose goodness will draw up to heaven with great rejoicing all who truly serve him.

PHILIP

I say we must join together, each and every one of us, in bearing witness that Christ is risen from the tomb. Let us answer the doubter with the united voice of our certainty that the Lord of heaven visited us and spoke to us.

(Cleophas and a companion walk about in the platea.)

CLEOPHAS

Friend, I've been hearing a great deal of talk today to the effect that Jesus the Anointed, having been crucified, has now returned to life and has actually come forth from his sepulchre.

COMPANION

If what you have heard is true, you and I must set out at once, bearing our offering to the tomb of him who was and is both human and divine.

CLEOPHAS

Faith, let us go this instant. I was close to despair when I saw the lance thrust through his side to his very heart, and his head close-bound with thorns. For truly he was the Son of God.

COMPANION

I still seethe with grief and indignation for his sake. Nothing could possibly have justified the slaying of God's Son!

JESUS

Why do you grieve? What is it that you mourn, robbed of all your cheer? Has some wonder come to pass?

CLEOPHAS

Unless you are a stranger[8] to these parts, it is wholly unnecessary to ask whether a wonder has occurred touching a certain holy prophet who was nailed to a cross, his arms outspread, his hands and feet torn.

COMPANION

And his soul rent by sorrows. After he was put to death, they buried him in a sepulchre. It is there we are going because we are told that he has risen again.

JESUS

Want of faith has turned your wits and deadened your spirits. Otherwise, you would understand that Christ had to die and, as surely, rise again on the third day.

CLEOPHAS

I do not doubt that he has risen, still bearing, moreover, many a wound on that body which we cherished. Frozen in our misery, we saw them tear the Lord's flesh on the cross, and there they martyred him.

JESUS

May you have peace and joy abounding, for indeed it is certain that like him you seek, you shall enter into sanctuary. But tell me, where had you planned to be by nightfall?

COMPANION

Because we share equally our bereavement and sorrow for the Lord's sake, we weren't intending to go far at all, merely to a village called Emmaus.

JESUS

Plainly, then, I shall journey farther than you this night. Nonetheless, have faith that he who died now lives again, miracle though it is. . . .

CLEOPHAS

The hour is late, good friend, and it is almost dark. Remain with us, for your words have brought great hope.

(Here bread is got ready.)

JESUS

I will abide with you, and your joy shall never fail. Seat yourselves so that I may break bread in your presence.

(Jesus shows his wounds.)

COMPANION

O Lord, healer who knows no equal, I see your wounds starkly gaping before me.

(Here Jesus shall depart from Cleophas and his companion.)

As soon as ever the bread was broken, I fully recognized the person of my beloved Christ!

CLEOPHAS

Ah, did not our hearts burn within us on the way as he opened to us the Scriptures, Jesus, Mary's son, and at the breaking of bread?

COMPANION

Our gloom was as intense as the burden of our trouble was heavy until he came and lifted us so soon to gladness. All need of the worldly life with its diversions left us when we gazed upon those gaping wounds laid bare.

CLEOPHAS

Well may we rejoice at having seen the Lord Jesus in his power and grace, and manifestly filled with the mercy which any man who prays to him shall obtain.

COMPANION

We will tell throughout the land that we spoke with Jesus, our dear Lord, and how we met him as we journeyed on the road this selfsame day.

(Cleophas and his companion go toward the apostles.)

(Here Thomas shall come to the apostles, and Peter says:)

PETER

The time has now come, Thomas, for you to take yourself in hand and believe that the Lord has risen, because he has actually been here with us. And anyone who doesn't believe it is unlucky ever to have been born.

THOMAS

It was you, Peter, who denied him on the very eve of his dreadful agony. In light of that, I refuse to credit what you say, asking instead that you stop lying and give up these attempts to spread idle rumors. Please!

JOHN

He isn't lying, absolutely not. Jesus Christ, the Son of God on high, came into this house, though every door was shut, and his words were, as before, "Peace to you all."

THOMAS

Oh, don't be childish! Your talk is breaking my heart. Jesus our Lord can never rise again, more's the pity of it. The thing is definitely and completely impossible.

JAMES THE ELDER

Believe, Thomas, believe. Pray in faithfulness of spirit to Christ, the heavenly one. He has undeniably returned from the grave, since today each of us spoke to him.

THOMAS

Wound me no further. My misery is already enough to have made me deadly sick through and through. Yet still greater is my sorrow that my Lord is dead, and I shall never, never see him again.

MATTHEW

Had you stayed with us today, you'd have seen him alive and well before your very eyes. The wonder is that though you hear the truth, you simply won't believe it.

THOMAS

Blessed Mary! If you'd listen to me, Matthew, you'd stop spinning these yarns of yours and making me out a clown. As far as I'm concerned, the wonder is that you feel no shame for the lies you tell.

PHILIP

He has told you no lies but has instead stuck to the literal facts. Christ, the king of mankind, was with us in this house today.

THOMAS

Oh, he was not, Philip, he was not! If you people don't stop your nonsense, I know for sure I'm going to get so furious I'll hit someone.

JAMES THE YOUNGER

Anger won't help your case in the slightest. Lord Christ the Merciful has risen, there's no room for doubt about it, and should you lose your soul, you will have been a very foolish man. You amaze me, Thomas.

THOMAS

It's scarcely amazing that I'm angry when you're all working together to make me miserable. What with grief at your talk and wretchedness over Christ's death, I may well find myself in a worse state than ever.

BARTHOLOMEW

If you've been sad at losing Christ, from this moment on you can be filled with gladness. Only believe that he has returned from the grave and you will have a happiness which never fails you.

THOMAS

How can I believe that the body of Jesus, which I saw dead, now lives again? Those villains spent their will on him with many and fearful tortures.

SIMON

Although you cannot profit from our advice, you can at least fear that hellfire will burn you for your unbelief and, what is just as great an evil, for going so far as to reject the joy that knows no end.

THOMAS

Those are strong words, Simon, but their value is trifling, and I am not afraid. I only wonder why, with Jesus so soon dead, the sorrow of it does not rend my heart in two.

JUDE

Oh, believe us who have seen him alive since his resurrection! He was here with us and gladdened us mightily, yet neither man nor woman unlocked the doors for him.

THOMAS

Your story doesn't hold water. If you have any affection for me, Jude, you'll go away and let me alone. A ghost, for example, can appear to decent people even when they are in their homes with all the doors shut.

ANDREW

Thomas, I think you're the most foolish man in the world, and that's too bad. If you're determined to doubt, beware of finding yourself in hell, burning there in fire and smoke.

THOMAS

You're mighty anxious, Andrew, to force me to believe something which cannot be true, namely, that Jesus has risen from the dead and returned to the world. It's you who are foolish, and how foolish!

(Here Thomas goes down.)

CLEOPHAS

Ah, Thomas, he's the one who's wise while you rant and rave, become so stubborn you won't credit even your brother apostles.

COMPANION

We were going to the village of Emmaus, that's the fact, and on the way we met Jesus himself, the Lord of grace. Now believe us!

THOMAS

Bah! Palmers who wander the countryside are notorious liars, gulling people with false yarns. I can't swallow any part of your claim to have talked today with my dear Lord Jesus.

CLEOPHAS

He revealed the Scriptures to us, making them crystal clear, from the beginning to Moses and on down through many other prophets. I'm convinced he's the Lord of this world and the next. It was sheer delight to talk with him.

COMPANION

In our presence the sublime Lord Jesus showed us his wounds as he broke a loaf of bread. We saw them all agape.

THOMAS

Silence, you rogues! Have you no shame? He wouldn't put himself on display for a dirty pair like you. By the Lord God of grace, I'm deeply suspicious of you, I mean it!

CLEOPHAS

Get rid of your suspicions in this case because the Lord spoke to us today in broad daylight. Have faith that he is risen, for if you don't, it's certain you'll never be saved.

THOMAS

There's no believing a couple of beggars with their clothes a rainbow of patches. You're simply lying imposters, knocking about from pillar to post broadcasting the latest insanities.

COMPANION

You're over the hill, Thomas, clean daft. You just don't want to believe us, far gone in doubt as you are. I'm tired of listening to you.

CLEOPHAS

You've become that very unfortunate thing, an unbeliever, Thomas, and may well come to grief for not believing in Christ's resurrection. Your heart is as hard as your will is unbending. Leave off the great defiance, for otherwise salvation will be impossible.

THOMAS

I don't know what I can do, alas. Unless I see my Lord, I will never believe him risen, regardless of how dreadful the consequences, never until with my hand I touch his very heart through his wounded side.

(Here Thomas moves toward the apostles, and Jesus, though the doors are closed, shall come in to them and salute them.)

JESUS

Although your doors are fast shut, O Apostles, I come into your midst to visit you. Let each of you keep the faith no matter what the future brings.

And you, Thomas, put your hand into the wound where I was pierced through the heart, likewise through hands and feet. Believe that my suffering has redeemed all who accept and follow me.

THOMAS

Lord, take pity on me! Well I know you to be the God of charity and of mercy. Forgive me that before this moment I thought you dead.

JESUS

Thomas, because you have seen my open wounds, your heart believes. Upon as many as shall not see me and yet have perfect faith, I call down the fullness of my blessing.

THOMAS

May you be blessed, Lord, whose overflowing grace is always ready to show mercy to those who serve you. He who can behold your face shall have unfailing joy. When my body returns to dust, preserve my soul from the Evil One.

Oh, God, what a fool I was when I would not believe that Christ was risen from the tomb although assured of it by many! I have greatly sinned. Lord, grant me your forgiveness.

JESUS

And now, my apostles, remain steadfast in your belief, knowing that inasmuch as I am risen from the dead, you shall have salvation, even as my angels, through the power of the Holy Ghost, shall summon on high all who believe in me and seek pardon for their sins.

My blessing remains with you. I must go to my own country, assuming there the seat which is prepared for me at the right hand of the Father. With the faithful everywhere I leave my grace that through it they may have life eternal and untroubled in my kingdom.

(And so ends the Resurrection of Our Lord.)

THE DEATH OF PILATE BEGINS[9]

(and Tiberius says:)

TIBERIUS CAESAR[10]

Although mine is the most exalted name in the world, admitting of no equal, I am, nevertheless, the melancholy victim of leprosy, ever asking myself what is to be done. If a cure proves impossible for me, my future becomes unthinkable.

COUNSELOR

Majesty, I offer you my soberest advice, which is as follows: dispatch a messenger to Pilate. Order the governor to send to you without delay Jesus Christ, the King of the Jews, who can cure any disease under the sun. He is none other than God, ruler of heaven and earth. He will heal you beyond the shadow of a doubt.

EMPEROR

Bless you, counselor, bless you! Lightfoot, my good and trustworthy messenger, you must at once go on a short errand for me.

MESSENGER

Here I am, my Lord Tiberius, Lightfoot himself, at your service. By my head, you have only to tell me what you require.

EMPEROR

Go to Pontius Pilate and request him to send us the Godhead, Christ, King of the Jews. The governor shall have our favor in exchange for his compliance.

MESSENGER

Your errand, my liege, will be done promptly and faithfully. I do not linger in your presence. Farewell. . . .

(The messenger says to Pilate:)

Good day to you, Lord Pilate. I bring you greetings from Caesar, who asks that you be at pains to send, even to the doors of the imperial residence, the supreme physician, Jesus Christ.

PILATE

Be so kind, messenger, as to stretch your legs for a bit in a stroll about the countryside. Meanwhile, I shall make it my personal business to find out whether Jesus is at present within my jurisdiction.

(And then the messenger shall go and walk about in the platea a little, and Veronica shall meet him.)

VERONICA

I beg you to tell me, my dear young sir, whom you seek as you walk.

MESSENGER

Why do you concern yourself? Surely you are in no position to be of assistance. The emperor has sent me to seek help in this region. He suffers from a grave disease and cannot find a doctor who is able to cure him. Tell me, please, where Jesus is to be found since he could restore the emperor to health no matter what malady was involved.

VERONICA

The Jesus you seek is dead, and gone, indeed, to the grave. Though he was our Lord, Pilate put him to death. Were he alive, he would make the emperor's health as sound as it ever was regardless of how ill he had been.

MESSENGER

What a pity that I ever set out on this mission! Were it not that Jesus is dead, my sovereign would be healed, but oh, God, as it is, with the emperor so sorely afflicted, I don't know which way to turn or what step to take!

VERONICA

I am one of Christ's followers and am willing to go with you to the emperor. Acting in the Lord's name, we shall for certain find a remedy that will completely cure the emperor, provided only that he has faith in Jesus as the God of heaven.

MESSENGER

I accept your offer gladly. Let us hasten to his majesty, and if he is healed, you shall have your freedom, be rewarded with gold, and have access to the imperial ear at all times.[11]

Sire, there is no cause for anxiety. It appears that the prophet you sought has been executed, but I have brought back with me a certain woman who, in the prophet's name, will rid you of your malady.

EMPEROR

Because, messenger, the prophet who could have restored me to health is dead, I shall abstain from food. However, woman, what have you to tell me? Let us hear anything that might cheer us in the slightest degree.

VERONICA

I exhort you to believe in Christ Jesus, and I will show you the imprint of his face on linen. It was his gift to me. And the moment you look upon him, he will heal you completely without the need of any other remedies whatsoever.

EMPEROR

What is your name, good woman? Should these claims of yours prove true, they will undoubtedly gain you great favor. You shall be rewarded and made lady over much land.

VERONICA

My name is Veronica. I have in my possession a likeness of Christ's face made by his own sweat. Whoever beholds it and has faith is bound to regain his health.

You must believe in Jesus, that he is our Lord, the Savior of mankind; whereupon you shall unfailingly be healed if your prayer rises to him from a whole heart.

EMPEROR

I entreat him with all my heart to send health to me even as he is truly the God of infinite grace. I acknowledge you, O God, as the one Lord of Creation and implore you, our Savior, speedily to help me.

Pray show me the likeness, the mere fact of which is such a marvel to me. And come nearer in your devotion to our majesty since I have more to say to you before you leave our presence.

VERONICA

Now look upon it, and you shall be cured of your disease; yes, quickly and easily. I say believe on him, the Redeemer of all souls, the God of heaven above.

(Then she shall show him the handkerchief, and he shall kneel, saying:)

EMPEROR

O Jesus, full of pity, your dear face I will kiss.

(He kisses the handkerchief.)

I put my trust in you, believing that you will cure me of the last taint of my leprosy. Christ, Lord of heaven and earth, may you be worshipped forever.

(He is healed of his leprosy.)

I am healed, completely healed! Blessed be the Lord, our Lord who was slain. Neither earth nor heaven contains a greater deity. He is God in the highest!

VERONICA

Now that you have been restored to health, you have ample reason to know that there is but one God, Christ Jesus, whom Pilate put to death. Without fail, therefore, avenge the Christ, the King of Heaven.

EMPEROR

Good Veronica, it shall be done, even as the Lord made me whole, cleansing me of all my disease. If Pilate is alive, he shall surely perish, he and as many as follow him.

Torturers, come to me! else you will feel the smart of punishment before the season changes. . . . I find myself so grieved, so appalled, I cannot think beyond the moment.

FIRST TORTURER

Here we are, my emperor, straightaway. Terrible was the thunder of your summons. I trembled and thought I might die of fright.

EMPEROR

Go, seek out Pilate for me, and as men of worth, take care you are not slack in your duty. Bring him to us that we may view him. As soon as we lay hold on him, he dies.

SECOND TORTURER

Let's hurry to find the hateful buzzard. He was always a bad one, never in his life ashamed of acting wrong.

THIRD TORTURER

He'll be brought to you, my lord, and that shortly, no matter how strong he is. I won't let him beg off regardless. We'll plant him right here where we're standing now. He won't have made any headway against us. . . .

FOURTH TORTURER

You, Pilate, you're to present yourself before the emperor, and it's no use to give us a lot of talk. You're going along with us in spite of yourself, you lying rascal!

PILATE

I have no objection to going with you. It will be a pleasure to appear before his imperial majesty, Tiberius Caesar, who is invariably courteous to everyone. In truth, I hold him in great affection. . . .

FIRST TORTURER

Here he is, Caesar, the man you know to have persecuted the prophet, Jesus. He condemned him to the cross, where he died, having suffered much for men's sake.

(The emperor comes down.)

EMPEROR

A hearty welcome, Pilate. As God is my witness, I have so strong a liking for you, I couldn't wish you harm either now or in future.

PILATE

Caesar, many thanks. Reporting to you is always a joy since your graciousness is exceeded only by your sovereign power, which is unmatched the world over.

SECOND TORTURER

Was it for the like of this that we hustled the fellow to you, only to have him made so all-fired comfortable? Come on there, worthless, outside with us double-quick!

(They grasp him.)

THIRD TORTURER

All right, come along, wonder-worker. Tell us, are you some kind of magician, seeing as how nobody can ever seem to get to you, weekdays or Sundays? Answer me and no stalling.

(The torturer shall release him, and he withdraws a moderate distance.)

FOURTH TORTURER

To my mind, we could go right ahead and kill him ourselves because of what that specimen has done. I'm telling you, bet my hat on it, he's butchered the greatest man who ever lived. By God, he has!

(Here the torturers absent themselves for a short time.)

EMPEROR

Oh, shame! shame! I must be on my guard, for unless Pilate is done away with as soon as possible, I shan't know what course to pursue. The wretch must pay for his crime, a crime that sickens me to the very heart.

Yet when he came forward, loathsome creature that he is, he spoke so winningly I gave way, unable to find the slightest flaw in anything he said or any conceivable reason to kill him.

Upon my soul, I believe the fellow is a wizard, a past master of the black arts unequalled throughout the length and breadth of the empire. Therefore, Veronica, as you love your emperor, hasten to tell him what is best to be done at this juncture.

VERONICA

It is my firm belief that you cannot touch him, much less kill him, even though he comes within your reach, as long as he wears about him the garment of the crucified Jesus.

He wears it next to his skin, so have him brought before you again and the garment removed from him. Otherwise you will never succeed in laying a hand on him.

EMPEROR

Bless you, Veronica! The facts being what they are, I shall seize the garment. Torturers, return to us at once, that our spirits may be restored and our work made safe from miscarriage.

FIRST TORTURER

Here we are, lord. Since we have often fared well in your service, you have only to inform us of your wishes, and we will speedily carry them out as is our duty.

EMPEROR

Fetch Pilate into our presence a second time. Through earlier oversight, we were deceived by him. Actually, he is a wicked man. I hate the evil-smelling beast, by my faith, hate him intensely.

SECOND TORTURER

I will fetch him at once. . . . You know, if I felt up to it, I'd personally hammer him into little pieces, I would. But just to see him is to find yourself liking him.

THIRD TORTURER

I don't care how much people love him, I'd as soon kill him as not. His singing days are over. Look, there he is! You're to come to the emperor right now, where you'll get a quick sentence to torture that'll be the real thing.

PILATE

I go to him gladly, as he is not only a powerful overlord but also a noble human being, a truly gracious man and ruler of a farflung empire.

FOURTH TORTURER

Take a good look at the fellow, Majesty. I'm thinking that now you have him before you, it will be impossible for you to harm him for as long as he's in your sight. I'm certain of it.

EMPEROR

Torturers, you will proceed into the city, all of you, and observe at every point whether there is any treasonous talk being raised against us. . . . And now, Pilate, I declare my intention of obtaining from you the seamless garment which you wear next to your flesh.

PILATE

The garment·I wear, my emperor, is not suitable for one of your station nor a worthy object of your desire. To tell you the truth, it is soiled, not having been washed for a long time.

In any case, it is unfit for a sovereign lord like you. I implore you not to require that I surrender it under present circumstances.

EMPEROR

Surely, Pilate, I could never be demeaned through assuming a garment which has been about the person of Jesus. Rather, since I find myself longing to possess it, I ask you in all seriousness to hand it over immediately and without further parley on this occasion.

PILATE

Your majesty, were I to take it off now I would be left as good as naked in your presence. To see me thus exposed before you would be indecent, and indecency violates the deference toward a king or an emperor which decorum entails.

VERONICA

You must command him, my lord, to strip off the garment without another word. So long as you give ground, he will simply not obey.

EMPEROR

Remove the garment at once. Further delay, on any pretext whatsoever, is denied; additional temporizing likewise. I will have the garment no matter how reluctant you are.

PILATE

Alas! since I must part with it, I recognize only too clearly that from this day forward I shall never know peace. Indeed I fail to see how my life itself is to be spared unless through payment of much gold.

EMPEROR

Away with you, infamous scoundrel! You have crucified Jesus, Our Lord and Savior. Let someone hand me my sword, that I may kill this insect as swiftly as the word leaves my tongue.

VERONICA

Hold off, sire! Do not allow him so easy a death. Seek for him rather the hardest, the most pitiless end a man can have because, limitless villain that he is, he has snuffed out the life of God's Son, who made us and all things else in heaven and earth.

Commit the abominable one to prison, there to await trial and lawful sentence of death.

EMPEROR

To prison he goes forthwith and to a merciless death, preceded by searching torments from which no man may shield him.

Ho, jailor, come forward! We shall have you strangled and quickly, too, if you don't. You and your boy are not to loiter but must carry out our commands on the instant.

JAILOR

Lord, we're ready. What are your wishes? No sooner said than done, whatever they be.

EMPEROR

Put this creature in the dungeon, there to rot in total darkness. He is a sorcerer. We shall ordain for him the most agonizing death it is possible to inflict upon the murderer of Jesus, our redeemer.

SERVANT

Majesty, I will put him in the bottommost pit among the rats, lice, and fleas, where he'll suffer plenty. They say young Lashbutt[12]—that's me—is pretty lively when it comes to getting ideas.

JAILOR

Take and throw him in the hole. Don't hold back or pay any attention to his noise, as he's of no account. And let's not have any grumbling from you. He's got to go the distance, definitely, and can't sidestep what's coming to him, never mind how slick he is.

SERVANT

Now here's where you're to stay and rot to the bone, and when you're sentenced, you'll go out the hard way, something you sure deserve. A dog is better than you.

PILATE

Tell me the sworn truth. What manner of death has been decreed for me? I know I am to die, know it well, yet am tortured by remorse.

JAILOR

Faith, you're to have the ugliest there is. It's already been decided. Don't imagine there's any hope for you in this world. You've got only a few days left.

PILATE

Even so, I can and will protect myself from a barbarous death at

the hands of any man alive. Into my own heart my own knife I here-
upon press home! Oh wretched, wretched. . . .

EMPEROR

As our loyal subject, Veronica, give us your views on the best
method of destroying Pilate in order that the wicked beast may perish
in an extremity of pain and rage.

VERONICA

Before proceeding further, my dear lord, it would be well to have
the jailor inquire into the prisoner's condition at this time. However,
I am honestly convinced that no amount of suffering could ever be
more than he deserves.

EMPEROR

Jailor, this should make you very happy. How is Pilate bearing up
under confinement? What is his appearance? Let us have a full report
on his present state of health.

JAILOR

Your majesty, Pilate is dead. In his anguish and despair, he stabbed
himself. With surprising suddenness, he drove a sheath knife clear
into his heart, seeking a baneful end.

EMPEROR

Now thanks be to Jesus for granting that arch-villain the world's
most frightful death. I hold it certain that no man can find a more
abandoned exit from life than suicide.

Immediately, therefore, take him by his two feet, jailor, you and
your boy, and bury him deep in the earth because many people, I am
firmly persuaded, are going to stand in dread of that corpse.

JAILOR

Take the head, Lashbutt, while by the heels I tow him to his grave.

SERVANT

That I will, master, by my arse. Vengeance on him and a bad end. So be it.

(And then the body shall be ejected from the earth.)

Oh, master, by my soul, this has got to be a devil with a curse on him, believe me! When he jumped out of the ground like he did, I'm telling you, I was so scared, I let one.

JAILOR

And I'm telling you, hollow-head, when he shot up from his grave, I ran scared, letting a whole string of them, for you'd have supposed he couldn't stir, packed down as he was.

SERVANT

Well, let's be big heroes; go back right now and stick him in the grave again. . . . Uh oh, he's turned black! Still, I figure he'll stay down this time, if he's on God's side, or else he's a devil.

JAILOR

And if he's not on God's side, it would take a whole village just to handle him and get him into the ground. Let's get a move on and rebury him.

(And then they shall put the corpse in the ground, and it shall be ejected a second time.)

SERVANT

He's one strong devil, I swear he is. Doesn't stay down any time at all. A bad lot without a single friend in heaven. Let's go tell the emperor about it this minute, the two of us.

JAILOR

Caesar, high lord, that fellow's corpse simply will not stay in the ground.

EMPEROR

We openly proclaim that he was a devil abroad in the world before ever he met his death.

SERVANT

Each time we bury him, the devils come and ruin our work. They keep tossing him up, splitting the earth that's over him, an awful sound to hear.

EMPEROR

Fie upon it, oh, fie! What is to be done unless we can make shift to dispose of the fiend somewhere? Failing Christ's aid, the stench of his carcass will fatally infect every soul in our empire.

VERONICA

To his sorrow and bafflement, my liege, he will not be able to escape from a strong iron chest sunk beneath the waters of the Tiber. From that place, it is certain he will never rise until doomsday.

EMPEROR

In faith, Veronica, you have given flawless counsel. Come to us, torturers, and that with all possible speed, lest your delay prove the death of us!

FIRST TORTURER

Your majesty, while returning from Spain, I had reached mid-Germany and was, as a matter of fact, at table there when I heard your call. Please reveal your wishes at once.

SECOND TORTURER

Tell us the occasion of this call to duty. If there is something which weighs on your mind, we will take care of it in a hurry, as we're not idle loafers.

EMPEROR

Take the corpse of that wicked fellow, Pilate—its damable stench pervades the land—and throw it, encased by an iron box, into a remote cove of the Tiber, where it may sink to the bottom.

THIRD TORTURER

Shortly, wearing an iron shroud, the loathsome thing will be heaved into the river where the water is very deep. From that moment, no man need ever fear it again.

FOURTH TORTURER

There's such a load of curses on the body, I honestly don't think the water will put up with it. It's too devil-ridden. Let hellfire burn it, so there'll be nothing left to come back and haunt people.

FIRST TORTURER

Seeing we have the strongbox, let's get the blasted meat into it, lay hold, and rush it to the water like madmen.

SECOND TORTURER

All right, the body's in. Now to the water with it. They couldn't pay me not to get rid of stuff so rotten-born, that's sure. There isn't gold enough.

THIRD TORTURER

To hell with him on the Devil's shoulders! He was and is accursed, no maybe about it. Let's make quick work of it, as I'm set on launching him into deep blue water.

FOURTH TORTURER

There you go, Pilate, damn you! on your way to the bottom, and everybody's curse goes with you, you who falsely condemned the Son of God, Mary's child.

(And then let them throw the body into the water.)

TRAVELER

In order to freshen up a bit, I'll step down to the river and wash my hands good and clean.

(And he shall wash his hands and shall die immediately.)

Ah, woe that I was ever born! My death is sudden, oh sudden! The water must have done it. I cannot live a moment longer.

MESSENGER

My liege, you must seek fresh counsel. No one is able to survive a passage of the Tiber. It has destroyed a multitude already. In God's name, let Pilate's corpse be removed from the river to some other place.

EMPEROR

Ah, dreadful, dreadful! What action shall we take? Unless you can help us, Veronica, we are without a remedy. The body is accursed. Give us your ready advice that we may have peace of mind.

VERONICA

As long as the corpse remains in the river, neither man nor beast can pass over it and escape death because, while he lived, Pilate was the epitome of evil. Nevertheless, I counsel against gloom.

Despite the cost in silver and gold, cause the body to be raised. Having acquired a boat at trifling additional expense, let the body be put aboard it and floated down to the sea. From there, the boat will transport it to hell. For that, your majesty, I hold myself answerable.

EMPEROR

Our dear lord, Mary's son, bless you even as I bless you, Veronica. Torturers! Torturers, come to us! Speed your steps and thereby cheer our spirits.

Oh, where are you, you wandering rogues? Awesome was the shout of our summons. God save us, grief and impatience strike us to the heart.

FIRST TORTURER

There's never a day when I like to loaf, so tell us straight off what we have to do.

EMPEROR

You are to proceed to the river and raise the body of Pilate, thereupon conveying it by boat to the sea. I shall give you much treasure as a reward for your services.

SECOND TORTURER

We'll pull him up at once. He as good as asked for hard punishment and a bad end when he passed that wicked false sentence on Jesus Christ, the King of Heaven.

THIRD TORTURER

Yes, let's fish him up, men, and earn our money. Lay a tight hold on him with grappling-irons so he can't possibly get away from us.

FOURTH TORTURER

I've got a pair of irons on him. Heavy as stone or not, the wicked carcass has got to come up. Put your back into it, everybody, and be careful.

FIRST TORTURER

Look, the putrid thing is rising, devil take it! I say we drag him right out on the bank, the son of a hellhound.

SECOND TORTURER

Into the boat with him fast, fast! Slide him aboard with the curse of God, angels, and holy men upon him.

THIRD TORTURER

There, the trim's perfect. Hoist the sail and let him go with the wind and with the curse of Heaven and all the blessed.

FOURTH TORTURER

Shove her off now. . . . I hear a hideous noise, and as he floats nearer to the seaward ledge, the water begins to churn around it. A horde of devils have come to get him; I know they have.

FIRST TORTURER

Quick, let's make for home, away from the fiends who gather for their quarry. You can hear the gleeful yells. Let's go this very second before we too get hurt.

LUCIFER

All devils, come with me, that swiftly we may fetch the soul and body of Pilate. He shall stand forever in a whiffling flame, ever agonized, ever crying out, and his unending song shall be, "Oh, woe to him who is born into the world."

BEELZEBUB

Because it is accursed, this body falls to us, found unworthy of a resting place either in earth or water, fresh or salt.

SATAN

Coffined in iron, he was put deep under Tiber's waters, where he brought death to many through sheer terror.

BEELZEBUB

Not a ship passed over him but what it foundered. Instead of joy, he has won for himself a skin of fire.

LUCIFER

Raised from the river, he was brought again to shore and put aboard a stout boat to begin his journey with us into the abyss.

SATAN

The boat was rigged with mast and sail which drove it from land and hurled it upon a reef, surrendering its passenger to our jurisdiction.

BEELZEBUB

As was ordained, the massive rock opened to receive him who by his own deed renounced the kingdom of heaven. There we welcomed him, his voice a horror on the ear amid the flame, the smoke, the red-hot glow, that will always linger in that stone.[13]

LUCIFER

We shall furnish him with searing heat, shivering cold, the wide-mouthed grins of devils—a complete assortment of never ending torments.

SATAN

You, deeply cursed body, shall with your soul be dragged to hell, your chant, "Woe to him!"

BEELZEBUB

Everybody now lay hold of this boat of his so as to get him under-way, and Tulfric, kindly begin for us the tail of a ditty.

TULFRIC

Yah! You can just kiss my tail instead,[14] since it sticks out far enough astern of me, for sure! Beelzebub, Satan, you two sing a mighty bass, and I'll carry me an elegant treble.

(And so ends the Death of Pilate.)

THE ASCENSION OF CHRIST TO HEAVEN BEGINS

(and Peter says:)

PETER

To what can we look forward, precious Lord, if you leave us again? We shall be desolate, finding no happiness in anything until we see you once more.

JESUS

Be of good cheer, Peter, and strengthen your brethren in the true faith. I go to my place at the right hand of the Father, leaving you the comfort of the Holy Ghost.

PHILIP

Dear Master, through the abundance of your grace, disclose to us the Father and that will suffice us. Mighty is your Godhead to all who in their need appeal to you for mercy.

JESUS

Ah, Philip, your faith grows lax, since otherwise, having been with me so long a time, you should know well the substance of right belief.

I say to you in all seriousness that whoever will have seen me, of necessity will have seen my Father.

Even as I am both God and man, it unalterably follows that the Father is in me and I in him. Inasmuch, therefore, as I go to my Father, do you stand fast in your faith that all may attain salvation.

JAMES THE ELDER

Lord, where should we go to find ourselves a place to live, a place to which we cannot be followed but where we can pray to almighty God, numbered exactly as we now are, the eleven of us and no more?

JESUS

At once betake yourselves to the Mount of Olives. There the Father will give ear to your petition. I shall come to you at that place and from it will ascend to heaven.

(The disciples proceed to the Mount of Olives.)

ANDREW

We will go this moment, Lord, for it is impossible to stay so much as a night in any community hereabouts because of the way the Jews continually harass and threaten us.

JOHN

Let us go, then, to Olivet, since it is there, as we read in our scriptures, that we are to await the coming of Mary's son, Jesus Christ, the light of the world.

BARTHOLOMEW

So be it! Let us make haste and may Christ Jesus, the King of Bliss, be with us. Woe to the man ever born of woman, who does not believe that the Lord is our Savior.

SIMON

O Christ, King on high, hear our prayer for deliverance from the lure of evil. Armed with the gift of divine grace, we fear no torment of man's devising.

JUDE

Perfect is our faith that the grace of Christ, born of Mary, abides with us. In the beginning, the Lord created us and in the end he has redeemed mankind with his blood.

JESUS

Now peace to each and all of you here present, you who wait for me. With the coming of night, forty days will have passed since I rose from the dead.

JAMES THE YOUNGER

If only it could be your resolve, Lord, never to leave us. For if you were with us, how great our joy, truly, and how serene our spirit!

JESUS

Can you be ignorant of the heart of the matter? I am with every man who lives in a state of grace. Let him say what he will, unless my flesh and blood dwell within him, he shall not attain to heaven.

THOMAS

Lord, what am I to do when you have ascended to the Father on high? Never again to behold you among us in your Godhead is to go ever sorrowing.

JESUS

You are to travel to India, Thomas, and shall preach in my name, winning converts to my service in a land where believers are few in number.

And likewise the remainder of you, go forth in pairs and preach the gospel over all the world. Whosoever believes and is baptized into the faith shall achieve salvation.

He who refuses to believe cannot enter my service, not were he to offer the world as payment. The truth is this: suffering shall be the sentence upon him who transgresses my will.

MATTHEW

Even as you are the maker of all things, Lord, we will proclaim that you alone are God. As for the unbeliever, his way to redemption simply does not exist.

(Here Jesus kisses them all.)

JESUS

My blessing I leave with you. Before your eyes, I now mount up to heaven itself, and there, the world redeemed through me, I shall sit at the right hand of God, my Father.

(Here Jesus ascends.)

FIRST ANGEL

Who may it be that in the perfection of his manhood and clothed in red[15] has come so swiftly to the kingdom? Great joy attends his arrival; it is manifest that heaven holds him dear.

SECOND ANGEL

I cannot say, since even though a mortal were to travel no less than forty miles a day for as much as seven thousand, seven hundred years, still he would not have reached this realm.

THIRD ANGEL

Who comes to us from earth, his head and shoulders, feet and legs, as red as blood? That he could be of human kind astonishes me since even angels cannot match the speed of his journey hither.

FOURTH ANGEL

He comes from Edom, and the wonder would be that he has not brought terror to a numberless host of evil spirits, for I believe he is none other than the Son who was sent hence, he who is the King of Bliss.

FIFTH ANGEL

What manner of being are you, your garments dyed so deep a crimson, here in the kingdom of heaven, where I am certain that no man, unless through full Godhead, takes his stand?

JESUS

I am a king who has done battle, my undivided cause the deliverance of Adam and his seed from their ruinous plight. I am the King of Bliss, whose victory was won in arms of red.

FIFTH ANGEL

Glory to the celestial King! All honor to our God, creator of heaven and earth! So great our joy, we shall never cease from singing Glory to God in the Highest.

(Then let all the angels sing "Gloria in excelsis Deo.")

SIXTH ANGEL

How is it that you are clothed in red, here on high where mankind has never set foot? The raiment of angels is as white as the sun on a cloudless day, nor have I yet seen them wear a different hue.

JESUS

Red is mine by right, seeing that my coat of mail[16] became a coat of blood, and the lash cut through to the skin from head to foot, driving deep into the flesh at points innumerable.

SIXTH ANGEL

Lord, I would not have rejoiced had I known the cruel torment you endured. When we witnessed your coming, I had no knowledge of your death or resurrection.

SEVENTH ANGEL

I beg you to reveal who you are. Red garments are unheard of. Why, then, do you wear them? I have never seen that color worn in this domain by anyone.

JESUS

To free Adam from Hell, I wore for hours a crown of thorns. When its barbs sank through the skull into the brain, my suffering was indeed great.

SEVENTH ANGEL

Alas, I was totally unaware that the Son of very God had absented himself from heaven. In the time he undertook to redeem the whole burden of Adam's sin, the torture he bore must truly have been intense.

EIGHTH ANGEL

As for me, Lord, I marvel that you, who are the King of Bliss, are nevertheless clad in red and how, your body having been so sorely racked, you could rise from earth by your own unaided strength.

JESUS

I am a king, just and powerful. From of old time man's sin has offended me, yet nothing now prevails against me. Hell's gate I broke, and delivered, from great evil, torment, and distress of spirit, the souls of those who did my Father's will. Them I brought to joy.

Though man, God, and sovereign together, my only bulwark was a wooden cross, my helmet a crown of piercing thorns. With my limbs wrenched from their sockets, I hung exposed to the general view. Through my side into the heart, my spear was couched to rest.

A ruffian skewered my feet with spikes, my gauntlets were huge nails driven through my hands. For tunic and breastplate I wore harsh and mocking purple girded around me, so that my blood cemented the flesh to the cloth as I stood before Pilate.

When the purple was snatched off by ready fingers, the flesh came away with the cloth, even to the bone. After my good works in men's behalf, I asked for drink. They proffered bitter gall, which I would nowise accept.

I perished with a spear-thrust to the heart, yet assuredly on the third day, I rose again from the dead.

EIGHTH ANGEL

Blessed is your name, O treasured Lord! We rejoice exceedingly in the knowledge that human kind have attained to heaven. God the Father, through the operation of the Holy Ghost, has sent salvation into the world, while above us God the Son shall dwell on high forever.

NINTH ANGEL

Lord Jesus Christ, we knew nothing of how, in the fullness of your grace, you journeyed to earth. The beauty of your tidings is a source of joy and through you we are made glad.

JESUS

Heavenly Father enthroned, now am I come to you from the world in the likeness of a mortal. With my heart's blood, I have redeemed mankind in order that none whom we created need be lost.

GOD THE FATHER

Welcome are you in heaven, my Son, twice welcome to me. Take your place at my right hand, you who have undergone surpassing toil and, in victory, have delivered the souls of men from the torment of perdition.

EMPEROR

Good people, you have witnessed the true circumstances of Christ's resurrection: how he broke the gates of hell, leading into bliss Adam and Eve and all those who did the Father's will. Very great, surely, was the love he bore mankind.

And Jesus ascended to heaven's joy. May he ever preserve you from the Devil and his train, and may the Lord's blessing descend upon each of you present here today and go with you as you turn your steps toward home.

Now, musicians, strike up a brisk tune that we may dance.

NOTES

Beginning of the World

1 In the Cornish MS (Bodley 791), the stanza which contains this passage is written on the flyleaf in a different hand and may not have been a part of the original. I have attempted to fit the passage into context as smoothly and consistently as possible through observing a distinction between heaven as the abode of God the Father and his angels and heaven (sky, firmament) as the vaulted canopy of the medieval earth, locus of celestial bodies and source of rain.

2 I have omitted from this stage direction a final clause, written in a later hand, which reads *hic ludit Lucifer de celo* 'Here Lucifer plays his part from heaven.' Although wholly inoperative as it stands, it should not be passed over in silence because it implies the onetime presence in *O.M.* of an episode or episodes still to be found in the English cycles and in the Cornish *Gwreans an Bys* (Creation of the World). These episodes deal with the creation of angels and the fall of Lucifer.

3 A literal rendering of the Cornish rather than a hopefully equivalent metaphor struck off by the present translator.

4 An older term than treble or soprano for the highest voice in part music. According to the *Harvard Dictionary of Music*, the practice of descant, which goes back to the 14th c., "was a method of improvisation to the plainsong melody." See also Carter, *A Dictionary of Middle English Musical Terms*.

5 At this point, the Cornish supplies two additional lines, which may be rendered as follows: "Happy is the lot of all who fill their days with well-doing." Several factors prompt their omission from the present work. They weaken God the Father's terminal speech to Cain; they constitute a moralistic tag not elsewhere characteristic of Deus Pater's utterances; they form more or less of a *non sequitur;* and above all they serve to conclude a corrupt stanza, atypical both in length and rhyme scheme. (For a discussion of the stanza, see Phyllis Harris, *Origo Mundi,* pp. 344-47.)

6 The Cornish has *se,* probably a borrowing from M.E. *se,* whose root meaning of 'seat, throne' yields an entirely sober reading literally, while it does not preclude such ironic secondary meaning as 'bishop's throne' and, by extension, his 'jurisdiction' or 'diocese.' This instance of irony, whether demonstrably conscious or not, is by no means unique in the *Ordinalia.*

7 These two lines in the original (*O.M.* 963-64) appear to be a contribution by the playwright that is independent not only of his primary source, the Vulgate (*Genesis* 6:16), but also *Cursor Mundi,* another important presumptive source, and such an analogue as the third Chester pageant. The two lines require that Noah shall reinforce the Ark's 'port' or door with wooden cross-members ('beams nailed athwart') in order that the door may not, presumably, be rendered unusable through damage by the wind-lashed waters of the Deluge.

The precise nature of the damage which God the Father seeks to forestall has puzzled translators because the final word in the passage can be assigned either of two opposed meanings. The Cornish word is *degees,* a participle, whose preponderant meaning when used elsewhere in the literature is 'closed.' If the prefix *de* is construed as an intensive, we get the literal rendering 'that it [door] may not be emphatically closed,' *i.e.,* 'closed tight.' On the other hand, Norris, in his *Ancient Cornish Drama,* gives 'that it may not be opened,' while Nance, in his annotated copy of Norris, can be seen to have temporized between 'closed' and 'opened,' finally settling upon 'opened.' Nance has left a pencil drawing that shows how he visualized the marine carpentry which Noah was called upon to execute. His sketch represents the cross-members as a reinforcement of the frame and exterior planking of the door against the action of the seas and not as an interior guard against premature or inadvertent use by the ark's passengers while it rode out the flood.

8 Another and striking departure from the Old Testament, here a matter of substitution rather than addition. The Vulgate *(Genesis* 8:4) reads: *Requievitque arca . . . super montes Armeniae;* the King James Version, "And the ark rested . . . upon the mountains of Ararat." The two names were formerly used to designate the same region. Whatever *O.M.* loses in terms of traditional plausibility or unanimity by bringing the ark to rest on Calvary instead of Ararat, it gains in terms of thematic unity through which the entire *Ordinalia* may be seen as the timeless drama of salvation, its supreme epiphany centered upon a cross outside Jerusalem's wall.

9 Responsibility for the qualifying pronoun is mine. It gives Pharaoh's messenger a touch of chauvinism, of invincible ignorance not explicit in the Cornish at this point, which bluntly makes a vessel of Judeo-Christian faith out of a pagan Egyptian with the literal phrase 'the law of God on high.'

10 If we accept Fowler's necessarily tentative conclusion that the *Ordinalia* was composed "somewhere between 1300 and 1375, or, more narrowly, between 1350 and 1375" ("The Date of the Cornish 'Ordinalia,'" p. 125), it becomes reasonable to expect some trace of topical influence upon *O.M.*'s dramatization of the plagues of Biblical Egypt by 14th c. England's experience with the Black Death, which reached Cornwall in 1348. Bodmin, the ecclesiastical center of the county, was severely hit, as was Truro, which appears to have been largely evacuated by its population in an effort to escape the epidemic. Admittedly, however, such topical influence on *O.M.* as there may be is conjectural.

For what it may be worth, one notes that the dramatist made no attempt to follow Scripture chronologically through the sequence of ten supernatural afflictions suffered by Pharaoh and his people as recounted in *Exodus.* The play contracts the Old Testament narrative into a mere pair of relatively short messenger speeches. The first is general, reporting great loss of life, the apparent result of the Hebrew God's displeasure. But the second messenger speech *(O.M.* 1558-64) attracts the eye in that it names a single, specific, naturalistic factor as the immediate cause for the sudden, high mortality among the Egyptians. The messenger informs Pharaoh that his subjects and their cattle are being struck down wholesale by poisoned water and poisoned grain, much as Edward the Third's Cornish subjects and their cattle, the latter through neglect, perished in the outbreak of bubonic plague (cf. Elliott-Binns, *Medieval Cornwall,* pp. 88-89). One of the results of this quite drastic condensation is that *O.M.*'s version of the plagues of ancient Egypt and history's version of the Black Death in medieval Cornwall resemble one another far more closely than either resembles the story as told in *Exodus*.

11 Although never beyond a few words at a time, the *Ordinalia's* spoken lines make occasional use of Latin, French, and Middle English. I have reproduced the Latin and the French essentially as they appear in the original text, except for a unique case *(O.M.* 1975-78) where two languages, Latin and Cornish, are so closely bound by the syntax that a net loss rather than a net gain of effectiveness would have resulted from a failure to translate both into English. The Middle English, however, has been modernized throughout, a somewhat reluctant decision because it obliterates one means employed by the dramatist to indicate differences of status among characters. (See Introduction, *The Cycle as Drama*.)

The ellipsis which follows the bit of French has been supplied by me, here as elsewhere, since no pauses or breaks are provided by the manuscript within a play as a unit.

12 *O.M.*'s first mention of Mt. Tabor is in a speech by God the Father ordering Adam to make sacrifice on the mountain. The second is contained in a stage direction which provides that Moses shall replant the Rods in the soil of Mt. Tabor. It is not until we encounter the name for a third time that Tabor acquires a specific location, namely, Arabia. This may come as something of a shock to readers familiar with the geography of the Old Testament, since the Mt. Tabor uppermost in their minds is to be found considerably less than a hundred miles northeast of Jerusalem and about six miles from Nazareth in Galilee. Is it, then, an author's error or a touch of romantic caprice that is responsible for dispatching King David from Jerusalem to Araby, an indeterminate and arduous journey whether in ancient or medieval times, when a comparatively modest local trip would have sufficed?

It appears rather that the dramatist is again intent (see note 8 above for an earlier instance) upon his double-stranded theme—the Oil of Mercy and the Rood Tree, a concern to which even sacred geography is willingly subordinated. Ancient Arabia (obviously the Sinai peninsula of *Exodus*) was far separated from Galilee in geographical terms, and the nomenclature of the Old Testament does not equate Mt. Tabor with Sinai or Horeb. But on the symbolic level frequently assumed by the *Ordinalia*, space becomes elastic and differences of identity are reconciled.

Thus *O.M.*, while it omits the giving of the Law to Moses on Sinai, does have him replant the sacred rods there or thereabouts, the rods which are destined in aftertime to furnish the wood of Christ's cross.

13 For reasons given above (note 11), both the Latin and the Cornish of this speech by King David have been rendered into English. The original lines *(O.M.* 1975-78) read as follows: *in nomine dei patris/a nef mennaf yskynne/eius atque spiritus/re-worro wyth am ene.*

14 While it is traditional that King David be able to itemize a variety of musical instruments trippingly on the tongue and incidentally emphasize the role of the harp, I have not scrupled to alter the poet's word order in this passage for the sake of easier articulation and more grateful phrasing in English. Nor have I

attempted to normalize the names of the less familiar instruments the king enumerates, save in two instances. Where the Cornish has M.E. *organs,* I have substituted the Italian *organetti,* the plural of *organetto,* a small, portable organ known to have been used in medieval processions. Where the Cornish has *symphony,* again Middle English, I have followed the O.E.D's alternate meaning of 'musical instruments in general.' (But see Vulgate, *Daniel* 3:5, 7, 15).

15 The MS reads *ballok* 'little balls (s).' The tone of this M.E. term is nicely adjusted to its context in the original, but in literal translation it threatens to become tautologic and, worse, coy. At the opposite end of the scale, the rendering, 'testicles,' seems inappropriately anatomical and polysyllabic, bringing to mind the familiar complaint that modern English is deficient in sexual vocabulary at a level between the scientific and the bawdy.

16 The suddenness with which King David shifts his address from Bathsheba to Uriah without pause or preparation beyond that of moving from one stanza to the next increases the tempo from rapid to headlong. The possibility that a bridge passage has been lost from Bodley 791 at this point is raised by a pair of tightly sequential circumstances in the MS: (1) the stanza containing the king's words to Bathsheba is shorter than those which precede and follow it; (2) the king's immediately following words to Uriah happen to come at the top of a new MS folio *(O.M.* 20a, 2139). The scribe could have inadvertently dropped transitional lines and even a stage direction accounting for Uriah's presence, as his copying moved to a fresh folio.

17 The Latin echoes the Vulgate *(Psalms* 50:3). Verses 1 and 2 are explanatory rather than devotional. They specifically assign the authorship to David and term the entire psalm an act of contrition for his sin as denounced by Nathan in *II Kings* 12.

18 *O.M.* follows tradition in naming the sacred tree, the Holy Rood, as the locus of composition of the Psalms.

19 King David's zealous and dram-loving (?) messenger is the first but by no means the last person or group of persons in the cycle to receive Cornish real estate as payment in kind for services rendered. Carnsew is a surviving place-name in the parish of Mabe and was, according to Henderson *(Mabe Church and Parish,* p. 31), "the chief place in the parish during the Middle Ages." It comprised the manor lands of the Carnsews, a prominent family in medieval times.

Trehembis was once part of the Carnsew holdings in Mabe.

20 Two of the place-names in this speech cannot be positively identified. Leland, archivist to Henry VIII, regards Bosvannah (modern spelling) as the early Cornish name for Bodmin, an important ecclesiastical centre in the Middle Ages. (See note 15, *Resurrection of Our Lord.)* While later historians who make the same claim as Leland may in general be merely following his authority, Whitaker claims to have seen documentary evidence in support (see Maclean, *Bodmin,* p. 1, n.). There is at present a small farm near Penryn named Bosvannah, but its cession seems to a degree inconsistent with such a major gift as Lostwithiel.

Lostwithiel is situated about six miles southeast of Bodmin. A coinage town in the Middle Ages, Lostwithiel was known as the king's town. Adjacent to it lay Restormel Castle (now a ruin), a favorite resort of the early Dukes of Cornwall. With Bodmin and Helston (see note 4, *Resurrection of Our Lord),* it forms a group of major cessions not, like a majority of the others, under the jurisdiction of the Bishop of Exeter.

Lanner may not be the correct representation of the Cornish word at this point. Under spellings not too unlike its MS form, *Lanerhy,* the name was attached to several medieval locations in Cornwall, including the bishop's manor in the parish of St. Allen. But linguistic evidence suggests that *Lanerhy* may be not a place-name but a common noun meaning 'forests,' referring in this case to those which formerly existed in the vicinity of Bodmin and Lostwithiel.

21 For the possibility that we may have here an early instance of a stock character, the allegedly bibulous Welshman, see Harris, *op. cit.,* pp. 391-92, and Hudson, *The Land's End,* p. 131.

22 At the risk of reading into *O.M.* a quality far more characteristic of 20th c. than 14th c. drama, I regard this speech by King Solomon to his messenger Griffin, as containing both conscious and unconscious irony on the king's part. The conscious humor is obvious, while the unconscious must be thought of as beyond Solomon's self-awareness—that for all his wealth and splendor he was not above the allure of petty economy. A second potential example of his close-fistedness will be forthcoming in the next scene.

23 The tongue-in-cheek atmosphere of Solomon's twin gift to his masons, a gift which provokes a broadly sardonic reply from Second Mason, could hardly have failed to amuse a local audience. For whatever may be the value of Budock and its fine old parish church today, we learn from researches of Henderson (MS Ecclesiastical Antiquities, I, p. 54) that the chancel, roof, and walls of the then mother church were ruinous in 1399 and that Budock during the later Middle Ages was thought of as eclipsed by its neighboring daughter church of Gluvias. Twentieth century Budock adjoins Falmouth; Gluvias lies on rising ground east of Penryn. The straightline distance between them is less than four miles.

The trend of Henderson's findings receives support from Thomas in his *Falmouth,* p. 61, when he states that Budock was reduced to the status of a chapel by 1664, the year in which contiguous Falmouth became an independent parish.

As for Seal Rock, it is identified by Leland *(Itinerary,* Vol. I, p. 321) as the local name for Black Rock in his time—first half of the 16th c. Present-day Black Rock appears on maps and charts as a sizable ledge situated at the mouth of Falmouth harbor. Covered by the sea at flood tide, it reveals itself on the ebb as a menace to unwary navigation, measuring approximately 200 by 100 feet, its sole crop a rectangular bed of seaweed. Its location is marked by a spindle topped with a beacon for the hours of darkness.

24 The language of the original is not specific enough for us to be certain about the precise structural location and function of the 'strong beam' *(gyst cref)* mentioned by First Carpenter as essential in order to make the 'house' sturdy *(O.M.* 2481-82). Norris passes over the ambiguity without comment, but Nance, as in the case of the small door in Noah's ark (see note 7 above), has left a record of his interpretation of the carpenter's opinion. At the foot of p. 189 of his annotated copy of Norris, Nance wrote: "It is not clear how the *gyst* that is to make the whole roof strong was put in position *after* the other timbers. It suggests a ridge timber, as it is the longest and straightest of all." *Gyst* is M.E. 'joist,'

commonly a horizontal member in the framework of a floor, or, as Nance reasonably assumes in the above context, roof.

He accompanies his note with a sketch that reproduces one of the simpler patterns employed in the roof timbering of early Cornish churches (cf. Pevsner, *The Buildings of England—Cornwall,* pp. 235-36; Cox and Ford, *Parish Churches,* p. 117). That the author of *O.M.* wrote from local observation, making no attempt to suggest the ecclesiastical architecture of pre-Christian Jerusalem, was obviously and properly taken for granted by Nance.

25 A representative portion of Bohelland Field may still be seen rising from the north shore of Penryn Harbor. When viewed in the spring of 1964 from a gate located on its upland side, the field consisted of a treeless expanse of enclosed pasturage.

26 No longer extant, Penryn Wood appears to have covered a hillside lying south of medieval Penryn in the direction of Budock. It was a feature of an extensive park, once the property of the bishops of Exeter. Park and wood have long since given place to the gradual expansion of the town. In his *History of Glasney Collegiate Church,* T. C. Peter supplies several allusions to Penryn Wood and the bishop's park. Each of them is supported either directly or indirectly by references to surviving medieval records, such as letters, patent rolls, the episcopal registers of the diocese of Exeter (throughout Glasney's existence embracing both Devon and Cornwall), and the Glasney College cartulary.

I quote in part (ellipses mine) from Peter's narrative of the year 1330 at Glasney (pp. 48-49) as follows: "In 1330, the bishop wrote to his bailiff at Penryn . . . that he had reason to believe that the malefactors who had recently committed outrage and despite in his park of Penryn, entered it by way of the enclosure of one of the canons, and passed on the easier owing to the gardens of the canons not being properly fenced. . . ." Farther on, Peter continues: "On 19 February, 1330, a mandate was issued against trespassers on the same park." He then quotes the mandate itself in English translation: "John, bishop, &c., to the provost of the collegiate church of Glasney, &c., greeting, &c. It has lately come to our hearing that certain sons of perdition, whose names and persons are unknown to us, but whose excesses are made plain by the evil they have wrought, with devilish daring entered the park belonging to our church and to us, publicly and openly and with mighty clamour, with a view to hunting, and did slay, take, and carry away our fallow deer and other wild animals kept therein; and did cut down and burn our trees and shrubs growing therein, in despite of ourselves and our steward, to the grave danger of their own souls and the prejudice and contempt of ourselves; shewing a pernicious example to others; by reason of which without doubt all and singular these malefactors have *ipso facto* to their damnation incurred the sentence of the greater excommunication, by the Holy Fathers in such case decreed. . . ." Bishop John Grandisson thereupon proceeds to detail how the excommunication shall be carried out by the provost.

In his catalogue of Glasney's canons and prebendaries, Peter has this to record of one Nicholas Stoke (p. 149): "He was accused to the bishop of cutting down timber in the woods pertaining to his prebend in Glasney without real necessity, and the bishop, 19 November, 1400, wrote to Benedict Canterbury, prebendary of the said collegiate church, directing him to inhibit Nicholas publicly from continuing this waste, and to take steps for preventing like waste in future. . . ."

27 An imaginary line which begins at Enys, runs south through Gwarder (and Penryn) to Kergilliack, and then angles east via Tregenver to Arwennack, would form a rough L. The total linear distance involved does not exceed four statute miles.

Enys, like Penryn Wood once the property of the bishops of Exeter, is now a major estate belonging to the Enys family. Gwarder was and is an estate lying south of Enys and just north of Bohelland Field (note 25). Kergilliack, said by the late Cornish scholar and linguist Henry Jenner, to have become a golf links in his time, was an estate in the Middle Ages. It is now divided into two large farms, Higher and Lower Kergilliack, situated about a mile and a half south of contemporary Penryn.

Turning east, we come to the still inhabited estate of Tregenver. Formerly a manor, it lies on the eastern border of Budock parish where the latter meets the landward edge of present-day Falmouth. Arwennack was a medieval manor and long the seat of the Killigrews, the founders of Falmouth. A part of the site is marked by a twice rebuilt mansion facing Falmouth harbor.

28 King Solomon's choice of his 'clerk of the privy seal' to be ordained 'overseer' (bishop, high priest) of the newly completed temple could be a topical reference. Data thus far accumulated point to Richard de Bury, author, canon of Exeter and Glasney, privy seal to Edward III, and subsequently Bishop of Durham, all within the first third of the fourteenth century.

29 The Cornish *(O.M.* 2651) reads: *crog rom-bo er an thewen,* literally 'may I have hanging by the thews.' It is the final word in the line, *thewen,* which has provoked the widest variation of rendering among translators and commentators. Norris construes *thewen* as 'gods.' Nance, following Loth, makes it 'jaws.' My version of the line, 'may I be pilloried like a naughty woman,' has been influenced by Fowler (unpublished gloss) and by Spargo's *Juridical Folklore in England,* Ch. I.

Professor Fowler suggests that the singular of the Cornish *thewen* is actually the Middle English word *thew,* which Spargo shows to have been loosely applied to several instruments of public punishment, chiefly for women, during the Middle Ages in Britain. These instruments appear to have included the pillory, the tumbrel, and the ducking-stool (cucking-stool, cocking-stool). Spargo (p. 20) quotes from Borlase, *The Natural History of Cornwall,* as follows in part: "Among the punishments inflicted in Cornwall of old time was that of the cocking-stool, a seat of infamy where strumpets and scolds, with bare feet and head, were condemned to abide the derision of those that passed by, for such time as the bailiffs of manors, which had the privilege of such jurisdiction, did appoint. . . ." According to a history of Penryn still in manuscript when shown to me (1964), the privilege of the tumbrel was restored to medieval Penryn in 1270.

My rendering of *O.M.* 2651 is based upon three dominant considerations. First, the Cornish says 'may I have hanging' (neck-stretching), which suggests the pillory *(collistrigium)* rather than either tumbrel or ducking-stool (see Andrews, *Old-Time Punishments,* for illustrations of all three devices). Second, humiliating public exhibition was the main object of the pillory and was not shared with immersion as in the case of the others. Third, this form of punishment is known to have been largely confined to women—scolds, prostitutes, blasphemers.

30 Not to be confused with Bohelland Field already bestowed upon his carpenters by King Solomon (note 25 above), Bohelland is the old name of the church of St. Gluvias, Penryn.

The place-name, Bosaneth, is still carried by a mill and a neighboring farm located in the parish of Mawnan approximately three and a half miles south of Falmouth and four and a half miles from the site of Glasney College.

31 Included by the bishop in the same context and almost the same breath as Bohelland and Bosaneth, the Canonry of the Close virtually has to be a reference to Glasney and not merely because the prelate lumps the three properties in the one gesture of episcopal largesse. Geographically viewed, the three places occupy the angles of a triangle whose longest side, Gluvias (Bohelland) to Bosaneth, measures under five miles, the shortest side, Glasney to St. Gluvias, about a mile. There is the further fact that Glasney is known from allusions in the episcopal registers (see note 26 above and item 1 in the Glasney Cartulary) to have housed the canons in separate yet apparently grouped and enclosed dwellings with gardens and fences. Peter (*op. cit.*, p. 48) mentions a wall that separated the houses and gardens of the canons from the bishop's wood, adding that traces of it remained at the time his book was published (1903). A sketchy map of Glasney, dating from the later years of the reign of Henry VIII and now in the British Museum (see Peter, *op. cit.*, facing p. 41), indicates that a substantial wall, furnished with battlemented towers commanding the seaward approach, girdled the entire precincts of the college before its suppression. Old deeds and copies of letters patent preserved at Enys (see note 27 above) contain specific allusions to the provost's house, the sexton's, *i.e.*, sacristan's house (at Glasney the office of sacristan ranking next to that of provost), the vicar of Mylor's house, the vicar of Bodmin's house (alluded to in the Glasney Cartulary also), styled in each instance as having been in former Glasney College. Since all these clerics were canons of Glasney, there can be small doubt that their dwellings and those of others like them composed O.M.'s *ol chenanry an clos* 'all the canonry of the close.'

32 The form is that of the Vulgate (*John* 5:2). The King James Version has *Bethesda*. Both texts are referring, of course, to the one body of water.

Christ's Passion

1 In his essay on the sources of the Cornish drama (MS, County Museum, Truro, p. 26), Jenner identifies these and the succeeding lines sung by the Hebrew boys as "a free paraphrase of the processional hymn in elegiacs attributed to Theodulph, a 9th century Bishop of Metz, '*Gloria, laus et honor tibi sit, Rex Christe Redemptor.*'" (This hymn is sung at the second station of the Palm Sunday procession; see Sarum Missal.) Although Jenner regards the author of *P.C.* as having been an accomplished Latinist, the Cornish does not abandon its native prosody for anything like a close imitation of Latin elegiac verse. The Cornish does, however, depart from its standard 7-syllable line in favor of the 4-syllable line during the stanzas sung by Fourth, Fifth, and Sixth Boys, the shorter line employed occasionally throughout the *Ordinalia* in lyric passages (see Introduction, *A Note on the Present Translation*).

2 Dramatic and thematic convenience are characteristically better served than historical precision at this point *(P.C.* 355-57); not that the dramatist and his medieval audience would have been either impressed or gratified had they known that modern archaeology places a temple, erected *c.* 130 A.D. by the emperor Hadrian and dedicated to Jupiter, on the traditional site of Solomon's Temple.

The same holds good for the later speech by Caiaphas *(P.C.* 575-80) wherein he not only swears by the blood of Mohammed but also proceeds to denounce Jesus for subverting the inhabitants of Jerusalem (ostensibly in the third decade A.D.) from their allegiance to the Prophet of Islam, whose followers under Caliph Omar did not, of course, capture the Holy City for another six centuries.

3 In the MS, this brief speech by Andrew seems to come too late, making it appear that the disciple either has not been listening to the exchange between Jesus and Judas Iscariot or does not believe what he has heard. Like Norris and Nance, I have been tempted to transfer Andrew's four lines to an earlier location immediately after *P.C.* 744-52, a speech which completes the Master's solemn warning of the fate in store for his as yet unnamed betrayer. This position would enable Andrew's now dangling stanza to serve as a coherent sequel to the words of Jesus and lead into those of Judas Iscariot *(P.C.* 753-56). It would also allow the dialogue to arrive at a natural pause before changing direction in order to dramatize Luke's version of the Last Supper, which tells of the contention among the disciples as to which of them is 'reputed to be the greatest' *(Luke* 22: 24-30). All this recommends itself on rhetorical grounds, but, unhappily, the rhyme-scheme would be disregarded by the proposed change.

A second, differently oriented rationale for the MS location of Andrew's remark stems from the possibility that he is not referring to what has been said but is anticipating what is about to be discussed—the question as to which of the Twelve is the greatest. Viewed thus, the text of the passage must be presumed corrupt though remaining recognizably directional.

4 By the medieval Cornishman even mildly sensitive to the ideological climate of his era, the two swords of this passage might well be interpreted as symbols of the twin powers, spiritual and temporal, of Church and State. These august brands were to clash in more than one local arena with the suppression of Cornwall's monastic and collegiate establishments, including, of course, Glasney. They had, indeed, already clashed in the person of Thomas à Becket, to whom Glasney was dedicated.

Another interpretation is, however, specifically recorded in the writings of the Patristic commentators. The commentary on Luke 22:38 *(Glossa Ordinaria, P.L.* Vol. 114, col. 340) says, *Duo gladii promuntur, unus Novi, alter Veteris Testamenti, quibus adversus diaboli munimur insidias:* 'The two swords represent, one the Old, the other the New Testament, by which we are fortified against the wiles of the devil.'

5 Norris has moved this speech by Annas and Judas Iscariot's reply to it from their original location after *P.C.* 999-1004 (Judas urges wariness when attempting to arrest Jesus) to an earlier position immediately following *P.C.* 959-64 (Caiaphas orders the torturers to go with Judas and seize the crazed pretender to divine origin). Nance accepts the change, as do I, because otherwise Prince Annas is made to refer to the Kiss of Betrayal before Judas has proposed it as an identifying token. There is also my feeling that the relocation improves the forward thrust of the dialogue where it occurs and compounds the sting of perfidy.

6 Norris construes *def* in this line *(P.C.* 977) as 'captain,' Nance making it 'son-in-law,' the meaning of the Cornish word as given by *The Old Cornish Vocabulary* (MS, 12th c.). Nevertheless, to identify Prince Annas as the son-in-law of Caiaphas runs counter to Scripture *(John* 18:12), which names Annas as the father-in-law of Caiaphas (Vulgate, *socer Caiphae).* I look upon this discrepancy as a clear case of author error and am adhering to what he wrote over what he should have written. This likewise holds for the play's other references to the kinship of Annas and Caiaphas *(P.C.* 570 and 989).

7 The MS *(P.C.* 1244) has *lappa,* a borrowed M.E. noun meaning, in general, extension.' Norris translates it 'lap,' yielding 'let him fan with his lap.' Nance comments (marginalia on Norris) to the effect that in the days of long skirted coats, to fan with the lap (of a coat) was the readiest way of blowing up a fire. This rendering is plausible enough on the literal level, but it fails to take into account the earthy source of the line (Third Torturer) and the potential for double-meaning which Jenner, among others, recognizes as present elsewhere in *P.C.* (note 16 below). I have therefore replaced 'lap' with a term which the O.E.D. circumspectly defines as 'a dangling appendage,' dating it from 1622. Partridge's *Dictionary of Slang and Unconventional English* is more specific while remaining decorous: 'The *membrum virile:* low; from ca. 1895. The term occurs in a somewhat Rabelaisian song. Ex. d-d., 'a dangling appendage.'

8 Cf. note 3, *Beginning of the World.*

9 Since asides are not indicated by the *Ordinalia's* stage directions, the likelihood of their occasional presence has to be inferred. Nance, consistently mindful of the plays as theatre, suspects that First Messenger's impudent answer to Caiaphas was addressed to the audience rather than the high priest, who is, nonetheless,

suitably undercut as a leading representative of the wrong side. The fact that Caiaphas cannot fully command the respect of one of his own subordinates is emphasized by First Messenger's radical deviation from the highflown, howbeit now and again suspect, deference paid by servants to masters throughout the trilogy.

10 The Cornish *(P.C.* 1695) reads *coth was gof,* literally 'old fellow smith.' Norris translates the phrase, 'old smith fellow.' Nance, who seems to ignore tradition by an additional degree, makes it 'old blacksmith fellow.' The Vulgate reads *fabri filius,* whose strict translation is 'worker's son,' and if any material or medium is indicated by the classical Latin, *faber* 'fabricator,' it is specified as 'any hard material' (Cassell's *Latin Dictionary).* Norris' 'smith' designates a worker in metals generally; Nance's 'blacksmith' denotes a worker in black metal, *i.e.,* iron.

Both translators were evidently influenced toward their respective renderings of the Cornish *gof,* 'smith,' by the prevailing circumstances when the word next appears in *P.C.,* the episode that deals with the legendary forging of the nails which fastened Jesus upon the cross *(P.C.* 2663-2742). Here there can be no question as to what kind of handicraftsman is involved. He is an iron worker, a blacksmith.

11 Of this serio-comic analogy, whose pungence I have not attempted to soften, Jenner wrote (MS lecture on the Cornish drama, County Museum, Truro, p. 93): "Two doctors of the law are introduced and argue before Herod for and against the claims of Jesus to be both God and Man. . . . The argument in favour . . . is curious . . . and may account for an emblem found in Cornish churches. . . . It was probably not as a mere ornament that a mermaid was carved on bench-ends . . . in Cornwall. It evidently symbolized the two natures of Christ, though the councils of Ephesus and Chalcedon might have found some fault with the advocate's way of expressing what is known in theology as the Hypostatic Union."

The County Museum also possesses a nearly definitive photographic collection of bench-ends still to be seen in Cornwall's churches, including three that exhibit mermaids. The example at Camborne (St. Meriadocus) shows a mermaid with a harp. In St. James, Kilkhampton, three mermaids are carved on a shield, two smaller ones above, the larger one below under a chevron. The third and best example is to be found in the church of St. Senara, Zennor.

It is the church at Zennor on the seacoast of southwest Cornwall whose proximity to St. Just and affiliation with Glasney College furnish a link, however tenuous, with *P.C.,* with the author who supplied First Doctor with his mermaid analogy, and with an audience able to identify and appreciate a local allusion. The church, about seven miles from the St. Just Round, was appropriated to Glasney College by Bishop Bronescombe in 1270.

12 This is the first of only three Cornish place-names occurring in *P.C.* as compared with fifteen or sixteen in *O.M.* The MS has *Tryger (P.C.* 1274), which Norris translates with no change beyond the adding of a vowel, 'Tryguer.' But Nance goes significantly further, construing *Tryger* as 'Trigg Hundred.' He appears to have followed Pedler, who offers an identical interpretation in his notes on the place-names in the *Ordinalia (The Ancient Cornish Drama,* Vol. 2, p. 502). In Britain, a 'hundred' signifies a subdivision of a county or shire.

Historical Trigg Hundred consists of 12 parishes lying anywhere from about 28 miles to more than 35 miles northeast of Penryn and a minimum of 6 miles north of Lostwithiel. The bulk of the hundred extends northward from Bodmin to Blisland, northwestward from Bodmin to Egloshayle near the estuary of the River Camel. Lostwithiel and Bodmin are the two locations mentioned in *O.M.* (though see note 20, *Beginning of the World*) which are much over half a dozen miles distant from former Glasney College, Penryn.

Assuming that the Glasney area is again the geographical center of reference for *P.C.* as it seems to have been for *O.M.*, an assumption which automatically makes the boy's mention of 'here' an allusion to the Budock-Penryn locality, his denunciation of his master becomes quite expansive. It carries all the way from what might be termed his New Jerusalem to a region that could have seemed to him and to the less travelled among his audience the metaphorical counterpart of the ends of the earth, *i.e.*, the eastern boundary of Cornwall. Pedler *(op. cit.,* p. 503) remarks: "The hundred of Trigg in the thirteenth century . . . comprised the district around Bodmin, but the ecclesiastical division of the deaneries of Trigg Major and Minor . . . comprehended . . . all the northeast part of the country from Bodmin to Stratton. The meaning of the passage in the text is obviously equivalent to saying 'from this place to the extremity of Cornwall.' "

Among a number of other possible identifications of *Tryger* is the "great episcopal fief of Tregeare" (see Henderson, MS Ecclesiastical Antiquities I, pp. 21, 297), which once included with other holdings the church of St. Just in Roseland (not to be confused with the St. Just of note 13 above) and its "whole parish," plus the church and parish of St. Anthony in Roseland. On this evidence, Boy's ultima Thule would be drawn in from the border country of Trigg Hundred to Powder Hundred (West), where St. Just and St. Anthony are to be found approximately four miles equidistant from Penryn, to the northeast and southeast respectively, across Carrick Roads and Falmouth Harbor (see note 23, *Beginning of the World*).

13 See note 10 above.

14 On a recent map of Cornwall (John Bartholomew & Sons, Edinburgh) "Marazion or Market Jew" may be found a short distance east of Penzance on the curving shoreline of Mount's Bay. The MS spelling of the name is *Marghes jow* or *yow (P.C.* 2668), literally 'Thursday market.' Henderson has written (MS Ecclesiastical Antiquities I, pp. 261-62): "Marazion and Market Jew seem to have originally been separate villages which coalesced at an early date to form a little town yet existing." Marazion was, during the Middle Ages, the property of the Benedictine Priory of St. Michael's Mount, itself a onetime daughter house of Mont St. Michel in Normandy. The great rock of St. Michael's Mount rises from the waters of Mounts Bay directly opposite Marazion. The village was once the southern terminus of the overland trade route from the port of Hayle in the north. Market Jew is situated in Penwith Hundred about 15 miles southwest of Penryn and Falmouth.

One of Nance's marginalia on Market Jew *(The Ancient Cornish Drama,* Vol. 2, p. 503) reads: "It was evidently thought likely to please a Penryn audience to make these 'unpopular' characters [the blacksmith and his wife] come from Penwith." On a subsequent page (505) of the same volume, Nance observes: "Marghesyou is far to the west of all these [*Ordinalia* place-names in the Budock-Penryn area]. The smith lives there. . . . It gives a rhyme for *kentrow [P.C.* 2665], which may be the only reason for this."

It appears that there could have been another, less mechanical reason. According to *The Encyclopaedia Britannica* (13th ed., *s.v. Penryn*), Walter de Stapledon, while bishop of Exeter from 1307 to his death in 1326, secured a Thursday market for his burgesses of Penryn. Assuming the correctness of this statement, which lacks corroboration by any other source at present known to me, and further assuming that the surviving version of *P.C.* was adapted to performance at Glasney, it follows that Fourth Torturer is not dispatched some 15 miles in order to obtain the required nails but virtually around the corner. Referring to this episode in *P.C.*, Jenner (MS lecture, The Sources of the Cornish Drama, p. 96) maintains there was a Market Street in Penryn, "not far from Glasney College, which is probably intended." This is a rather loose identification, however, its value largely depending upon how long the street can be shown to have borne the name. The former name of the present Market Street seems to have been Our Lady Street.

15 The Cornish itself *(P.C.* 2697-98) yields this pun, a rare occurrence in the *Ordinalia.*

16 The presence of bawdy double-meanings in this speech by the smith's wife *(P.C.* 2714-20) and in the exchanges which follow between her and First Torturer while the nails are being made seems to me intentional although not, of course, unavoidable, as Norris' rendering demonstrates *(The Ancient Cornish Drama*, Vol. 1, pp. 437, 439). The fact that Jenner reaches a conclusion similar to mine, in substance if not in spirit, is clear from his remarks on this nail-making passage: "The scene in the Cornish drama has a good deal of inappropriate ribaldry" (MS Sources of the Cornish Drama, p. 17).

17 If Second Torturer's boast can be taken at face value, it is as empty as King Solomon's gift of Seal Rock (see note 23, *Beginning of the World)* proved barren. Modern Hayle lies, as it did in the Middle Ages (see note 14 above), on the east side of the Hayle river estuary yet so far west in the county as safely to eliminate the greater part of his eligible competition, an inverted hyperbole which gives the torturer's quip its point.

Since the Cornish word *heyl* 'river' is patently a ubiquitous term in a region where rivers are as plentiful as they are in Cornwall, it would not be difficult to bring forward a number of rival claims, but to what profit? Irony would evaporate and the county-wide range of the place-names in *P.C.* would shrink toward the more parochial limits characteristic of *O.M.*

18 As they stand in the surviving MS, the 12 lines *(P.C.* 2849-60) which attempt to carry through on this stage direction are impossible to translate intelligibly even though their general purport is clear—a drawing or distribution of lots among the four torturers, one of whom has been blindfolded. I have amended the passage, endeavoring to make the implicit more explicit while retaining as much of the original as possible. I give Nance's literal rendering (unpublished manuscript, *Passio Christi*, p. 79) for comparison.

Fourth Torturer

See, I have three lots!

First Torturer

Take this one, put it with them,
and that is a fourth!

Second Torturer

Now unblindfold, and say
which is the lot that possesses without doubt
the coat of Jesus of Nazareth.

Third Torturer

It's that one's, for certain!
you all know
which lot it is.

Fourth Torturer

By Saint Jove, it's mine!
Let each take his own share:
let him carry it home.

For Norris' construction of the passage, see *The Ancient Cornish Drama*, Vol. 1, p. 119.

19 The Vulgate (*John* 19:26) says only *Mulier ecce filius tuus* 'Woman, behold thy son,' whereby Jesus referred to John and not to himself as he clearly does in the Cornish (*P.C.* 2925-27). The Scriptural reference is followed by most analogues in England, the sole exception among the better known being two manuscripts of the *Northern Passion*. The Welsh *Passion* (Gwenan Jones, ed., *A Study of Three Welsh Religious Plays*, 1939) reads in translation: "Behold, woman of unhappy condition, / thy son before the dread scene / and instead of thy son now, / take John the Evangelist" (345-48).

The Cornish dramatist, not content merely to depart from Scripture, has also introduced a hunting or baiting metaphor: *benen a welte the flogh / myl wyth dyghtye ages brogh / gans nep mylgy*, which Nance, following Loth, translates, 'Woman, seest thou thy child / a thousand times worse served than a badger / by any greyhound?' If the figure is construed as a reference to hunting rather than baiting, one can hardly fail to be reminded of the canons of Glasney, whose notorious enthusiasm for the chase is memorialized in the recorded protests of the bishops of Exeter (see note 26, *Beginning of the World*).

20 I have followed the amended sense of this stage direction in the MS, which originally read *tunc venit iosep baramaeus et nichodemus et petient corpus ihu* 'Then comes Joseph of Arimathea and Nicodemus, and they shall beg for the body of Jesus.' Scribe B has over-corrected the first clause by striking out *et nichodemus* but improves matters in the second clause by altering *petient* to *petiet*. When

'Joseph' is supplied to give *petiet* a subject in the second clause, the stage direction is reconciled with what actually proceeds to take place in the version of *P.C.* which survives.

21 The play omits the Scriptural mention of alabaster as the material of the box containing precious ointment with which Mary Magdalene anoints Jesus at the supper in Bethany *(P.C. 485-88)* yet chooses to specify it here *(P.C. 3136)*, where the Gospels offer no basis for it. They speak only of a rock-cut tomb, a burial chamber large enough to be entered by several persons at one time; for example, the two Marys and the Angel in *Mark* 16:5. But it should be kept in mind that the representation of a Jewish entombment would very likely have struck a lay audience in medieval Christian Cornwall as outlandish and hence pagan. The dramatist therefore presents the familiar, accepted burial mode, a coffin or sarcophagus, generically a box. The Christian audience would recognize a white alabaster sarcophagus as handsome and precious, a fitting object of reverence and, quite possibly, a status symbol for Joseph, the convert as man of property in *Matthew* 27:57. (See also note 3, *Resurrection of Our Lord*.)

22 If the reader finds himself in any doubt as to the nature of the tomb which Joseph of Arimathea has just described to security-minded Pilate, this stage direction should dispose of it. The language of the MS is brief but adequate: *paratur sepulcrum et lapis superponitur* 'A sepulchre is prepared, and a stone put upon it.' A marginal note by Nance in his copy of *The Ancient Cornish Drama* (Vol. 1, p. 471) observes: "This must be on the plain." As usual, Nance is alert to considerations of staging (he was convinced that the surviving MS of the *Ordinalia* is a producer's version), and there is something to be said for the view that, religious considerations aside, a sarcophagus with a removable lid would reveal the action where a representation of the Biblical chamber tomb with its opaque shell and low portal would tend to obscure it.

23 Reproducing the "English Alabaster Convention," Nance has left a drawing (his copy of *The Ancient Cornish Drama*, Vol. 1, p. 473) of the Entombment as, he appears to imply, it was presented in *P.C.* The sketch shows John, Mary Jacobi, Mary Salome, and Nicodemus on one side of the tomb, facing Joseph of Arimathea and Mary Magdalene (she kneeling) on the other side. The Virgin Mother bends over the body of Jesus which lies as if upon a slab. The dramatic fullness of the scene, for which *P.C.* does supply the cast of characters and the setting, is approximated by the Hegge play but not by any other of the English dramatic analogues, while the most detailed of the Gospel accounts *(John* 19:38-42), although including both Nicodemus and the enbalming, must be considered bare by comparison.

1 Carminow and Merthen, like Kennall, were sizable, non-contiguous manors numbered among the holdings of the powerful Carminow family in 14th c. Cornwall, Kirrier Hundred. They are still to be found as properties in the county. Kennall Wood is situated about two miles northwest of Penryn, Carminow some ten miles and Merthen approximately six miles southwest of it.

Henderson (MS Ecclesiastical Antiquities II, p. 106), citing the Assize Rolls, notes that Glasney College tried in 1318, 1320, and 1321 to recover lands in Merthen.

2 Henderson (MS Ecclesiastical Antiquities I, p. 481) supplies evidence from records now at Exeter of a Dansotha, "the down near Four Burrows" (barrows), which was included in a grant of land comprising "nearly all Perran, all St. Agnes, and part of Illogan parishes." This identification, while it cannot be considered definitive, is supported by the findings of Gover *(Place-Names,* p. 363) and has at least the merit of locating Dansotha at no great distance from Perranzabuloe, the site of Cornwall's best preserved medieval playing place.

Of Crukheyth, research to date has come up with several possibilities but has not been able to reduce any of them to a certainty. Fowler *(op. cit.,* p. 102) writes: "Probably this is Grugwith (or Grugith) in the parish of St. Keverne (Gover, p. 544), as Pedler suggests (Norris, II, 497 f.), although the form is unusual." Should this view ultimately prove correct, Crukheyth would lie some eight miles south of Penryn, Dansotha being on the order of ten miles north of Penryn. Since the two properties are bestowed upon the soldier by Pilate in one and the same line *(R.D.* 377), so great a geographical spread as 18 miles in itself suggests the need for further investigation. A point certainly to be considered is the fact that the *cruk-* of *Crukheyth* signifies 'hill,' 'mound (hence barrow)', whereas Dansotha is identified as a spot near barrows.

3 Although with these lines *(R.D.* 521-22) the *Ordinalia* evidently again departs from the Vulgate's specification of a traditionally Hebraic rock-hewn burial chamber, another source not only supports the sarcophagus concept but also couples with it the sheltering enclosure of a chamber tomb. Writing on the subject of the Lord's Sepulchre, Bede, as cited by Comestor *(Historia Scholastica, P. L.,* Vol. 198, col. 1634) may be translated as saying in part: 'It was a circular room excised from subjacent rock of such height that a man with extended hand could hardly touch the top, having entrance from the east, at which a great rock was placed before the door. In its north part the coffin of the Lord's body was made of the same rock, having seven feet in length. . . . The coffin was not opened from above but from the southern side, whence the body was inserted . . . and was as it were a sarcophagus inclined on its side, having an entrance from the side. The color of the tomb, indeed, and of the coffin is said to be rubicund and white mixed.'

Aside from his designation of a sarcophagus, howbeit with features not par-

265

alleled by the *Ordinalia,* Bede's commentary, in reporting the material of the sepulchre to be mixed red and white stone, appears to have fixed upon alabaster, the same mineral from which Joseph of Arimathea's new tomb had allegedly been fashioned in *P.C.* (3136). The color discrepancy (the alabaster of Joseph's tomb is 'white as milk,' whereas Bede's envisioned sepulchre is a mixture of 'rubicund and white') can be accounted for by the circumstance that while true alabaster at its purest, as distinguished from Oriental alabaster, is a soft, translucent, uniformly snow-white variety of gypsum, its color is often modified by the presence of iron oxide, which results in a reddish clouding or veining (Bede's *permistus* 'mixed') in the stone.

4 Pilate's bribe of the soldiers in return for their silence as self-proclaimed eye-witnesses of the Resurrection constitutes the *Ordinalia's* last gift of Cornish real estate at the hands of ancient Hebrew kings (David and Solomon), a Jewish "bishop," and here a Roman official. The gift was, as Fourth Soldier says of it *(R.D.* 675), a generous one in medieval terms and times. Penryn and Helston were alike valuable ports, coinage towns, and chartered boroughs in the Middle Ages, the former in the hands of the bishop of Exeter, the latter in those of the Duke of Cornwall.

5 The MS renders this poignant little lyric in Middle English. I have made a quatrain of the original couplet, which reads *(R.D.* 733-34, *et seq.): ellas mornyngh y syngh mornyngh y cal / our lord ys deyd that bogthe ovs al.*

6 Set off to the right between *R.D.* 874 and 875, the MS supplies the Latin notation *mulier noli me tangere* 'Woman, touch me not.' Since it cannot be classed as a routine stage direction and is immediately duplicated by the Cornish of *R.D.* 875, I have omitted it from the translation. The only other instances of this practice in the *Ordinalia* occur later in *R.D.* and are noted below.

Except for the added word *mulier, R.D.'s* notation is quoted verbatim from the Vulgate *(John* 20:17). While there is no positive clue to the function of the notation, there is the circumstance that Bodley 791 is probably a playing or production version in which the convenience of a prompter may have figured. It is also possible that this bit of Vulgate text was forthwith sung, a lingering vestige of an Easter trope.

7 The verbal ingredients of Thomas' threat of physical violence to Mary Magdalene, a threat which I have ventured to wrap in a pun, are supplied by a combination of medieval legend and the literal meaning of the Cornish *(R.D.* 920-23). Legend (for instance, *Legenda Aurea*) credits Mary Magdalene with ownership of a castle at Magdala (el-Majdel), a town on the west shore of the Sea of Galilee three miles northwest of Tiberias. After naming Castle Maudlin, *stout awos castel maudlen,* literally, 'stout though Castle Maudlin [be],' Thomas goes on to assert, again literally, 'I will break thy head to thee from above' or 'for thee atop' (. . . *me a ter the pen / thys awartha*).

For an extended English treatment of the Mary Magdalene legend in dramatic form, see *The Digby Mysteries* (ed. F. J. Furnivall), "Mary Magdalene."

8 Again set off to the right between *R.D.* 1260 and 1261, the MS carries the Latin notation *tu peregrinus es* 'Art thou a stranger?' Likewise between *R.D.* 1320 and 1321 there appear the words *nonne cor nostrum ardens erat nobis in via* 'Did not our heart burn within us in the way?' I have omitted these from the

translation for reasons identical to those given in note 6 above.

9 Earlier students of the *Ordinalia* have tended to regard the Death of Pilate as a break in the continuity of *R.D.*, as a separate, unrelated episode awkwardly interposed between the Resurrection and the Ascension. Norris observes (*op. cit.*, Vol. II, p. 443): "But although we have only three pieces in form, they are four in fact; the third, which should have been called the 'Resurrection and Ascension,' being interrupted by the 'Death of Pilate' . . . the action of which is entirely detached. The Editor [Norris] would perhaps have done better if he had printed the Death of Pilate as a separate piece, but the immediate connection of the first and last divisions did not strike him until the whole was in print."

Jenner, who takes it upon himself to subdivide each of the three plays of the trilogy into theoretically designated acts and scenes, writes of *R.D.* (MS essay, The Cornish Drama, p. 110): "The second act is entitled *De Morte Pilati* . . . taken from an early legend *Cura sanitatis Tiberii*, the original form of which goes back to the 8 C. at least . . . This drama [episode] may or may not be an original composition, but I do not know of any other drama on the subject." Actually this material does not appear in either the English cycles or the *Northern Passion,* not even in *Cursor Mundi.* The dramatist could have found more than one version, however, in *Legenda Aurea.* (For other versions, see *Siege of Jerusalem*, E.E.T.S., O.S., Vol. 188.)

As for Nance, he complains in a marginal note to be found in his personal copy of Norris (at *R.D.* 1586 f.) that the Death of Pilate, although in his view a separate composition not worked in with the rest of *R.D.,* nevertheless lacks an appropriately separate title (cf. Jenner's claim above). On the other hand, he continues, the Ascension, which has been accorded a title of its own in the MS stage directions, is actually an unbroken continuation of the prior Resurrection episode, detouring the Death of Pilate and going straight into Peter's reply to the speech with which Jesus had concluded the Resurrection more than 700 lines earlier *(R.D.* 1571-86 to *R.D.* 2361-66).

Examination of the MS stage directions fails to bear out either Nance or Jenner with respect to the alleged presence or absence of episode titles as such. Without departing from the usual style, the Latin rubric falling between *R.D.* 1586 and 1587 (juncture of the Resurrection and the Death of Pilate) reads: *et sic finitur resurrectio domini et incipit morte pilate et dicit tiberius caesar* 'And thus the Resurrection of Our Lord is concluded, and the Death of Pilate begins, and Tiberius Caesar speaks.' Similarly, between *R.D.* 2360 and 2361 (juncture of the Death of Pilate and the Ascension), the direction reads: *et sic finitur mors pilati et incipit ascensio Christi in celum et dicit petrus* 'And so is ended the Death of Pilate, and the Ascension of Christ to heaven begins, and Peter says—'

While one can agree that the transitions between the Death of Pilate and the episodes that flank it are not of the smoothest, it is something else to maintain, as Nance does, that the dialogue at the close of the Resurrection drives straight on to the opening lines of the Ascension in total disregard of the 773 lines, devoted to the fate of Pilate, which intervene. To my ear, the cadence of Christ's final words before the break is shaped to a semi-close, marking a pause in the drama that parallels a like interval which tradition has established between the Resurrection and the Ascension on the fortieth day after Easter. *R.D.* specifically confirms the tradition in the words of Jesus himself *(R.D.* 2436-39).

The view that the episode amounts to a separate composition, an opinion to which both Norris and Nance, if not Jenner, subscribe, appears subject to modification on several grounds: for example, the sharing of characters in common. Pilate, of course, figures not only in the Death but also in the first portion of *R.D.,* taking a prominent role in the action of *P.C.* as well. Two other characters, the jailor and his boy, Lashbutt, reassume the identities in the Death of Pilate (see note 12 below) which they introduced in *P.C.,* and the emperor Tiberius, having opened the episode of Pilate's death, pronounces the epilogue of *R.D.* as a whole. Lucifer, Satan, Beelzebub, and Tulfric must likewise be added to the list of repeaters in the Death of Pilate, all save Tulfric frequenting the *Ordinalia* from early in *O.M.* onward.

Further considerations that support the concept of interaction between the Death of Pilate and the other divisions of *R.D.* are a matter of function. They become apparent the moment one explores the consequences of omitting the Pilate episode. Without it, *R.D.* would, for instance, become disproportionately short, as Nance seems to appreciate, and scarcely adequate to its assignment as the third day's play (see epilogue of *P.C.).* Again, the cut would materially weaken *R.D.* as spectacle, as catharsis via Pilate the scapegoat, the arch-hero in mocking and sulphurous reverse. The depth of his descent to an eternity among the damned adds by contrast to the measure of his erstwhile victim's ascent on high into the company of the forever blessed, which so soon follows.

10 History records that Tiberius was Roman emperor from 14 B.C. until his death in 37 A.D., a reign which could have witnessed both the Crucifixion, traditionally assigned to the year 33 A.D. at the latest, and the legendary suicide of Pilate, which may be thought of as having taken place during the forty days between Easter and the Ascension (see note 9 above). Hence *R.D.* names the appropriate Roman emperor as a participant in the action, but its account of his conversion to Christianity is, of course, an anachronism.

11 Unlike a similarly abrupt transition in *O.M.* (see note 16, *Beginning of the World),* the MS of *R.D.* displays no evidence of error or confusion in this passage, where the setting shifts from one location to another and Messenger switches from a dialogue with Veronica to addressing the emperor Tiberius within the one speech *(R.D.* 1673-84). The transition is marked in the MS, however, by a paragraph sign.

12 The significant point is not, of course, that a stock character designation like jailor's boy or servant should be the same in the latter two of the three plays. It is rather that the boy's nickname is carried over from *P.C.* into *R.D.* without change. The Cornish has *whyp an tyn,* which Norris bowdlerizes as 'Sharp-whip' *(P.C.* 2239) and 'Smart-whip' *(R.D.* 2081), whereas Nance first hit upon the more literal 'Whip Behind,' later substituting the rather cumbrous 'Whip o' the Breech.'

So exact a carry-over of an epithet in the Cornish suggests authorial continuity between the two dramas, if not with respect to initial authorship, at least in the course of subsequent revision when, conceivably, the vein of popular humor was broadened. This would apply particularly to the surviving version of *P.C.,* of which Jenner has written (MS lecture, The Cornish Drama, p. 95): "Then follows a quite unnecessary comic dispute between the gaoler and his servant, which is not in the least interesting, and is no doubt original." Jenner's comment, a characteristic linking of a conservative opinion with a bold assumption, refers to *P.C.* 2253-2342, a passage of almost a hundred lines. The analogous sequence in *R.D.* (2081-2116) is grimmer, much less digressive, and a little over a third as long.

13 Is Beelzebub alluding here to a volcano? Volcanic phenomena are not to be associated with Cornwall, save at an exceedingly remote period in its geological history, but the ostensible setting of Pilate's catastrophic fate is Italian rather than Cornish. If *R.D.'s* author was familiar with the encyclopedic commentary of Rabanus Maurus (*c.* 776-856), as he might well have been, he would have been aware of fire-mountains in general and Sicily's notorious Mt. Etna in particular. Of the latter, Rabanus observes *(P.L.,* Vol. 111, col. 363): *Mons Aetna ex igne et sulphure dictus, unde et gehennna* 'Mt. Etna, on account of its fire and sulphur, is spoken of as a Gehenna.' Thus *R.D.* can be understood as committing the corpse of Pilate to a welcome by underworld princes in the fiery throat of the New Testament hell.

14 The obscene jocularity of this bit of word play between Beelzebub and Tulfric hinges on what is made of the term *pen pusorn (R.D.* 2353). Norris construes *pen* as 'end,' Nance as 'head,' the Cornish denoting either end of something, *i.e.,* 'extremity.' When *pusorn,* 'burden' or 'refrain,' is added, Norris reads 'end of a song,' Nance, 'head of a refrain,' later revised to 'head-burden.' The choice favors Norris on several counts: his version runs with the grain of the Cornish, falls in with the sense of the passage, and provides the occasion for Tulfric's earthy rejoinder. In this case, admittedly a rare one, the opposite holds true for Nance's final version, which coins a musical term not to be found in the vocabulary of the period and leaves Tulfric with no tinder for his spark.

Norris, however, proceeds to lead bravely into a play on the word 'end' or 'tail' (of a song), only to lose courage when he comes to Tulfric's punning reply and retreat behind a footnote *(op. cit.,* Vol. II, p. 177): "These lines [*R.D.* 2355-57] are necessarily paraphrased." I have judged it equally necessary to render Tulfric's still current vulgarism without the Norris disguise ('I wag my tail at ye'), which Loth *(Revue Celtique,* Vol. 26, p. 266) was to characterize as "de la pure fantaisie."

15 The garment-of-red motif (see also Introduction, *Staging*), introduced by First Angel at this point *(R.D.* 2489) and echoed by other angels and by Christ as the Ascension scene unfolds, has its primary source in the Vulgate. *Isaiah* 63:1-2 reads: *Quis est iste, qui venit de Edom, tinctis vestibus de Bosra? Iste formosus in stola sua, gradiens in multitudine fortitudinis suae. Ego qui loquor iustitiam, et propugnator sum ad salvandum. Quare ergo rubrum est indumentum tuum, et vestimenta tua sicut calcantium in torculari?* 'Who is this that cometh from Edom, with dyed garments from Bosra, this beautiful one in his robe, walking in the greatness of his strength? I, that speak justice, and am a defender to save. Why then is thy apparel red, and thy garments like theirs that tread in the winepress?' (Douai). *Revelation* 19:13 reads: *Et vestitus erat veste aspersa sanguine: et vocatur nomen eius: Verbum Dei.* 'And he is clothed in a garment sprinkled with blood, and his name is called The Word of God.' (Douai).

16 The Cornish words, *ow hobersen (R.D.* 2536), 'my habergeon,' introduce what

is probably the most powerful and unquestionably the most extended metaphor in the *Ordinalia*. Beginning with an ironic reference to the habergeon, a short high-necked jacket of mail, usually without sleeves, the replies of Jesus to the wondering angels continue to develop a surcharged contrast between the victimized Son of Man, stripped and defenseless on the cross, and the triumphant Son of God, clothed in the matchless armor of divinity. This medieval concept of the Christ-knight is sustained through a total of 60 lines.

BIBLIOGRAPHY

BIBLIOGRAPHY

Anderson, Mary D. *Drama and Imagery in English Medieval Churches.* Cambridge [Engl.]: University Press, 1963.

—————. *The Imagery of British Churches.* London: John Murray, 1955.

Andrews, William. *Old-Time Punishments.* Hull: W. Andrews & Co., 1890.

Ashton, John. *The Legendary History of the Cross.* London: T. Fisher Unwin, 1887.

Beunans Meriasek. Edited by Whitley Stokes. London: Trubner & Co., 1872.

Boase, Charles William. *Registrum Collegii Exoniensis.* (Oxford Historical Society, XXVII). Oxford, 1894.

The Bodmin Register. Bodmin: Liddell & Son, 1827-30.

Borlase, William. *The Natural History of Cornwall.* Oxford: Printed for the author by W. Jackson, 1758.

—————. *Observations on the Antiquities, Historical and Monumental, of the County of Cornwall.* London: W. Jackson, 1754.

Camden, William. *Britannia.* Edited by Edmund Gibson. 2nd ed. London: Awnsham Churchill, 1722.

Carter, Henry Holland. *A Dictionary of Middle English Musical Terms.* Edited by George B. Gerhard. (Indiana University Humanities Series, No. 45). Bloomington, Ind., *c.* 1961.

Chambers, Edmund K. *The Mediaeval Stage.* 2 vols. Oxford: Clarendon Press, 1903.

Chapman, W. E. *History of Gluvias.* [Unpub.]

The Chester Plays. Edited by H. Deimling and Dr. Matthews. (EETS ES, 62, 115). London: K. Paul, Trench, Trubner & Co., 1893.

The Cornish Church Guide. Truro: Oscar Blackford, 1925.

Cox, J. C. and Ford, C. B. *Parish Churches.* London: B. T. Batsford, Ltd., 1961.

Craig, Hardin. *English Religious Drama of the Middle Ages.* Oxford: Clarendon Press, 1960.

Cursor Mundi. Edited by Richard Morris. (EETS OS, 57, 59, 62, 66, 68, 99, 101). London: K. Paul, Trench, Trubner & Co., 1874-93.

The Digby Mysteries. Edited by F. J. Furnivall. (New Shakspere Society). London: N. Trubner & Co., 1882.

Elliott-Binns, L. E. *Medieval Cornwall.* London: Methuen, 1955.

Emden, A. B. *A Biographical Register of the University of Oxford to A.D. 1500.* 3 vols. Oxford: Clarendon Press, 1957-59.

Fowler, David C. "The Date of the Cornish *Ordinalia.*" *Mediaeval Studies,* XXIII (1961), 91-125.

Frank, Grace. *The Medieval French Drama.* Oxford: Clarendon Press, 1954.

The Glasney Cartulary. MS, Cornwall County Record Office. Abstracted, *Journal of the Royal Institution of Cornwall,* XXI (1879), 213-63.

Glossa Ordinaria. P.L., CXIII, CXIV.

The Golden Legend of Jacobus de Voragine. Translated by Granger Ryan and Helmut Ripperger. London: Longmans, Green & Co., 1941.

The Gospel of Nicodemus. In M. R. James, *The Apocryphal New Testament.* Oxford: Clarendon Press, 1953.

Gover, J. E. B. *The Place-Names of Cornwall.* (Typescript). Truro Museum. [1948].

Guthrie, A. "The Plain-an-Guary, St. Just, Cornwall—an Exploratory Excavation," *Proceedings of the West Cornwall Field Club,* Vol. II, No. 1 (1956-57), 3-7.

Gwreans an Bys. Edited by Whitley Stokes. Berlin: Published for the Philological Society by A. Asher & Co., 1863.

Halliday, F. E. *A History of Cornwall.* London: Gerald Duckworth & Co., 1929.

————. *The Legend of the Rood.* London: Gerald Duckworth & Co., 1955.

Harris, Phyllis Pier. *Origo Mundi, A New Edition.* Ann Arbor, Mich.: University Microfilms, 1964.

Henderson, Charles. *Ecclesiastical Antiquities of Cornwall.* 2 vols. (MSS, Truro Museum). In large part edited by H. L. Douch, *Journal of the Royal Institution of Cornwall,* special issue (1955); Vol. II, Pt. 4 (1956); Vol. III, Pt. 2 (1958); Vol. III, Pt. 4 (1960).

————. *A History of the Parish of Constantine in Cornwall.* Edited by G. H. Doble. Long Compton: King's Stone Press, 1937.

————. *Mabe Church and Parish.* Long Compton: King's Stone Press [1931].

————. MSS, Vols. II, III, VII, VIII, IX, X, XV. Truro Museum.

History of the County of Cornwall. Edited by William Page. (Victoria History of the Counties of England, Pt. 6). London: Archibald Constable & Co., 1924.

Hone, William. *Ancient Mysteries Described.* London: William Reeves, [1823].

Hooper, E. G. R. "An 'Ordinalia' Place Name." *Old Cornwall,* VI, No. 6 (Spring, 1964), 262-63.

Hudson, W. Henry. *The Land's End.* London: J. M. Dent & Sons, 1908.

The Itinerary of John Leland the Antiquarian. Edited by Thomas Hearne. 9 vols. Oxford: J. Fletcher, 1770.

Jeffery, H. M. "The Early History of Falmouth." *Reports of the Royal Cornwall Polytechnic Society,* No. 54 (1886), pp. 94-102.

————. "Glasney College, Penryn." *Ibid.,* No. 57 (1889), pp. 100-104.

————. "A Map of the River Fal and Its Tributaries, from a Survey Made in 1597, by Baptizta Boazio." *Journal of the Royal Institution of Cornwall,* IX (1886-89), 165-70.

————. "On a Map of Part of the Parishes of Budock and Mylor, Drawn About A.D. 1580, with a Notice of Arwennack House." *Ibid.,* pp. 160-64.

Jenner, Henry. "The Cornish Drama." *Celtic Review,* III (1906-1907), 360-375; IV (1907-1908), 41-68.

————. "The Cornish Drama" (revised version). MS, Truro Museum.

————. "Perran Round and the Cornish Drama." *Reports of the Royal Cornwall Polytechnic Society,* No. 79 (1912), pp. 38-44.

————. "Sources of the Cornish Drama." MS, Truro Museum.

Jones, Gwenan. *A Study of Three Welsh Religious Plays.* [Aberystwyth]: R. Evans & Son, 1939.

Jubinal, Achille (ed.) *La Passion de Notre Seigneur* in *Mystères inédits du quinzième siècle.* 2 vols. Paris: Techener, 1837.

Keigwyn, John. Translation of the *Ordinalia.* MS. Bodl. 28556B (now Corn.e.2).

Kempthorne, G. A. "Notes on the Collegiate Churches of Cornwall." *Old Cornwall,* III, Pt. 3 (Summer, 1938), 89-99.

Lanyon-Orgill, P. A. "The Cornish Drama." *The Cornish Review,* I, No. 1 (Spring, 1949), 38-42.

LeBraz, Anatole. *Le théâtre celtique.* Paris: Calmann-Levy [1905].

Legende. See Meyer.

Longsworth, Robert. *The Cornish Ordinalia: Religion and Dramaturgy.* Cambridge, Mass.: Harvard University Press, 1967.

Loth, Joseph. "Études corniques IV: Remarques et corrections au Lexicon Cornu-Britannicum de Williams." *Revue Celtique,* XXIII (1902), 237-302.

————. "Etudes corniques VI: Corrections à divers textes corniques." *Ibid.,* XXVI (1905), 218-67.

Ludus Coventriae, or the Plaie Called Corpus Christi. Edited by K. S. Block. (EETS ES, 120). Oxford: Oxford University Press, 1922.

Lysons, Daniel and Samuel. *Magna Britannia III: Cornwall.* London: Printed for T. Cadell and W. Davies, 1814.

Maclean, John. *The Parochial and Family History of the Deanery of Trigg Minor.* 3 vols. London: Nichols and Sons, 1873-76.

————. *Parochial and Family History of the Parish of Bodmin.* London, 1870.

Madan, F., and H. H. E. Craster. *A Summary Catalogue of Western Manuscripts in the Bodleian Library at Oxford.* Vol. II, Pt. 1. Oxford: Clarendon Press, 1922.

Meyer, Wilhelm. "Die Geschichte des Kreuzholzes vor Christus." *Abhandlungen der königlich bayerischen Akademie der Wissenschaft, Phil.-Hist. Klasse,* XVI (1881), 103-160.

Nance, R. Morton. "The Cornish Miracle Plays." MS, Truro Museum.

————. *The Cornish Ordinalia in Unified Spelling.* (Typescript). Truro Museum.

————. *Gwryans an Bys.* Padstow [Engl.], n.d.

————. "Painted Windows and Miracle Plays." *Old Cornwall*, V, No. 6 (1955), 244-48.

————. "The Plen an Gwary or Cornish Playing-Place." *Journal of the Royal Institution of Cornwall*, XXIV (1935), 190-211.

Nasmith, James. *Notitia Monastica*. Cambridge: University Press, 1787.

Norden, John. *Speculi Britannie Pars: A Topographical and Historical Description of Cornwall*. London: William Pearson, 1728.

Norris, Edwin (ed.) *The Ancient Cornish Drama*. 2 vols. Oxford: Oxford University Press, 1859.

————. R. M. Nance annotated copy, Truro Museum.

The Northern Passion. Edited by Frances Foster. (EETS OS, 145, 147, 183). London: K. Paul, Trench, Trubner & Co., 1913-16.

Ordinale de origine mundi; Passio Domini nostri Jhesu Christi; Ordinale de resurrexione Domini nostri Jhesu Christi. MS. Bodl. 791.

Pascon agan Arluth. Edited by Whitley Stokes. *Philological Society Transactions* (1860-1861), pp. 1-100.

Peter, Thurstan C. *The History of Glasney Collegiate Church, Cornwall*. Camborne: Camborne Printing and Stationery Co., 1903.

————. MSS, Truro Museum.

————. "Notes on the Church of St. Just-in-Penwith." *Journal of the Royal Institution of Cornwall*, XIV (1900), 173-90.

————. *The Old Cornish Drama*. London: E. Stock, 1906.

Petrus Comestor. *Historia Scholastica*. P.L., CXCVIII.

Pevsner, Nikolaus. *The Buildings of England—Cornwall*. Hammondsworth: Penguin Books, 1951.

Polwhele, Richard. *History of Cornwall*. 2 vols. London: Printed by T. Flindell for Cadell and Davies, 1816.

Prosser, Eleanor. *Drama and Religion in the English Mystery Plays*. Stanford: Stanford University Press, 1961.

Pryce, William. *Archaeologia Cornu-Britannicum*. Sherborne: Printed by W. Cruttwell, 1790.

Quinn, Esther. *The Quest of Seth*. Chicago: University of Chicago Press, 1962.

Rabanus Maurus. *De universo*. P.L., CXI.

The Register of John Grandisson. Edited by Francis Hingeston-Randolph. 3 vols. London: G. Bell, 1894-99.

Roddis, R. J. *Penryn*. Truro: D. Bradford Barton, 1964.

Sandys, William. "On the Cornish Drama." *Journal of the Royal Institution of Cornwall*, I (1865), 1-18.

The Sarum Missal, Edited from Three Early Manuscripts. Edited by J. Wickham Legg. Oxford: Clarendon Press, 1916.

Scawen, William. *Antiquities Cornubrittanic*. MS. Acc. 833, Cornwall County Record Office.

Smith, A. S. D. (Caradar). MSS, Truro Museum.

Snell, Lawrence S. *Documents Towards a History of the Reformation in Cornwall.* No. 1, *The Chantry Certificates for Cornwall;* No. 2, *The Edwardian Inventories of Church Goods for Cornwall.* Exeter: James Townsend & Sons, n.d.

Southern, Richard. *The Medieval Theatre in the Round.* London: Faber and Faber, 1957.

Sowell, C. R. "The Collegiate Church of St. Thomas of Glasney," *Journal of the Royal Institution of Cornwall,* I (1865), 21-34.

Spargo, John W. *Juridical Folklore in England.* Durham, N.C.: Duke University Press, 1944.

Stokes, Whitley. "A Collation of Norris' *Ancient Cornish Drama.*" *Archiv für celtische Lexicographie,* I (1898), 161-74.

Sullivan, Sister John. *A Study of the Themes of the Sacred Passion in the Medieval Cycle Plays.* Washington: The Catholic University of America Press, 1943.

Tanner, Thomas. *Notitia Monastica.* London: Printed by William Bowyer at the expense of the Society for the Encouragement of Learning, 1744.

Thomas, R. *History and Description of the Town and Harbour of Falmouth.* Falmouth: J. Trathan, 1827.

Torrey, Charles Cutler. *The Apocryphal New Testament.* New Haven: Yale University Press [c. 1945].

The Towneley Plays. Edited by George England and Alfred W. Pollard. (EETS ES, 71). London: K. Paul, Trench, Trubner & Co., 1897.

Tregarthen, J. C. "The Badger in West Cornwall." *Journal of the Royal Institution of Cornwall,* XXIII, Pt. 2 (1930), 256-64.

Whitaker, John. *The Ancient Cathedral of Cornwall Historically Surveyed.* 2 vols. London: Printed for John Stockdale, 1804.

—————. MSS, Truro Museum.

Whitley, H. Michell. "The Church Goods of Cornwall at the Time of the Reformation." *Journal of the Royal Institution of Cornwall,* VII (1882), 92-101.

Wickham, Glynn. *Early English Stages, 1300 to 1660.* Vol. I. London: Routledge and Kegan Paul, 1959.

Williams, Arnold. *The Drama of Medieval England.* [East Lansing, Mich.]: Michigan State University Press, 1961.

The York Plays. Edited by L. Toulmin Smith. Oxford: Clarendon Press: 1885.

Young, Karl. *The Drama of the Medieval Church.* 2 vols. 2nd ed. Oxford: Clarendon Press, 1951.